Transforming Exclusion

Transforming Exclusion

Engaging Faith Perspectives

Edited by

Hannah Bacon and Wayne Morris
with
Steve Knowles

t&t clark

Published by T&T Clark International
A Continuum Imprint
The Tower Building, 11 York Road, London SE1 7NX
80 Maiden Lane, Suite 704, New York, NY 10038

www.continuumbooks.com

British Library Cataloguing-in-Publication Data
A catalogue record for this book is available from the British Library

ISBN: 978-0-567-23638-8 (hardback)
           978-0-567-27374-1 (paperback)

Typeset by Newgen Imaging Systems Pvt Ltd, Chennai, India
Printed and bound in Great Britain

Contents

Preface

The concept of a book that sought to address exclusion from faith perspectives began as a conversation between a team of academics at the University of Chester in 2008. This group met to talk about what interests them in the study of theology and religion, and to discuss the projects and publications each member of the group was working on. As the conversations ensued, it became evident that one of the concerns that united many of us was a commitment to engaging the study of theology and religion with the contemporary world. With Emilie Townes, there was a recognition among the participants in this conversation 'that what should drive our research in large measure is that we are exploring traditions that have driven people to incredible heights of valor and despicable degrees of cravenness.'[1] But more than simply sharing such motives for research in theology and religion, there was a recognition that one of the principal tasks of the study of theology and religion is to transform unjust ideas and practices that marginalize and exclude many people within religious communities and organizations, and in society more widely. Part of this task involves naming and deconstructing the ways that religions can themselves exclude people, how they can contribute to and have shaped unjust ideas and practices in society but, at the same time, recognizing that religions can also be major forces for cultural, social and political change. They have the potential not only to exclude, but to be culturally, socially and politically transformative.

As the concept of this book developed, a number of important issues became clear. First, any book that seeks to address exclusive ideas and practices must recognize its own limitations. It cannot address every area of exclusion, and of those it does address, it cannot hope to transform entirely. It can, however, seek to make a contribution to shaping both thinking and practice in those questions it does seek to address. This collection focuses on a number of groups and communities who experience exclusion, and aims to make a contribution towards the transformation of such exclusion. Secondly, it was agreed that conversation with people outside of the academy was important, in particular with those people who experienced exclusion directly or who worked alongside those who are excluded. As a result, much of what is included in this collection emerges out of fieldwork with excluded individuals, communities and groups. Further, in October 2009, a symposium was organized involving the main contributors to this collection, who presented works in progress to other contributors, academics from other institutions and those working alongside those who experience exclusion. As we shall see

---

[1] Emilie Townes, 'Walking on the Rim Bones of Nothingness: Scholarship and Activism'. *Journal of the American Academy of Religion* 77: 1 (2009), pp. 1–15 (9).

shortly, conversations between chapter authors and other experts, both from the academy and from practice, has been a central feature in the formation of all the chapters contained in the book.

The title of this book, *Transforming Exclusion*, sets out the two main focal points of this text's discussion: 'exclusion', here referring to a process by which particular bodies, experiences and voices are marginalized, abandoned, and even demonized through the promulgation of certain attitudes, beliefs and practices; and 'transformation', here referring to the need not simply to challenge such exclusive behaviours, but to radically reconfigure the dynamics of exclusion altogether. The subtitle of *Engaging Faith Perspectives* reflects the authors' basic conviction that exclusion should not be left unchallenged and that faith demands a constructive response.

The Dynamics of Exclusion

So what more can we say about the meaning of exclusion or the 'dynamics' of exclusion? In *Exclusion & Embrace*, Miroslav Volf argues that exclusion has two interrelated features, both of which transgress against God's activity in creation; the first transgresses against the creative principle of 'binding', and the second against the creative principle of 'separating'.[2] For Volf, creation in Genesis 'exists as an intricate pattern of "separate-and-bound-together" entities'.[3] God separates light from dark and binds humans to the rest of creation as stewards; God separates water from land, sea creatures from land animals, and binds humans together as perfect companions for one another.[4] Both separating and binding operate alongside one another in a process he refers to as 'differentiation'.[5] Sin, then, amounts to the reconfiguration of what God separates and binds together; a manipulation of creation's patterns of interdependence.[6] Within this setting, exclusion takes on two dimensions, either as the inability of human creatures to see themselves as bound to others, where the self is considered sovereign and independent (a transgression against binding), or an inability of human creatures to respect or even recognize difference (a transgression against separating). Whereas with the former, the other becomes an enemy who must be firmly kept away from the self, with the latter the other is consumed so as to become identical to the self. Both are exclusive practices, since the former serves to *eliminate* the other and the latter to *assimilate* the other.[7]

[2] M. Volf, *Exclusion & Embrace. A Theological Exploration of Identity, Otherness, and Reconciliation* (Nashville: Abingdon Press, 1996), pp. 65–7.
[3] Ibid., p. 65.
[4] Ibid.
[5] Ibid., pp. 64–5.
[6] Ibid., p. 66.
[7] Ibid., pp. 74–5.

Both elimination and assimilation are important dynamics of exclusion, and we see them at work in the named examples discussed within this text. They both serve the same goal of stabilizing the identity of the self, either by forcing difference outside the space in which the self operates or by homogenizing the other so there is no outside space. Either way, the unity and stability of the self are kept intact. In both cases, the self is reinforced as normative and the other as threat. Such dynamics may then, for example, reinforce the able body as normative or secure the supremacy of the human animal over the non-human animal, the dominance of the so-called developed world over the developing world. They function on the understanding that whatever disrupts or interferes with the accepted boundaries of our own identities (whether the religious other, the young person, or the fat person) must be controlled. As such, the other is either pushed out of 'our' space (and so seen as weird and freakish or as an imposter, facilitating an 'us' and 'them' mentality) or dissolved into our space (and so made to be the 'same' as me, facilitating a 'we' mentality).[8] In both instances, the integrity of the normative centre is maintained.

The Problem with 'Inclusion'

'Inclusion' is avoided within the title of this book for good reason. Not only does this term raise a number of questions about what this actually means, it also may operate within the interests of exclusion, mimicking the dynamics of exclusion previously addressed. If to include means to bring what is outside or marginal into the centre, then in what sense does this really challenge the legitimacy of that centre? Does it not instead reinforce the power and normative nature of that centre, and in so doing, fail to destabilize or challenge patriarchy, heterosexism, anthropocentrism and colonizing approaches to sustainability, and so on. Indeed, inclusion read this way translates as an acceptance of the other on the grounds that they become like 'us'. We 'accept' disabled persons, for example, but try and ensure they are 'able' to live a 'normal' (that is, able-bodied) life; we embrace the religious other, but only on the grounds that they share similar views to our own. Such a reading of inclusion does not respect or truly affirm difference; instead, it continues to uphold particular features of identity as normative and 'includes' by trying to make that which is different the same. In this sense, the dynamics of inclusion are exposed as the dynamics of assimilation and homogenization.

In addition to this, however, inclusion is problematic because it may promise too much. Although this book's emphasis on 'exclusion' may seem like a negative framing of our discussion, it at least allows us to speak about a set of problematic dynamics which serve to marginalize, assimilate, dominate or eliminate the other, and which are manifest in a number of ways and contexts. Although we are met with an assumption – that someone or a particular group of people are being left out – this is an accurate assumption which is intended. When we speak about

---

[8] Ibid., p. 78.

'inclusion', however, we are immediately met with an assumption that may not be altogether accurate – that no one and no group of people are being left out.

It is true that some liberation theologies have struggled with this difficulty. Latin American liberation theology, for example, although seeking to speak for the poor and downtrodden in Latin America, was exposed as being, in some cases, a heavily academic project, somewhat removed from the lived realities of the poor and the oppressed themselves;[9] feminist theology, in its appeal to women's experience as source and norm, was exposed as assuming such experience to be white and middle class.[10] Although such theologies were intending to challenge exclusive attitudes, beliefs and practices (whether the oppression of the poor or of women) through seeking to include the voices of those who had previously been ignored and abandoned, this very agenda turned out to overlook particular voices and was, in the end, revealed to be exclusive.

Given these difficulties, and because the meaning ascribed to inclusion can be ideologically driven, we have opted to speak about 'exclusion', seeing this as a less dangerous path to tread. What, though, does it mean to 'transform' exclusion, and what might this mean for how we treat the other, whoever that might be?

Transforming Exclusion

It should be clear from what has already been said that we did not intend this book to be a straightforwardly 'academic' text. As well as being accessible to those outside the academy, we were very keen to make sure that the book was not overly theoretical at the expense of engaging with concrete examples of exclusion. We also wanted the chapters to say something not only about the nature of exclusion, but also about how it might be transformed. Such a desire for transformation reflects, in part, the liberationist sensibilities of us as editors and our conviction that the best theology is that which engages meaningfully with the concrete social, political and economic realities of oppression so as to make a difference to these circumstances. Our task was then not to engage with exclusion so as to theorize about it, but to ultimately aim at challenging the oppressive status quo in the various examples we discuss. Our concern was to ask, what does exclusion mean in these various contexts, what are the effects, and how can it be challenged and overturned?

Of course, transforming social attitudes and behaviours, religious beliefs and practices is no easy task! It may seem that a book such as this presents itself as a manual for the transformation of society. If this were so, as has already been discussed, the book would not fulfil its own remit, for such a huge brief is impossible to fulfil through the writing of a text. Although the text is intended to provide practical, helpful insights into how people of faith, as well as those of no faith,

---

[9] Cf. J. Moltmann, 'An Open Letter to José Miguez Bonino', in A. T. Hennelly (ed.), *Liberation Theology: A Documentary History* (Maryknoll: Orbis Books, 1990), p. 198.
[10] See, for example, J. Grant, *White Women's Christ, Black Women's Jesus* (Atlanta: Scholars Press, 1989).

might respond to exclusion, its main focus is to promote change in communities, whether in thought, word or deed. In this sense, the real work of transformation takes place outside the text, not within it.

But what does it actually mean to transform exclusion, and what might this mean for how we treat the other? It is probably important to say, first of all, that transformation does not mean conformity to the accepted boundaries of the centre. It is not about 'including' the other in the centre so they become like me (a process of 'normalization'), so together we can be 'we', but on 'my' terms. It is about uprooting the very logic of exclusion which seeks to eliminate, dominate or assimilate the other, instead allowing alterity (otherness) to thrive. The dynamics of transformation thus, in contradistinction to the dynamics of exclusion, demand that I share space with the other and let the other be in spite of what it might mean for me; that I listen to and value the experiences of the other, and perhaps most importantly, that I recognize my own need for the other. Volf is right when he states that 'The self is dialogically constructed. The other is already from the outset part of the self. I am who I am in relation to the other'.[11] We cannot be our 'selves' without each other. This interdependency, for Volf, is part of the binding and separating dynamics God establishes in creation and which were addressed earlier. However, Volf is clear that because God also separates, togetherness can never be about annihilating difference, but must instead always be about preserving and valuing it.

If then we propose with Volf that the two dominant dynamics of exclusion are one that expels difference from the self and another that reduces difference to be the same as the self, then transformation, put bluntly, must be about living *with* difference. This is not to tolerate difference or to put up with difference, but to actively *welcome* difference and to respect and protect its life. The symbol of 'embrace' suggested by Volf is therefore a helpful one, since it identifies that our approach to the other must always begin with open arms, in full recognition of our need and desire for the other; that we must also wait patiently for the other to respond, not forcing the other to comply; that we must close our arms to gently hold the other so that the host becomes the guest and the guest also the host, but without threatening the integrity of the other; and finally, that we must reopen our arms in order to let the other return to themselves and to ensure I retain my own identity. In essence, this final act symbolizes that 'the alterity of the other may not be neutralized by merging both into an undifferentiated "we"';[12] that although demanding proximity to the other, the practice of embrace and the journey towards the transformation of exclusion does not demand that we become the other. It is this distinction which provides the key to transforming exclusion.

The Structure of This Volume

The fundamental conviction of all the contributors to this volume was that not only should each chapter represent a specific engagement with an area of what is

---

[11] M. Volf, p. 91.
[12] Ibid., p.145.

perceived to be exclusion, but also that each contribution should be the catalyst for further discussion. On the basis of this, it was decided that, in order to facilitate and encourage valuable discourse, each chapter would be tripartite in structure, consisting of

- a main essay
- a short response from an academic or practitioner other than the author of the main essay
- a final concluding comment made by the author of the main essay.

With this in mind, suitably qualified dialogue partners were sought who would provide constructive and critical analysis of each respective contribution. These partners were selected on the grounds that they would advance the conversation, and thereby push the respective debates and conversations forward. Moreover, although very familiar with the subject areas in which they were selected to offer commentary, many of the respondents brought to the table very different perspectives. Thus, what we have is an analysis that attempts to trigger further reaction and thought in order to promote further exchanges of ideas and discussion for the author (and indeed the readership) to deliberate.

Finally, and in furthering the dialogical flavour of this project, each author has the opportunity to reply to points raised by the respondent. What is contained in these pages is the fruit of this immensely helpful set of constructive conversations, which not only provides discussion and debate between dialogue partners, but also provides a platform for further and wider reflection.

It is hoped that this tripartite structure does indeed serve as a stimulus to each respective debate, and that it provides a genuine attempt at fostering and furthering advances in matters of exclusion through the lenses of a variety of perspectives. The expectation is that the wider readership will collaborate and further these conversations, thus extending the dialogical nature of this project and the broader issue of exclusion in contemporary society. In other words, each chapter and its contents is not intended to be the final word on any area addressed, but rather the beginning of the conversations and deliberations.

Chapter One, authored by Steve Knowles, suggests that postmodernism provides religions with 'reasons to be cheerful'. Rather than being seen as an enemy to Christianity, challenging the major claims this religion makes about itself, Steve suggests that postmodernism should be understood as providing a space for multiple practices of various 'Christianity(ies)'. In so doing, the possibility of the coexistence of such multiple practices may challenge exclusive attitudes and practices that have insisted on only one form of Christianity being legitimate. Further, postmodernism provides a space for a greater openness to and engagement with culture that can make the voices and contributions to society of Christianity(ies) make more of a difference and seem more relevant to those outside of the churches.

In Chapter Two, Mohammad Seddon presents a discussion of how developments in regard to the 'other', within theology and religious studies, might contribute to a transformation of attitudes towards relations between Muslims and Christians in multicultural Britain. The 9/11 terrorist atrocities and other subsequent attacks, together with the issue of migration into the West by Muslims, Mohammad reflects, have both had a debilitating affect upon Western perceptions of Muslims and Islam, which has served to intensify the minority status of these communities. Drawing on the development of Western understandings of Muslim identity and post-colonial scholarship, together with analysis of two early Muslim migrations, Mohammad argues for a complete revision of how Islam is framed and understood in the West, and in particular, in contemporary Britain.

From an evangelical protestant perspective, Tom Greggs seeks to influence the preaching of evangelical Christians in relation to the religious other in Chapter Three. To do this, Tom focuses on the specifically Christian doctrine of providence and suggests that a deeper understanding of this doctrine will lead to a greater appreciation of the universality of God's grace. Tom draws upon the work of Karl Barth to assist in this task. Taking the unusual step of having Barth as his interlocutor in relation to matters of the religious other and exclusion, Tom argues, will lead to a far more profound understanding of this doctrine that will serve the church in a world marked by religious divides. Moreover, the realization of the sheer breadth of God's grace will, Tom hopes, go some way in helping to alleviate some of the separationist and exclusivist claims within the evangelical community.

In Chapter Four, Celia Deane-Drummond asks whether the concept of 'sustainable development' has a future. Identifying the notion of sustainable development as a western imposition that assumes economic growth and prioritizes the needs of human creatures over those of the non-human, she asks whether this conflicts with the principle of 'sustainability', which might demand the curtailment of growth in order to secure the future of the planet and its inhabitants. Drawing on the work of Martha Nussbaum and Aquinas, she argues that sustainability needs to be grounded in the principle of solidarity and in an awareness of the interconnected relationships between different peoples, other creatures and the shared resources necessary for flourishing. Of central importance, she suggests, is the need to act in ways which support the common good and flourishing of *all* creatures.

In Chapter Five, David Clough argues that the notion of human equality serves to exclude non-human animals. Critiquing the notion of equality understood as 'equal regard', he draws particular attention to the problem of 'boundary matching'. If based on humanity's capacity to reason, he argues, the notion of equal regard potentially serves to exclude those who do not have this capacity, but who we consider to be human and worthy of being treated with equal regard. If based on humanity's capacity to enter into social contracts, this serves to exclude those who are unable to consent to such contracts. David therefore promotes a theological ethics which is informed by Martha Nussbaum's capabilities approach, and which seeks to affirm all creatures (not just humans) as being worthy of moral consideration. He stresses the need to ground a notion of equal moral regard on the capabilities specific to particular creatures and to therefore act in ways which allow individual creatures to flourish. For David, this is grounded on a theological conviction that all creatures were created by God and that all, therefore, form part of God's good purposes for the created world.

Chapter Six, by Hannah Bacon, examines how the role of Christian theology might have helped perpetuate the negative link between 'femininity' and body size. Dividing the chapter into two halves, Hannah first examines one of the giants of Christian theology, Augustine, and argues that his influence on Christian thought has contributed to a deep theological suspicion toward the human body. Furthermore, drawing on fieldwork carried out in a UK slimming club, Hannah suggests that resonances of such suspicion toward the female body have filtered through to contemporary secular society. In the second part of the chapter, Hannah suggests how we can transform this negative suspicion of the body by arguing for a 'theology of abundance' that is embedded in the Trinitarian and incarnational identity of God.

In Chapter Seven, Wayne Morris considers how an understanding of salvation as 'flourishing' might challenge and transform approaches which present the able body as normative, and consequently stress faith as a prerequisite for salvation. According to Wayne, this kind of theological agenda privileges the able-bodied through its insistence on *confessing* the gospel, *hearing* the word and *intellectually* responding to it. Confirming the able body as the only 'normal' body, such theologies, he maintains, reproduce 'tyrannies of exclusion' by denying the place of disabled people in God's kingdom or by assuming that healing is in some way necessary for salvation. In response, he proposes a universal account of salvation. Through its stress on flourishing, this account identifies that all are entitled to 'life', to be treated with dignity, to experience freedom and inclusion, and to engage with the Spirit in whatever ways are appropriate to them. Rather than constructing the disabled person as 'other', those with disabilities are here affirmed as inherently valuable in their own right.

In Chapters Eight and Nine, Dot Gosling and Richard Turner focus on the experiences of exclusion of young people in churches and society. They use insights from theology and youth work practice to develop attitudes and practices towards young people and the practice of youth work that can contribute not only to altered experiences for young people, but also altered societies and churches. Dot focuses on the issue of the participation of young people in churches, arguing that too often young people are excluded from churches because attitudes, practices and structures work against their full involvement. Drawing on core values from within youth work practice, she argues for a model of participation that would transform churches and the contribution that young people can make to churches. Drawing on case studies from practice, Richard focuses on the importance of reflective practice in youth work, arguing that reflective practice and critical theological reflection on practice by practitioners in churches can lead to a new set of attitudes and practices towards young people.

This book is offered in the hope that it makes a contribution towards the transformation of exclusive practices in those areas it seeks to address.

Hannah Bacon and Wayne Morris with Steve Knowles

Acknowledgements

First of all, the editors would like to express their gratitude to colleagues in the Department of Theology and Religious Studies at the University of Chester. Many of these colleagues have made contributions to this collection, and it is only because of their enthusiasm for – and commitment to – this project that this book has been possible. A number of colleagues contributed to the early stages of this book, and although they did not submit a chapter to the final publication, their involvement in the project has been invaluable. In particular, we would like to thank Dr Fabrizio Ferrari and Dr Eric Christianson. Other colleagues who have been supportive and instrumental in this project include Dr Ruth Ackroyd, Professor Robert Warner and Robert Evans.

The editors would like to thank those who have been willing to be 'respondents' to main essays in this collection. Without them, the conversational structure of this collection would not have been possible, and the book would have lacked the depth of engagement we desired.

In October 2009, we held a symposium at Gladstone's Library in Hawarden, at which a number of external participants to the symposium helped chapter authors to form their ideas. Thank you in particular to Dr Kate Bacon, Dr Jo Carruthers, Carolyn King and Maxine Green, who attended this day and shared their wisdom with us. We would also like to express our gratitude to Gladstone's library for hosting us, and to Nathan Paylor and Emily Pennington, who each made important contributions to the organization of this event.

The editors would like to thank Tom Kraft at T&T Clark for his patience with us as we have sought to finish the editing of this collection and submit it for publication.

Finally, this project was made possible because of a grant from the University of Chester's Research and Knowledge Transfer Office, and for this, the editors are immensely grateful.

List of Contributors

Hannah Bacon is Deputy Head of Theology and Religious Studies at the University of Chester and teaches in the areas of Christian theology and feminist theology. She has published on feminist approaches to the Incarnation and Trinity and is author of *What's Right with the Trinity? Conversations in Feminist Theology* (Ashgate). Her current research focuses on theological approaches to the 'body' and considers the ways in which Christian motifs inform the practices and principles of secular diet programs.

Chris Baker is Director of Research for the William Temple Foundation and is Senior Lecturer in Public and Urban Theology at the University of Chester. He has researched and published extensively on the role and contribution of religion to public life in the UK, including public policy, social welfare, urban regeneration, happiness and well-being, and political economy. His latest book, *Postsecular Cities – space, theory and practice*, will be published by Continuum in 2011.

Susy Brouard works for CAFOD (Catholic Agency for Overseas Development) in the areas of adult education, theology and justice. She is currently studying for a Professional Doctorate in the area of Catholic Social Teaching.

Mahmood Chandia is Senior Lecturer in and Programme Leader of Islamic Studies in the International School for Communities, Rights and Inclusion at the University of Central Lancashire. His research interests include Islamic Manuscripts, Islamic Jurisprudence and Thought, Muslims in Britain, Muslim Studies, Islamic Philosophy and Mental Health Well-being and Islamic Finance.

David Clough is Professor of Theological Ethics at the University of Chester and teaches in the areas of theology and ethics. His current research is on the place of animals in Christian theology and ethics. Earlier publications include works on Christian approaches to war and the ethics of Karl Barth. He is a Methodist Local Preacher and has been part of national ecumenical working groups drafting reports on the ethics of modern warfare and climate change.

Celia Deane-Drummond is Professor in Theology and the Biological Sciences at the University of Chester and is Director of the Centre for Religion and the Biosciences. She is Vice Chair of the European Forum for the Study of Religion and Environment. Her more recent relevant books include *The Ethics of Nature* (Blackwell); *Ecotheology* (DLT); *Christ and Evolution* (SCM Press); *Creaturely Theology: On God, Humans and Other Animals*, edited with David Clough (SCM Press); *Seeds of Hope: Facing the Challenge of Climate Justice* (CAFOD); and *Religion and Ecology in the Public Sphere*, edited with Heinrich Bedford-Strohm (Continuum).

Dot Gosling is Senior Lecturer in Christian Youth Work at the University of Chester. She is currently working towards a Doctorate at the University of Birmingham on the participation of young people in churches. She is also an ordained minister in the Church of England and a qualified Youth Worker.

Elaine Graham is Grosvenor Research Professor of Practical Theology at the University of Chester. Her publications include *Making the Difference: Gender, Personhood and Theology* and *Transforming Practice: Pastoral Theology in an Age of Uncertainty, Representations of the Post/Human, Words Made Flesh* and (with H. Walton and F. Ward) *Theological Reflection: Methods.* Throughout her career, she has maintained an interest in the relationship between theology and social issues, including work on gender, technology and urban life and faith. She is currently working on a book on public theology in a 'post-secular' society.

Maxine Greene is a former national youth officer for the Church of England and has published widely. Among her publications are: (with David Green) *Taking A Part: Young People's Participation in the Church* (Church House Publishing) and (with Chandu Christian) *Accompanying: Young People on their Spiritual Quest* (Church House Publishing).

Tom Greggs is Professor of Systematic Theology at the University of Chester and teaches and researches broadly in the area of Christian Doctrine. He is the author of *Barth, Origen, and Universal Salvation* (with OUP) and *Theology against Religion* (forthcoming with T&T Clark), and is the editor of *New Perspectives for Evangelical Theology* (with Routledge). Tom is secretary of the Society for the Study of Theology, and co-chair of Scriptural Reasoning at the American Academy of Religion. He is actively engaged in interfaith work between Muslims, Jews and Christians.

C. T. R. Hewer is Fellow in Christian–Muslim Relations at St. Ethelburga's Centre for Reconciliation and Peace. He is author of *Understanding Islam* (SCM Press).

Lisa Isherwood is Professor and Director of Theological Partnerships at the University of Winchester. She is a liberation theologian and has published widely in her distinguished career. Among her many important publications are: *The Fat Jesus: Explorations in Boundaries and Transgressions* (Darton, Longman and Todd) and *The Power of Erotic Celibacy* (T&T Clark). Professor Isherwood is an Executive Editor and founding editor of the international journal *Feminist Theology* and serves on the editorial board of the *Journal of Feminist Studies in Religion*. From 2007–2009 she was Vice President of the European Society of Women in Theological Research and is co-founder (1990) and Director of the Britain and Ireland School of Feminist Theology. She is on the theological consultancy board for Caritas and is a board member of the Animal Ethics Centre in Oxford.

Steve Knowles is Lecturer in Theology at the University of Chester and teaches in the area of theology and philosophy of religion. His current research interests include examining the interface between religion and popular culture, with a more specific interest in spirituality and popular music. He is the author of *Beyond Evangelicalism: The Theological Methodology of Stanley J. Grenz* (Ashgate).

Wayne Morris is Deputy Head of Theology and Religious Studies at the University of Chester and Senior Lecturer in Contextual and Practical Theology. His major publications include *Theology Without Words: Theology in the Deaf Community* (Ashgate) and (with Roy McCloughry) *Making a World of Difference: Christian Reflections on Disability* (SPCK). He continues to work on theological questions and the experience of living with disability, and is also currently working on developing a practical theology of salvation in light of the experience of living in a multi-faith world.

John Richardson has worked with young people in both voluntary and statutory youth settings since 1974. In 1980, after qualifying as a youth and community worker in Yorkshire, John worked for a number of years in an Afro-Caribbean centre in Bradford and various youth projects in and around Leeds. He has lectured in social policy and sociology at Ilkley College and taught youth and community work at St Martin's college (now the University of Cumbria). From 1994–1997 he developed the work of the Foxton centre in Preston and successfully bid for substantial lottery funding for the centre and the local community. John now works as a parish priest, youth worker and chaplain to Preston College. Having published a number of articles around youth and social work for both national and international audiences, John's academic interests are centred around the theory and practice of 'helping relationships in a globalised world' in youth, social and community work.

Mohammad S. Seddon obtained his PhD in Religious Studies at the University of Lancaster and is currently Director of the Centre for Applied Muslim Youth and Community Studies (CAMYCS), Lecturer in Muslim Studies and Honorary Research Fellow at the Department of Theology and Religious Studies, University of Chester. He is a former Research Fellow at the Islamic Foundation, Leicester, and is an Executive Member of the Association of Muslim Social Scientists (UK). His research interests are historical and contemporary issues relating to Islam and British Muslim communities. He has published a number of related works and books including, *British Muslims: Loyalty and Belonging, British Muslims Between Assimilation and Segregation: Historical, Legal & Social Realities*, and *The Illustrated Encyclopaedia of Islam*.

Richard Turner is Senior Lecturer on the JNC Christian Youth Work programme at the University of Chester. He worked as a Youth Advisor in London from 1984–1988 and for 14 years as a Youth Officer for Liverpool Diocese. In 2001, Richard was seconded to the University of Chester to help establish the JNC Christian Youth Work programme and returned as programme leader in 2002. He has experience working with young people from a variety of life experiences; training at local, regional and national levels; supporting and supervising full-time and volunteer youth workers; organizing youth events and international exchanges; and establishing numerous youth work projects.

1 Postmodernism: Reasons to be Cheerful!

Steve Knowles

The term postmodernity is variously used to describe the differing strands, themes and ideas, not all interrelated, that have developed as a form of critique and reaction to modernity. It is a description for the *zeitgeist*. Such reaction has been stimulated, in general terms, by a loss of faith in the progressivist and speculative discourses characteristic of the Enlightenment programme. This stultifying legacy (according to most postmodern theorists),[1] with its emphasis on the authoritarian nature of reason, and inflexible, fixed and totalizing agenda, is giving way to ideas from the postmodern vantage point which, in contrast, include fragmentation, diversity, instability, ephemerality, otherness and discontinuity.

To attempt, with any precision, a definition of postmodernism is notoriously difficult. David Harvey notes, 'No one exactly agrees as to what is meant by the term, except, perhaps, that "postmodernism" represents some kind of reaction to, or departure from, "modernism".[2] Indeed, arguably, the attempt to define it is antithetical to that which is deemed postmodern. There are two main reasons for this. First, it is due in part to the ambiguous nature of the term. Does it refer to a break with modernity (Foucault)? Does it show a continuous link with modernity (Lyotard)? Perhaps it refers to a stage within a degenerative modernity (Habermas)? Or does the prefix 'post' simply question the influence of modernity as we know it (Lyon)? The whole situation is made even more difficult when one considers that there is a certain amount of confusion as to what modernity itself

---

[1] Laurence Cahoone notes, 'Philosophical opinion regarding the postmodern family is deeply divided. For some, postmodernism connotes the final escape from the stultifying legacy of modern European theology, metaphysics, authoritarianism, colonialism, patriarchy, racism and domination. To others it represents the attempt by disgruntled left-wing intellectuals to destroy Western civilization.' See *From Modernism to Postmodernism: An Anthology* (Oxford: Blackwell, 2003), p. 1.
[2] D. Harvey, *The Condition of Postmodernity* (Oxford: Blackwell, 1989), p. 7.

actually refers to.[3] Furthermore, it is important to remember that postmodernity cannot be explained as if it was one process, state or attitude. It is not. Many postmodern thinkers would reject the idea because, for them, no one thing or idea is monolithic. All is open to further fragmentation and interpretation.

With the above in mind, it will come as no surprise that many ideas associated with the postmodern turn have been interpreted in a variety of ways. Moreover, postmodernism has been understood by many to be a direct threat to the Christian religion. In this chapter, two specific areas will be explored. First, I will examine one trait of postmodern thought that has become something of a slogan for the postmodern intellectual ferment and centres upon the so-called demise of the metanarrative. The demise of the metanarrative is seen by many theologians to constitute a complete undermining of the biblical story. I will argue that this is not as clear cut as many believe, due to the ambiguous nature of the term. I will suggest that a fresh reading of Jean-François Lyotard, the key thinker in regard to metanarratives, shows that Christianity and postmodernism are not as incompatible as some would argue. There is, I conclude, a case for arguing that Christianity does not constitute a metanarrative. This will help in alleviating a sense of exclusion from dialogue within the postmodern climate. Secondly, and on a more practical note, I will analyse the concept of the decentred self, which will in turn provide a link to the concept of community and its importance in postmodern times. The purpose of this is (a) to demonstrate that postmodernism is not the bane of Christian faith (or religion in general), as has been reported by some theologians; and (b) to propose that 'doing' theology at a local level will help in alleviating the spectre of exclusion by incorporating certain postmodern ideas.

The Demise of the Metanarrative

In 1979, the French philosopher Jean-François Lyotard published a slim volume, entitled *The Postmodern Condition: A Report on Knowledge*. The substance of this volume was to report on the current state of knowledge in the most advanced societies. The significance of his work is his insistence that we have a crisis of narratives which, indeed, defines the postmodern situation. In particular, Lyotard sought a break with any narrative of science. Lyotard suggests that science is not satisfied simply with seeking the truth; rather it is compelled to legitimize itself by its own narrative. He succinctly defines postmodern in the following way: 'Simplifying to the extreme, I define *postmodern* as incredulity toward metanarratives.'[4] This statement sets the tone for Lyotard's critical analysis of what he understands to be the biggest difficulty with the modernist world view. Primarily, Lyotard has in mind

---

[3] See H. Bertens, *The Idea of the Postmodern* (London: Routledge, 1996), for a good introduction to this issue.

[4] J. F. Lyotard, *The Postmodern Condition: A Report on Knowledge*, trans. G. Bennington & B. Massumi (Manchester: Manchester University Press, 1997), p. xxiv.

Enlightenment thought that, in simplistic terms, constitutes the idea that science acts as the great emancipator of humanity, because of its ability to legitimize itself through the discovery of knowledge. Gary Browning observes that 'Lyotard picks out science and the justification of scientific knowledge as emblematic of a legit-imating absolutist *modern* self-image.'[5] Lyotard uses 'the term *modern* to designate any science that legitimates itself with reference to a metadiscourse . . . making explicit appeal to some grand narrative, such as dialectics of Spirit, the hermen-eutics of meaning, the emancipation of the rational or working subject, or the creation of wealth.'[6] Here we have Lyotard citing what can be described as quintes-sential modern metanarratives. They are the Hegelian idea of the Absolute Self, the Marxist hope for the future, and Adam Smith's notion of wealth creation which has developed into a capitalist narrative of liberation from poverty via, among other things, techno-industrial development. The crux of the problem, for Lyotard, lies in the legitimation of such knowledge. For Lyotard, the two key types of metanar-rative that he singles out for treatment in *The Postmodern Condition* are that of the 'speculative' variety and the metanarrative of 'emancipation'. A brief examination of what Lyotard says about these two paradigm examples will now be undertaken.

The central motif of the speculative metanarrative that Lyotard notes can be found in the thought of Hegel. Lyotard notes how Hegel's project of totalization is an example of a rational (meta)narrative that attempted to link the sciences and progress towards becoming 'spirit', thus resulting in a metanarration of a uni-versal history of spirit, 'spirit is "life", and "life" is its own self-presentation and formulation in the ordered knowledge of all its forms contained in the empirical sciences'.[7] In a nutshell, for Hegel (as understood by Lyotard), humanity makes progress through the increase of knowledge. This knowledge then finds legitimacy within itself, with the ramification that knowledge then dictates to society. All claims to knowledge are collected under the umbrella of this metanarrative and, depending on how they correspond to it, will be judged accordingly. It is this holis-tic approach to knowledge and how knowledge itself conforms to such a specu-lative metanarrative that determines its legitimacy. According to Lyotard, 'True knowledge, in this perspective, is always indirect knowledge; it is composed of reported statements that are incorporated into the metanarrative of a subject that guarantees their legitimacy'.[8] Because the status of knowledge is now so unbal-anced and fragmented, with the result that legitimacy itself is under question, the speculative metanarrative has broken down.

The other metanarrative to be scrutinized is that of emancipation. It is a narra-tive that has 'humanity as the hero of liberty. All people have a right to science'.[9]

[5] G. Browning, *Lyotard and the End of Grand Narratives* (Cardiff: University of Wales, 2000), p. 27.
[6] Lyotard, *The Postmodern Condition: A Report on Knowledge*, p. xxiii.
[7] Ibid., p. 34.
[8] Ibid., p. 35.
[9] Ibid., p. 31.

It is the educational policies of the French republic that kick-started such an out-look. After the French Revolution, the ideal was to enable the masses to partake in education: education for the masses, instead of just the dominant and privileged few. This type of emancipatory narrative that found liberation through education became vital for the Marxist narrative. Instead of the self-legitimation of know-ledge found in the progression of the empirical sciences, there is the hope of lib-eration (emancipation) of the proletariat through revolution. Legitimacy is found from within the people.

These two examples of narratives (myths), both speculative and emancipatory, are what Lyotard considers to be the major paradigm examples of metanarratives which have lost credibility in the current postmodern climate. Moreover, the pro-liferation of disciplines within the sciences illustrates that unity can no longer be assumed in an overarching scientific narrative, which means overall authority is no longer possible. Scientists are therefore forced, within their own respective communities, to assert their own disciplinary boundaries. This has the knock-on effect of demolishing appeals to a central legitimating authority. Science no longer has the ability to liberate humanity by means of absolute knowledge.

It is, however, for Lyotard, these two metanarratives of speculation and eman-cipation that give legitimation to others. As a consequence, the meaning of such narratives is in line with reference to the dominant metanarrative, and they receive their legitimation in relation to how far they are compatible with them. These smaller narratives are integrated through the progress of science and knowledge into the unified historical setting in which the grand narratives gener-ate. Moreover, delegitimation is underway. The explosion of technologies since the Second World War has, for Lyotard, shifted the emphasis 'from the ends of action to its means',[10] from a future hope of the betterment of society to dealing with the here and now.

I think it is clear from analysis thus far that Lyotard's aversion to metanarra-tives is not based specifically on their actual scope – how big a story – but on the nature of their claims; where their legitimation has its roots. What is clear from the main metanarrative examples that Lyotard cites is that he clearly has in mind those that are a product of modernity (one could be more specific and suggest the Enlightenment). They are those narratives that find their legitimation in their 'appeal to the universality of reason'.[11]

It is important to note from the outset that in *The Postmodern Condition*, Lyotard does not explicitly mention Christianity as a metanarrative. I have highlighted above the main targets that Lyotard has in mind. In the words of David Lyon,

[10] Lyotard, *The Postmodern Condition*, p. 37.
[11] Ibid., p. 96. In an illuminating paper, Justin Thacker argues that here Lyotard is not talk-ing about metanarratives. This is technically true, in that the actual word 'metanarrative' is not mentioned. However, a cursory reading of the short extract in which this passage is sit-uated clearly indicates that he is. See Thacker's, 'Lyotard and the Christian Metanarrative: A Rejoinder to Smith and Westphal', in *Faith and Philosophy* 22:3 (2005) pp. 301–15.

'Lyotard's book plunges right into the fate of Enlightenment thought in an age of globalized high technology.'[12] For sure, the Christian story is as big a story as they come. However, when the term 'meta' is used in philosophical discourse, it refers to a difference of level, rather than purely the size, of that discourse. This is a valuable point that the Christian philosopher Merold Westphal makes. Westphal argues that Christianity is a *mega*narrative, rather than a metanarrative. Furthermore, he categorically claims that Christianity is not a metanarrative.[13] This conclusion is based upon three points that are designed to simultaneously describe what a metanarrative is and highlight why Christianity does not qualify as such. The first two are straightforward interpretations of Lyotard's own understanding and have already been referred to above. That is that 'meta' is not a description of size, but of level of discourse, and secondly, that metanarratives are narratives that find their legitimation in some sort of overarching universal reason. Westphal argues that Christianity fits with neither of these. The third point, however, could be construed to be more contentious. Westphal writes, the 'difference between the Christian story and modernity's metanarratives concerns origins. The former has its origin in revelation, not in philosophy, and most especially modern philosophy, grounded in the autonomy of the human subject.'[14] What Westphal is deliberately trying to do is separate the Christian story (narrative), through examination of its origins, from the two types of metanarrative that Lyotard majors upon, as explicated above. That is to say, contrary to the narratives of emancipation and speculation that are a direct result of the Enlightenment, the Christian story has its genesis in an authority outside of humanity. The main problem with this idea is that Lyotard, elsewhere, suggests that metanarratives find their legitimacy not in their origin, but in their aims or *telos*. In a collection of letters written by Lyotard and published in English in 1988, entitled *The Postmodern Explained*,[15] he writes that metanarratives 'look for legitimacy, not in an original founding act, but in a future to be accomplished, that is, in an Idea to be realized'.[16] In other words, rather than the important issue being the origin, as Westphal claims, in Lyotard's view it is the future aim or promise of a narrative that makes it as such. On this basis, I think Westphal's argument appears to be flawed. That said, although the future is, of course, an important issue for Christianity, and much theology done today is echatologically orientated, origins are equally important.

This does not help Westphal's case at this point. I would, however, defend Westphal's basic claim regarding revelation by suggesting that this element is

---

[12] D. Lyon, *Postmodernity*, 2nd edn (Buckingham: Open University Press, 1999), p. 16.

[13] M. Westphal, *Overcoming Onto-Theology: Toward a Postmodern Christian Faith* (New York: Fordham University Press, 2001), p. xiii.

[14] Ibid., p. xiv–xv.

[15] The original title of this collection is *Le Postmoderne Expliqué aux Enfants* (The Postmodern Explained to Children).

[16] Lyotard, *The Postmodern Explained: Correspondence 1982–1985*, trans. D. Barry, B. Maher, J. Prefanis, V. Spate and M. Thomas (Minneapolis: University of Minnesota Press, 1993), p. 18.

purely of God's own doing. Revelation, by definition, is God breaking into the world and making himself known. Justin Thacker argues that Lyotard's premise is that we are linguistically conditioned, in our own cultural bubbles, unable to step out of our context to grasp reality or revelation.[17] This may be the case, but it is God that breaks into our cultural context – the cultural bubble, not vice versa. Revelation, in turn, is grasped through faith. This turns the epistemological tables somewhat. Instead of conforming to the pattern of metanarrative delineated above, the Christian story does not resort to any of the authorities of modernity. Gone are the self-legitimating bastions of knowledge that were synonymous with modernism. Instead, there is an appeal by faith to a God who breaks into our world and who delegitimizes the metanarratives of humanity.

Westphal goes on to claim that Christianity is not Lyotard's target.[18] From an examination of *The Postmodern Condition*, this appears to be true. One only has to scan the index to see that there is no reference to it, nor, for that matter, the word religion. The focus of this work is an attack on the metanarratives of modernity. However, Lyotard does specifically list Christianity in the later publication, *The Postmodern Explained*. He writes, 'The "metanarratives" I was concerned with in *The Postmodern Condition* are those that have marked modernity'.[19] Referring to the usual metanarrative suspects (as cited above), Lyotard interposes his list by suggesting Christianity as a fourth possible example, adding, 'and even – if we include Christianity itself in modernity (in opposition to the classicism of antiquity) – the salvation of creatures through the conversion of souls to the Christian narrative of martyred love'.[20] The list then continues with a description of Hegel. Now, certainly, very few will want to disagree with the very brief statement that Lyotard interjects regarding Christianity. There are, however, two points to make regarding this statement. First, the 'if' that Lyotard uses to start his conclusion concerning the inclusion of Christianity, I think, shows that Christianity is not regarded by Lyotard to be of great importance in the so-called order of metanarrative merit, especially in light of the fact that he makes no mention of it in *The Postmodern Condition*. Moreover, the version of Christianity that he talks about is 'Christianity in modernity itself'. The term 'modernity' has proved to be a rather protean concept. In the context that Lyotard describes, the current intellectual climate (postmodern), one would assume that he is referring to the modernity found in the form of the European Enlightenment of the eighteenth century, the influential fragments of which can still be seen today. If this is so, then Lyotard's Christianity is but a narrow expression of that which has existed for nearly 2,000 years. Even allowing for a broader understanding of modernity (from Descartes to the mid-twentieth century) would still mean a relatively limited understanding of the Christian faith. I think that the Christianity Lyotard

[17] Thacker, p. 306.
[18] Westphal, *Overcoming Onto-Theology*, p. xv.
[19] Lyotard, *The Postmodern Explained*, p. 17.
[20] Ibid., p. 18.

presents us with is far too narrow. What he refers to is a version of Christianity that attempted to rationalize the faith; a Christianity born of the Enlightenment and shackled to Enlightenment principles. It is based upon a theology that flirted with commonsense philosophy and which became inebriated with the progress of science and rationalism. Even the liberal theology pioneered by Schleiermacher and influenced as it was by Romanticism, itself a reaction to the Enlightenment, can be traced to a core universal religious experience.[21] This appeal to an inner universal religious feeling betrays the influence of the Enlightenment.

Thus, I would argue that Lyotard targets Christianity indirectly: as an afterthought. It is not on his initial 'hit list' of metanarratives as expounded upon in *The Postmodern Condition*. Indeed, it is quite a way down the pecking order.[22] The form of Christianity that Lyotard eventually includes is the 'modern version'. Given the context of Lyotard's work in *The Postmodern Condition*, where he is defining a range of factors that have culminated in an intellectual reaction termed broadly and ambiguously as postmodern – a reaction to the modern – it would seem reasonable that a modern version of Christianity would fall under the rubric of his criticism.

This now begs the question, does this then mean that Christianity per se has to be tarred with the same metanarrative brush? The answer has to be no. Of course, there are many examples that fall into the metanarrative trap from the modern period, including much Protestant theology, both liberal and conservative. However, much Christian theology, since the demise of the modern period, has moved on, with a variety of imaginative and engaging approaches to doing theology in a postmodern era. Non-foundationalist routes have been taken that understand the Christian traditions within communitarian terms.[23] More emphasis has been put on the experiential, rather than the rational, elements of faith and religion, which fits well with the widespread upsurge in spiritual interests.

That said, there is one issue which we still need to deal with, and this concerns that idea that a metanarrative is deemed as such if it has some sort of 'future hope'. In other words, returning to the seemingly flawed point Westphal made, it is not what constitutes a story's origin that makes it a metanarrative, it is its *telos*. Moreover, if this is indeed the case, does that mean that the postmodern condition is a hopeless condition? Is it a condition that by definition must be hopeless? Without any sort of recourse to the grand narratives which have lost all credibility, how do we now navigate the perils inherent in a constantly fragmenting postmodern world? Lyotard offers his readers a glimpse of hope. In chapter 13 of *The Postmodern Condition*, entitled 'Legitimation by Paralogy', Lyotard attempts to clear a way

---

[21] See George Lindbeck's penetrating critique of both the cognitive and experiential understanding of religious faith, in *The Nature of Doctrine* (London: SPCK, 1984).

[22] This is contrary to Thacker's understanding, in which he positions Christianity as one of Lyotard's main targets.

[23] See, for example, S. J. Grenz & J. Franke, *Beyond Foundationalism: Shaping Theology in a Postmodern Context* (Louisville: Westminster John Knox Press, 2001).

forward through the debris of the defunct metanarratives. After some discussion, he concludes that we cannot rely on the principle of consensus, because it is inadequate and falls back on the metanarrative of emancipation.[24] Consensus can never be reached. 'Consensus has become an outmoded and suspect value. But justice as a value is neither outmoded nor suspect. We must thus arrive at an idea and practice of justice that is not linked to that of consensus.'[25] This contradictory statement reveals a possible way through this complex situation.[26] Instead of metanarratives, we now have little narratives (language games) which are heteromorphous in nature.[27] Having a multiplicity of language games will, as a consequence, result in 'a multiplicity of finite arguments'[28] which will operate as temporary contracts. Lyotard closes with the words that 'this sketches the outline of a politics that would respect both the desire for justice and the desire for the unknown'.[29]

I suggest that the Christian hope would follow a somewhat similar line that Lyotard alludes to here. In the first place, I would reiterate the idea that most narratives would have some sort of hope that is contingent upon them having a purpose for existing in the first place. This is confirmed with Lyotard's desire (hope) to appeal to justice. The appeal to justice is particularly pertinent, as one of the primary concerns that many Christians have is a desire to see justice done and injustice overturned. Many theologies have developed out of the need for justice according to their own context. This is most apparent in the plethora of liberation theologies that have developed over the last 40 years. These theologies have grown as a reaction to the context in which Christian communities have found themselves. A second point concerns 'the desire for the unknown'. Christian theology is a theology of hope. Despite the myriad of eschatological studies over the centuries, there is still a plethora of hypothetical conclusions as to what form the *eschaton* will take; what Lyotard might call 'a multitude of finite arguments'. The pluriform situation in eschatological studies is due to the limitations that a finite humanity intrinsically possesses. It also serves to bring to the fore the plurality of communities, who adopt different viewpoints and approaches to doing theology as they respond to the demands of their situation. To put it succinctly, the Christian hope has an element of the unknown to it. Furthermore, there are as many different viewpoints on eschatology as there are theologians, which highlights a lack of consensus. This lack of consensus, although not to be defined as paralogy as such, is a good example of how a postmodern Christianity can function in light of Lyotard's concerns. This sort of model can be used to good effect in a postmodern

[24] Lyotard, *The Postmodern Condition*, p. 60.
[25] Ibid., p. 66.
[26] It seems to me to be contradictory, because Lyotard is suggesting that we can have an idea of justice that can be applied across the multitude of language games, which, I suggest, presupposes some sort of universality, or indeed constitutes a metanarrative.
[27] Lyotard is indebted to the philosopher Ludwig Wittgenstein for his idea on language games. See Wittgenstein's *Philosophical Investigations* (Oxford: Blackwell, 2001).
[28] Lyotard, *The Postmodern Condition*, p. 66.
[29] Ibid., p. 67.

approach to Christian theology and is already underway. Moreover, it would not be a Christianity shackled to Enlightenment ideas.

In summary, thus far, it has been argued that in light of the demise of metanarratives, which, according to Lyotard, defines the postmodern condition, only a narrow understanding of Christianity need be included. This is a Christianity informed by and influenced by the Enlightenment. This means that room exists for the practice of postmodern Christianity(ies), with the welcome reminder that those who belong to the plethora of communities that are labelled Christian are finite. All knowledge is to be held lightly and understood as temporary.

In the meantime, what difference does it make for the Christian faith in the postmodern climate if it is no longer considered to be a metanarrative in Lyotard's understanding of the term in *The Postmodern Condition*? It is simply not enough to state this and then do nothing. First and foremost, this approach assists in disarming secular and theological commentators who understand Christianity to be a metanarrative and, as a consequence, argue that this leads to scepticism towards the status of the Christian faith. This position is now tenuous. A reason some theologians attempt to dismiss postmodernism is directly connected to their understanding of metanarrative. Because the biblical story is an all-encompassing story, from the dawn of creation to the hallelujah chorus, they presume that it must be a metanarrative, simply because of size. Furthermore, because the concept of universal truth is seen to be at stake, their position becomes entrenched.

A good example of this can be found in the writing of the American scholar Douglas Groothuis. As well as suggesting that postmodernism equates to nihilism, he argues that, 'Truth decay is a cultural condition in which the very idea of absolute, objective, and universal truth is considered implausible, held in open contempt, or not even considered seriously.'[30] Postmodern thinkers, generally, do not deny the possibility of truth or that we can know anything objectively. What many postmodern thinkers actually object to is that we can know with any degree of certainty what truth is. Groothuis has simply taken a caricature of what he understands postmodernism to refer to and attached as many negative connotations (influenced by Enlightenment principles) as he can muster. This type of scaremongering does little to inform readers of the merits of postmodernism. However, it is easy to see how, from the demise of metanarratives, one can draw conclusions as to how this in turn jeopardizes the idea of truth. Contrary to Groothuis's claim that postmodernism ultimately leads to truth not being taken seriously, quite the reverse is true. Postmodern theorists take the question of truth seriously enough to go back to the drawing board and re-examine what truth can mean. Importantly, the reality that progress has been halted (in the Enlightenment sense) brings sharply into focus that what we claim to know should be held lightly. Humans are finite beings. Lyotard and company offer a timely reminder as to the

---

[30] See D. Groothuis, *Truth Decay: Defending Christianity against the Challenges of Postmodernism* (Downers Grove: IVP, 2000), p. 22.

temporariness of our claims and, with the aid of some pertinent reasoning, guide us away from the charade that was liberation through knowledge.

The rise of postmodern attitudes and, in particular, the demise of metanarratives, in theory, gives the Christian faith a level playing field upon which to dialogue with other narratives. Simply put, every community has a valid voice. This is something that another French philosopher, Michael Foucault, also sought in his critique of metanarratives. Foucault fought against what he considered to be the oppression of metanarratives. Metanarratives silence and suppress the voice of the minority through various forms of repression. Foucault was particularly interested in the relationship between that of knowledge and power. He argued that the obsession with first principles in Western society had led to a 'will to knowledge' that put the vested interests of either the Institute or the State as the motive for articulating discourse (the influence of Neitzsche is evident here). For Foucault, the appeal to objective truth was simply untenable, because it was intrinsically linked to this 'will to knowledge' relationship, which in the end is a fallacy that only produces so-called versions of the truth. One of the strengths of postmodern theory has been to allow space for the disenfranchised, the oppressed, those who are regarded as a minority and whose ability to be heard has been removed.[31] The postmodern condition gives a real hope for a remedy(ies) to this situation(s).

With this in view, it must always be borne in mind that there are two sides to the same coin, which must be acknowledged. First, equality is not unilateral. Tolerance is of paramount importance, not only in terms of having one's own voice heard, but also in terms of allowing a diverse range of opinions the space to be heard. The realization that we inhabit a postmodern world which champions diversity should be heralded as a good thing from a Christian perspective. That said, it should be noted, although there is not the space to say more here, that a repercussion of allowing a plurality of voices to be heard has resulted in some communities tightening their boundaries. Thus, there has been a rise in fundamentalisms. David Lyon comments, 'the choice overload from consumerism (with its slack of guidelines and reference points), and unease with trivialization of choice – offer a chance of retrenchment and trust in new authority figures, absolute truths, and fixed certainties.'[32]

Our attention will now turn to the importance of the emergence of community in a postmodern climate.

The Decentring of the Self and the Importance of Community in a Postmodern Context

The nineteenth century was a time that produced a vast amount of optimism in the belief of progress. Reason and observation could be utilized to full effect and

[31] See, for example, M. Foucault's, *Discipline and Punish: The Birth of the Prison* trans. Alan Sheridan (London: Penguin, 1991).
[32] D. Lyon, *Jesus in Disneyland* (Cambridge: Polity Press, 2000), p. 50.

assist in the power to self-improve, which seemed to be endless. Humanity had risen above superstition and ignorance. As a result, such optimism paved the way in presenting the self as autonomous. The grand narrative of modernism had seemed to have mapped out the destiny of humanity. Human beings were self-reliant, independent and thoroughly rational (so the Enlightenment myth would have us believe). However, this anthropological assuredness has been undermined and exposed as the sham it is. The hegemony of modernity has collapsed. Kenneth Gergen notes that 'both the romantic and the modern beliefs about the self are falling into disuse, and the social arrangements that they support are eroding. This is largely a result of the forces of social saturation.'[33] As a consequence, new ways of expressing the concept of the self have developed, with some more extreme than others. The trust and security that was present with the modern self has been replaced with a decentred and destabilized self. The new self faces a plethora of choices in life. Indeed, some argue that we are left in a permanent flux of relativity as a direct result.[34] In many cases, (though not all), postmodern anthropology seems to go to the other extreme. Instead of certainty and purpose, there is now play; for determinacy, there is indeterminacy. The postmodern self is not anchored to anything. It is a self that floats upon the waters of postmodern currents like a piece of driftwood, tossed about by the latest cultural whims, fads and fascinations.

The glut of choices now available is a direct consequence of the consumerist culture that manipulates almost every aspect of western society. Zigmunt Bauman succinctly posits that, 'consumer conduct moves steadily into position of, simultaneously, the cognitive and moral focus of life'.[35] Promoted and supplemented by new technologies and the media, consumerism affects who we are, how we perceive others and what we deem important. The upshot is that the modern frameworks that guided and limited how life was practiced are replaced by a free-flowing consumerist approach, where, like the disposable supermarket carrier bag, frameworks are temporary and last for as long as the consumer sees fit. If a framework shows signs of wear and tear, it can be modified (or postmodified!).

The significance of this is that values and beliefs are, in turn, being commodified.[36] Religion is not immune to such sociological factors. The proliferation of the New Age movements is, in part, a result of the postmodern pick and mix, consumerist approach to life. The benefit of this is that the consumer can simply adapt elements of spirituality/religion that suit their own current needs. This often results in an eclectic mix of elements from mainstream religion that is often coupled to interests in what has previously been seen to be fringe spiritualities. Here I refer to alternative spiritualities whose many ingredients include eastern

[33] K. Gergen, *The Saturated Self: Dilemmas of Identity in Contemporary Life* (New York: Basic Books, 1991), p. 6.
[34] D. Lyon, *Postmodernity*, 2nd edn (Buckingham: Open University press, 1999), p. 28.
[35] Z. Bauman, *Imitations of Postmodernity*, p. 49.
[36] See B. Smart, *Postmodernity* (London: Routledge, 1993).

mysticism, paganism and even elements of the occult. This illustrates that, in contrast to what some commentators believe, Western society is not undergoing a radical secularization, but quite the reverse. What we are witnessing can be called a re-enchantment of the Western world.[37] We will return to this shortly.

What is ironic about this decentring of the self is that, in some cases, it has led to a repackaged, autonomous self. The so-called free choices available to the postmodern consumer cannot mean what they imply. Every choice that is made rules out a host of other alternatives. With this in mind, a communitarian turn has emerged as being a viable route through the intellectual malaise.

Culturally, the last 40 years or so have proved to be tumultuous times. The way we understand ourselves, others and the world in which we live has undergone radical revision. Postmodern theories have helped us become more aware than ever before that our approaches to life, the decisions we make, the relationships we form are shaped by the context in which we are situated. We have become aware that there are a multitude of ways of being-in-the-world. Indeed, in contrast to Enlightenment reasoning, we cannot comprehend the 'world as it is', because of our cultural baggage. We cannot step outside of our social/cultural bubble to have an objective view of reality. Indeed, everything we do is in some sense contextual. Here, I argue, the importance of community is key to this discussion.

There is a certain degree of ambiguity to the concept of community, and this has been increased with the proliferation of so-called cyber communities and the advent of new media. For our purposes, 'a communitarian perspective recognizes both individual human dignity and the social dimension of human existence'.[38] Moreover, community 'is a group of people who are socially independent, who participate together in discussion and decision making, and who share certain *practices* . . . that both define the community and are nurtured by it'.[39] Coupled with an awareness that knowledge is socially situated, underlines the notion that the world is experienced through particular communal spectacles. Communities implement specific linguistic and symbolic materials to aid in constructing and describing the world in which they are situated. This understanding sits well in a postmodern climate in which the dismantling of universalist ideas has been replaced by local narratives that tell local stories that are specific to the local community who share and develop them. Moreover, it serves to counteract the extremities of the decentring of the (postmodern) self.

An important voice in the explication of how communities are formed and develop is Alister MacIntyre. Although some of his analysis in this area is nearly 30 years old, it is still highly pertinent in today's context. MacIntyre argues that humans are essentially story-telling beings. In place of the universal rationality, we

[37] See C. Partridge, *The Re-Enchantment of the West*, vol. 1 (London: T&T Clark, 2004).

[38] A. Etzioni (ed.), *The Essential Communitarian Reader* (Maryland: Rowman & Littlefield, 1998), p. xxv.

[39] R. Bellah et al., *Habits of the Heart: Individualism and Commitment in American Life*, 3rd edn (Berkeley: University of California Press, 2008), p. 333.

now have tradition-mediated rationalities, which nullify the individual rationalism as exemplified in the work of such philosophers as Kant and Locke. Indeed, 'facts, like telescopes and wigs for gentlemen, were a seventeenth-century invention.'[40] What is crucial for our understanding here is that traditions are inherent to communities. Traditions are shaped by how the particular community moulds, shapes and develops them. Moreover, traditions within communities are constantly being modified or even discarded as those communities grapple with their changing context. Traditions flourish or die depending on how they deal with what MacIntyre refers to as 'epistemological crises.'[41] Epistemological tentativeness and openness to the possibility that ideas can be supervened, acknowledges the humility that should accompany knowing and recognizes that it is in communitarian contexts that this takes place. Being continuously critically aware, with a dialectically orientated approach toward traditions, is something that needs to be further encouraged today.

To summarize thus far, versions of the postmodern self have ensured that the positive, autonomous self of the Enlightenment has been dealt a mortal blow. In place we have a variety of decentred selves who, influenced by consumerism, among many other factors, have adopted a pick and mix attitude to life. Moreover, while this has developed, a surge in interest in community and the dynamics associated with it has ensured that the knee-jerk reaction of extreme examples of the decentring of the self thesis has been combated with a more balanced approach.

In contemporary society, the traditional institutions of Christendom are finding it increasingly difficult to be heard. Moreover, this is further reflected in the general trend in mainstream church attendance, which suggests that this is still very much in decline. The voices that, 100 years ago, the majority of the population would turn to are being ignored. This is not to say that this is due to a lack of interest in spiritual matters; on the contrary, people are awakening to alternative forms of spirituality. Some would argue that we are actually in the midst of another religio-cultural milieu.[42] In view of this re-enchantment taking place in Western society, it is up to those who are part of Christian faith communities to engage with the opportunities that this postmodern climate undoubtedly presents.

So what form do these opportunities take, and how can they buck the trend of a seemingly declining interest in Christianity and a marginalization of this faith? First, the realization that theology is carried out by the community, in a particular context, will, I hope, encourage a more local approach to doing theology. The words of Terry Veling are particularly apt here, when he makes the point that 'Practical theology is more "verb-like" than "noun-like".'[43] It is the performing

---

[40] A. MacIntyre, *Whose Justice? Which Rationality?* (London: Duckworth Press, 1988), p. 357.
[41] Ibid., p. 361.
[42] Partridge, *The Re-Enchantment of the West*, p. 4.
[43] T. Veling, *Practical Theology: On Earth as it is in Heaven* (New York: Orbis Books, 2005) p. 4.

of local theology for the local audience that the postmodern condition is tailor-made for. There are many examples of this approach already successful in meeting the needs of the broader community.[44] Liberation theologians, in particular, have been doing theology in this manner for a number of years. Indeed, they can be described as being the epitome of a contextual approach to doing theology, in their attempt to bring transformation to the lives of the poor. In a similar fashion, Christian communities in the Western world should adopt a more fluid approach to 'doing theology'. No longer fettered to Enlightenment traditions, but reading their context through specific communal lenses and equipped with a Christian narrative that meets the needs of those around will ensure two things. In the first instance, it will go some way in helping to alleviate an almost subconscious exclusion of others. That is to say, preconceived ideas as to how others should conform to certain Christian principles should be jettisoned. Instead, the Christian narrative should be constantly being retranslated according to the audience it finds itself presented with. There are multifarious language games/narratives that demand different approaches. In this respect, there could well be as many translations of the Christian narrative as there are listeners. The second point is that this, I think, will lead to Christian communities becoming more influential in the broader community in which they are situated. This will help reverse the other side of exclusion. Society cannot reject a Christian narrative that is relevant. The Christianity of the late twentieth century and into the twenty-first has, in many ways, become irrelevant because it has failed to meet the concerns of society. In this respect, it has justifiably become marginalized and is seen, by some, as simply old-fashioned, the product of a bygone era. The postmodern condition has brought this into sharp focus. That is not to say that there is a lack of interest in spiritual matters; I have claimed that the reverse is true. With one eye on postmodern sensibilities and another on the spiritual hunger that seems to resonate in society, embedding the Christian story in culture will enable a greater degree of synthesis between the Christian narrative presented and the context or world view of the respondent. Of course, this leaves the door open to accusations of dilution of the Gospel and a loss of Christian identity. However, these accusations usually come from those in the corridors of power, not those at the coalface.[45]

One final point to be made concerns another level that the myriad of Christian communities need to operate on, which is the global level. It is impossible for the local community to be heard on a national or international level. However, the vast matrix of Christian communities, whose primary concern is the local, must recognize the need to form a web of belief that can, when necessary, transcend the local to appeal on a broader spectrum. This web of belief will consist of a huge amount of local narratival interpretations of what it means to be Christian. Picture, if you will, the Olympic rings that are linked together, only instead of five,

---

[44] See some of the case studies in C. Baker, *The Hybrid Church in the City* 2nd edn (London: SCM Press, 2009).
[45] See R. Schreiter, *Constructing Local Theologies* (New York: Orbis Books, 2008).

there is a multitude. Moreover, they are not all directly linked/in contact with one another as in the Olympic model. What they have in common is that they represent Christian narratives. To be heard beyond the local, the eclectic mix of local Christian communities need to cooperate. I would call this two-tier approach a glocalized outlook.[46] Glocalization is simply a portmanteau of local and global and is a term that simultaneously refers to the two-tier mission that the multifarious blend of Christian communities should participate. Of course, it would not be through matters of doctrine that unison would be heard, as they represent such diverse understandings of what it is to be Christian. What I am suggesting concerns matters that relates to social ethics. Debates concerning marginalization and injustice will be primary issues.

In summary, in this chapter I have attempted to show how the postmodern condition offers new opportunities for the Christian faith. Examining the theoretical understanding of metanarratives, I have argued that only a modern version of Christianity can be properly understood to constitute a metanarrative. Moreover, I suggest that the emphasis on community in a fragmented climate best connects with a postmodern, post-industrial landscape. Understood together, both aspects aid in facilitating Christian praxis and counter myopic tendencies to exclude the 'other' and alleviate the experience of exclusion.

I. Response to Steve Knowles

Chris Baker

First of all, I admire the tenacity and optimism of Steve's desire to recouple Christian mission and theology with the diversity and plurality inherent within the postmodern condition. Steve is right to imply that much of the rather pessimistic and disparaging tone of some branches of Christian thought in relation to the postmodernist tradition is somewhat akin to having one's cake and eating it, too. That is to say, the Radical Orthodoxy scepticism (including some of its new, more evangelical allies) is often happy to join forces with postmodernity's critique of modernity and secularism, with their misplaced faith in human narratives of salvation. It then turns the tables on postmodernity itself in order to expose the allegedly hollow and nihilistic heart that lies within. Within this model of out-narrating the narratives of postmodernity,[47] it is ultimately quite hard to know what sort of transformation of society is expected to flow from this one-sided hermeneutical encounter.

---

[46] The term 'glocalization' has its roots in Japanese business practice and has been used to describe the way business is adapted to local markets.

[47] J. Milbank, *Theology and Social Theory; Beyond Secular Reason*, 2nd edn (Oxford: Blackwell, 2006).

The church usually ends up feeling quite good about itself, portraying itself as a countercultural force untainted by compromise or adjustment to the supposed political neutrality of both State and the Market.[48] Or we tend to enter the rarefied world of divine metaphysics, where Eucharistic symbolism re-enchants the fallen urban world through sheer force of autonomous (and theologically positivistic) references to salvation or debates about relative degrees of ontology.[49] In the first approach, the world ceases to be read as a space of God's revelation and truth and, therefore, as something by which the church itself can be transformed. In the second approach, the world of day to day messy compromise and material fallibility tends to be devalued as it becomes deployed in the role of pedagogical cipher or doctrinal teaching point. While I acknowledge the importance of a distinctive Christian theological and political apologetic, both approaches taken in isolation are, I believe, inadequate tools for engaging with and redeeming the startling and ineluctable diversity of our contemporary world. God's world has moved on – in many ways, the church and theology still struggle to keep up.

A more fruitful quest in recent times has been the shift towards the search for a distinctively Christian form of ethics and values by which to effect the change of political and social structures and so thicken and enhance the transformative potential of the public square. The approach here is more dialogical with the world, seeking partnerships – but also honest disagreement and challenge – with those of other faith or secular traditions whose values, *telos* and methods overlap. This approach recognizes that all ontologies matter, but that one's belief in the superior ontology of (say) Christianity over other ontologies is not a preclusion to working in partnership or witnessing (if that is the preferred word) to alternative structures outside the mainstream consensus. Neither, crucially, should it be a preclusion to working from within the mainstream as well. One could argue this is a transformative model based more on *interdisciplinary* methods (i.e. an open but critical engaging with those of other disciplines and world views for the sake of shaping a common good). This is different to an *intra-disciplinary* model, which tends to resolve moral and political challenges by funnelling information and ideas through its own internal resources and hermeneutical methodologies.

However, it is important to stress that even in the interdisciplinary context, a sense of distinctive Christian identity and narrative is vital. We don't engage in the world to deny who we are. Rather, in the spirit of John 12.24, we engage in the world – we risk our Christian identities in the world – in order to find out who we really are. This approach, it seems to me, transcends the stale dichotomy of the Evangelical versus Liberal debate which Steve has already begun to unpick in his critical account of the work of US evangelical public theologian Stanley Grenz,

[48] See, for example, A. Paddison, 'On Christianity as Truly Public', in J. Beaumont and C. Baker (eds), *Postsecular Cities: space, theory and practice* (London: Continuum, 2010) and S. Hauwerwas, *A Better Hope: Resources for a Church Confronting Capitalism, Democracy and Postmodernity* (Grand Rapids, MI: Brazos Press, 2000).
[49] See, for example, G. Ward, *Cities of God* (London: Routledge, 2000).

who was keen to articulate a non-foundationlist methodology which attempted to reposition evangelical theology in line with the concerns of postmodernity.[50]

Second, therefore, what do I find to be the strengths and potential weaknesses in Steve's analysis? Let us begin with Steve's interesting discussion on the relationship between postmodernity and the metanarrative. He shows that the 'incredulity towards metanarrative' (as defined by Lyotard) has been interpreted by many within theological circles as an assault on the integrity of biblical revelation. This is because under Lyotard's definition, any totalizing system that claims supremacy via appeal to its own internal discovery of truth and knowledge collapses under the weight of its own reported forms of knowledge, because they eventually contain irreconcilable contradictions. Although Lyotard's later work appears to add Christianity to Hegel, Marx and Adam Smith, Steve is right to point out the contested and distinctly hazy thinking Lyotard applies to this. The main point Steve makes is that if Christianity is not a metanarrative, then postmodernity offers no threat to it. In this assertion, Steve therefore potentially opens up a new and creative space between Christian thought and mission and the diversity and plurality of postmodern society.

So far so good, but I wonder if this rather technical debate is somehow missing the point of how religion actually functions in practice; that is, as a controlling narrative at a moral (i.e. teleological) and functional level in the life of the individual believer. So if one wants to create the postmodern political conditions around which values associated with justice and the common good might be operationalized (as Steve suggests in the second half of his chapter), then it is essential that people still behave as though their religion is a metanarrative. In my opinion, a deeply held religious metanarrative that is able to be translated into a performative local or national politics is one of the few things powerful enough to stand up to the one metanarrative that clearly is still in town – namely, that of consumption and choice, which is based on what Steve rightly calls the decentred self. This decentred self is far more insidious than political secularism, since, in its appeal to the gratification of the present moment with no regard to the future or the past, it saps the moral and political will of all, religious or non-religious alike. The result is either widespread apathy and cynicism regarding the possibility of social transformation, or the dereliction of mainstream politics in favour of more extreme (and sometimes extremist) forms of political expression. My question to Steve is – is the focus on metanarrative in relation to the condition of postmodernity the right one to pick, if, as I suggest, religion functions in practice as a metanarrative anyway? I would also suggest that it's quite important, for the sake of diverse and contested public space, that it continues to do so.

Following a critique of the commodification of religion as an extension of the decentred self, Steve then argues, borrowing from Lyotard, that we can at least share with our neighbour a commitment to the value of justice and other virtues

---

[50] S. Knowles, *Beyond Evangelicalism: The Theological Method of Stanley. J. Grenz* (Aldershot: Ashgate, 2010).

and (after MacIntyre) express it through a recommitment to find new forms of community. It is, after all, in local communities where traditions are formed, reformulated and finally jettisoned. This, Steve claims, is a more fluid approach to 'doing theology', whereby centralized, one-size-fits-all models of Christianity are 'jettisoned' in favour of 'narratives that are constantly being retranslated according to the audience it finds itself presented with.' In this respect, he admits, there could be as many translations of the Christian narrative as there are listeners, or world views. In order for these many local narratives to cohere, Steve argues there needs to be a theological equivalent of what Roland Robertson calls 'glocalization', by which local and global forms of Christian identity are connected.

I share Steve's commitment to developing a local performative theology in which the Christian church translates the experience of a specific community into an indigenous form of religious expression, complete with languages and symbols by which to embed a community of disciples in that physical locality. To that extent, I also share his wider thesis, that the condition of postmodernity offers exciting opportunities and challenges to Christianity to evolve these creative and dynamic expressions of community and theology. I share his implicit frustration that the general mind-set of the church and Christian theology generally is stuck in a modernist, rationalist past that is fearful of change and the risky encounter with the Other, whose identity is expressed as much in diversity and immanence, as it is in stability and transcendence.

However, I do detect certain imbalances in Steve's argument in the second half of his chapter. The first is the lack of a proper recognition of an ongoing role for institutional modernity – namely, the institutions of the church and the historical legacies of art, argument and architecture that have shaped and continue to shape contemporary postmodern experience.[51] Institutional familiarity can also be a useful calling card to play in situations in which people's fear of change, transition and newness can be paralyzing.

In other words, modernity (and particularly its bureaucratic forms) continues to play an important role. At their worst, of course, bureaucracies smother innovation and rigorously control sanctioned argument. They respond particularly badly when threatened with extinction and tend to revert to default positions of shoring up the known at the expense of riskily investing in the unknown. There are many mainstream churches in the UK for whom this *modus operandi* is becoming more prevalent. At their best, however, institutions will support new initiatives with both finance and skilled personnel, and establish feedback loops whereby innovation and learning from the periphery is allowed to influence the strategic direction of the centre. As I have commented elsewhere,[52] and following

---

[51] See, for example, J. Garnett, M. Grimley, A. Harris, W. Whyte and S. Williams (eds), *Redefining Christian Britain – post 1945 perspectives* (London: SCM Press, 2007).
[52] C. Baker, *The Hybrid Church in the City – Third Space Thinking*, 2nd edn (London: SCM Press, 2009).

Pete Ward's work on liquid and solid church,[53] the new postmodern space is not a totally liquid one in which all solidity is washed away, but a new Third Space in which both liquid and solid elements combine to create new forms of identity and performance.

Linked to this approach is the need for Steve to further develop the concept of 'glocalization'. Robertson, a sociologist, developed the term in response to Japanese business practice by which global brands were adapted to meet local cultural expectations and needs. It is true to say, therefore, that this term does validate a shaping role for 'the local', but one needs to sound a note of caution when one of the most commonly cited examples of effective glocalization is McDonald's. They allow some of the menu to reflect local customs and taboos (lamb burgers instead of beef burgers in India, for example, and more vegetarian options), but the essential brand remains intact, as does its impact on local eating and buying habits. In other words, the idea of glocalization is a contested one that can, in fact, suggest the ability of the global market to subsume local difference into a metanarrative of increased consumption and homogeneity of brand. Are there signs of this dynamic within the UK religious market? And is there not an ongoing role for the institutional church to act as a bulwark against this trend as a non-market global institution, but only if capable of acting in the manner I suggest above? Either way, the term glocalization needs more theological work done on it, or else a new and more convincing term needs to be found.

Finally, there is perhaps too much of a utopian element to Steve's cheerfulness. By which, I mean that the option of risk involved in stepping into and engaging with local conditions of plurality and diversity is often costly and contested. The model can lead to burn-out and emotional exhaustion and, without a strong sense of identity and institutional support, one can easily fall into the trap of what Derrida calls 'being eaten', rather than 'eating well'.[54] By which he meant that hospitality towards an encounter with the Other often produces opportunities for eating well; that is, 'an opportunity to enjoy new experiences and ideas that deepen and refresh your own identity and sense of mission or purpose'.[55] The downside is that an encounter with the Other also produces opportunities to get eaten; in other words, 'one's identity and mission . . . is overwhelmed and one is left feeling disempowered by the experience of working in new partnerships and new forums of participation'.[56]

So does postmodernity offer Christian theology and mission reasons to be cheerful? Yes, because, as Steve suggests, it offers new spaces of engagement and creativity – and therefore transformation – to both the church and the wider community. My only critique is one of tone – there are indeed reasons to be cheerful,

[53] P. Ward, *Liquid Church* (Carlisle: Paternoster Press, 2002).
[54] J. Derrida, 'Remarks on Deconstruction and Pragmatism', in S.Critchley et al., *Deconstruction and Pragmatism* (London: Routlege, 1996).
[55] Quoted in Baker, *The Hybrid Church in the City*, p. 140.
[56] Ibid., p. 140.

but that cheerfulness is often costly. The conditions under which it operates and the transformations it creates are more hard-fought for than one might initially think. To conclude with a concept from Deleuze, postmodern space may well be smooth and frictionless, but if it is too smooth and frictionless when it comes to Christian engagement, then something is probably going wrong!

II. Concluding Comments

Steve Knowles

I am very grateful to Chris for his analysis of my proposal. While he agrees with the overall thrust of my argument, he thinks that this view is rather utopian in outlook. I hope that brief explication of two issues that he raises will go some way to alleviating this judgment. The twin foci of this reply will be upon the role of metanarratives and the term glocalization, though I will concentrate more on the latter.

Chris asks if selecting metanarratives in relation to postmodernity is the right one to pick, if 'religion functions in practice as a metanarrative anyway' (p. ?). My response to this is yes, on two counts. First, as I have stated, the Christian faith should be judged as a *mega*narrative – a big story. If the Christian proclamation is not a metanarrative in a technical sense, then it strikes me as being crucial that, given postmodern pressures, the Christian proclamation is repositioned. This helps to alleviate the stigma attached to such a label that undoubtedly is out of favour in postmodern times. Rather, we have a big narrative that aids in guiding life; a story that has its genesis in revelation, and not reason. Moreover, I would argue that this does not fundamentally affect the teleological (and functional) level that we both see as being of great importance, although it would differ from the modernist teleology that many argue is defunct. This steers a middle ground between modern and postmodern positions.[57]

Secondly, the demise of metanarratives is due, in part, to the denial of difference – one of the seeds from which postmodernism has germinated. Instead, the postmodern incredulity toward them, in the words of Dirlik allows for 'localized consciousness, and points to the local as the site for working out "alternative public spheres" and alternative social formations'.[58] This point is key for preparing the ground for a revised understanding of glocalization and how I will employ it.

One final point to note is that Chris claims that it is necessary to argue for a religious metanarrative which is robust enough to fend off the 'one metanarrative

---

[57] Although there is not the space to develop this here, I would seek to demonstrate a 'MacIntyrian' approach in regard to ethics, which would avoid, I hope, the accusation of relativism.

[58] A. Dirlik, 'The Global in the Local', in B. Ashcroft, G. Griffiths and H. Tiffin (eds), *The Post-Colonial Studies Reader*, 2nd edn (London: Routledge, ,2004), pp. 463–7 (465).

that clearly is still in town – namely, that of consumption and choice' (p. ?). In response to this, I would want to argue that consumerism is a defining feature of the postmodern, rather than a metanarrative. If postmodernity, in Lyotard's words, is incredulity toward metanarratives, and consumerism is a key defining feature of the postmodern (at least in its contemporary cultural form), it would seem to me to be incoherent to claim that consumerism per se is a metanarrative.[59] I think that we have to avoid what Heelas calls the blanket coverage application of consumerism to the contemporary landscape.[60]

Glocalization

Roland Robertson has attempted to describe some of the complexities of the global-local markets by introducing the term glocalization. In a nutshell, the term is derived from the adoption of local strategies by global companies. Chris is right when he states that a good example of this is McDonald's, who has successfully implemented local menus for local people, while at the same time maintaining and promoting the brand and its controlling stake in the global market. Furthermore, glocalization is intrinsically linked with globalization, and it is rather ironic that the recognition of the local (the other), and the rise in interest in it, has come about as a result of the failure of the homogenizing attempts of modernity and globalization. Indeed, it can be argued that a paradoxical consequence of the failure of globalization's homogenizing attempts is the recognition of the diversity of the world.[61] Featherstone argues that globalization makes us far more aware of new levels of diversity, as opposed to the cultural uniformity that one would expect.[62]

Given the close links with the global, it could be construed that using this term for theological purposes would be problematic, particularly as I am arguing, in part, for a breakaway from such tendencies. However, I would like to briefly highlight two points. First, my use of the term operates in a slightly different manner than that of the common understanding of Robertson's model. That is to say, the plurality of Christian denominations and independent churches/communities around the globe, and the continued expansion thereof, means that more and more often we see indigenous expressions of the Christian faith: expressions that are contextually developed. Consequently, my starting point is the local. It is the local that is the focal point in regard to doctrine and practice. Instead of what

---

[59] Consumerism is not a new phenomenon, and it would be wrong to consider consumerism as a specifically postmodern development. However, the postmodern climate has brought about an intensification of consumerism in contemporary society, due in large part to the technological revolution that is exemplified by the internet.

[60] P. Heelas, *Spiritualities of Life: New Age Romanticism and Consumptive Capitalism* (Oxford: Blackwell, 2008).

[61] M. Featherstone, *Undoing Culture: Globalization, Postmodernism and Identity* (London: Sage Publications, 1997).

[62] Ibid., pp. 12–14.

Chris rightly describes as the global subsuming of local difference within a controlling metanarrative (i.e. McDonald's), what we have are indigenous expressions of Christianity influencing society and the wider context.

In doing this, I want to make very clear the distinction between what can be referred to as a 'critical localism' and a localism that is understood as simply an ideological extension of global capitalism. A critical localism is a position that develops and changes out of the organic nature and context of the community: it is self-critical. The things that it holds dear are also held lightly. In this sense, this becomes part of an epistemologically critical realist position.

Secondly, and to reinforce the above, to maintain a link with other Christian communities, the community is part of a wider web of belief,[63] or put another way, a chain of connectedness. This is especially pertinent given what I have already said about metanarratives. A glocal approach sits well in a postmodern climate that has dismissed metanarratives as controlling and overbearing devices. However, a glocal understanding acknowledges the presence of other Christian communities outside its own boundaries and their right to be called Christians. What emerges here is more a coherentist and fluid approach to the Christian faith. The local and global spheres within which communities operate need to stand in dialectical relationship.[64] Indeed, the local and global are mutually dependant.[65] Employing the term glocal simultaneously flags up both the local distinctiveness and the global commonality of various expressions of Christianity, and this enables oscillation between the two.[66]

Finally, regarding the suggestion that I have shown a 'lack of proper recognition of an ongoing role for institutional modernity – namely the institutions of the church', I would counter that it is not simply that I have failed to give them proper recognition; on the contrary, it is because I have noted that some institutions (in this case ecclesial institutions) are not only struggling to be heard in the public space, but openly have ongoing internal differences and interpretations of the Christian faith that demands such an investigation. This illustrates the necessity for such a glocal understanding and approach. This inability to 'sing off the same hymn sheet' is but one example that reinforces the need to get beyond what many understand as the decaying edifices of modernity and fully recognize that the postmodern climate in which we find ourselves is a result of the failure of the modern project.

---

[63] The phrase 'web of belief' is taken from W. V. O. Quine and J. S. Ullian, *Web of Belief*, 2nd edn (New York: Random House, 1978).

[64] R. Robertson, 'The Conceptual Promise of Glolocalization: Commonality and Diversity', retrieved from http://artefact.mi2.hr/_a04/lang_en/theory_robertson_en.htm, 12.03.2010.

[65] D. Lyon, 'Wheels within wheels: Glocalization and Contemporary Religion', retrieved from http://webjournals.alphacrucis.edu.au/journals/aps/issues-23/wheels-within-wheels-glocalization-and-contemporar/, 13.03.2010.

[66] The downside of such an approach is that decentralization sometimes results in the growth of fundamentalism.

2 Negotiating Negation: Christians and Muslims Making a Space for the Religious 'Other' in British Society

Mohammad S. Seddon

Introduction

This chapter seeks to examine developing approaches in theology and religious studies in transforming attitudes to the religious other and how they might enhance relations between Christian and Muslim communities in the context of multicultural and religiously plural Britain. The current discourses on Muslims in Britain and the West are largely circumscribed by two particular occurrences that have irrevocably changed Western perceptions of Islam and Muslims for the foreseeable future. These two specific landmark phenomena are: the migration and settlement of minority Muslim communities across the northwestern hemisphere; and the terrorist outrages of 9/11, 7/7 and the Madrid bombings, committed by Muslim extremists. While Muslim migration and 'Islamic terrorism' have their own particular sociological and political drivers and impacts, their relative heuristic proximity has appeared to funnel the two unattached events into a single reception or understanding of 'Islam in the West' as irredeemably problematic. This false metonymy of Muslims and Islam as inherently pathological is continuously evidenced by the seemingly dysfunctionality of Muslim communities across Britain, Europe and America, which is coarsely measured by an acknowledged reluctance to assimilate into the countries to which they have migrated and settled. Further, serious questions pertaining to the loyalty and belonging of British Muslims are being asked in the wake of the 9/11 al-Qaida attacks and continued threats of 'Islamic extremism', resulting in an increasing securitization of British and Western societies. But the present negative framing of Muslim minorities is not simply a result of contemporary events and their placing as the paradigmatic other within modern, liberal Western societies. It is actually the outcome of a series of complex historical theological, political, social, geographical and cultural interactions. This claim is not new, nor is it intended to undermine the sad reality of a degree of social ineptitude and acts of religious terrorism on the part of a small but significant number of Muslims. Rather, it is undertaken in order to address the unfortunate marginalizing of a religious tradition and community, who are largely envisaged as culturally homogenous, socially impaired and menacingly belligerent across the spectrum of British public life. As stated, the othering of Islam and Muslims transcends contemporary typologies and fixities located in the narratives of 'social cohesion' and 'disenfranchisement', and exists instead as a complex historical continuum. What I am proposing here is a Foucauldian coupling of the past to the present as an archaeology of religious and civilizational encounter,[1] throughout which Islam remains permanently located outside the possibility of being the collective 'us' or 'we', who are 'Western', as both a territorial place of civilizational exclusivity and theological space of religious negation. Again, my claim is not new, and it relies heavily on Edward Said's thesis on the discourse of Orientalism as a Western knowledge/power discipline on the East.[2] Succinctly, Said asserted that Western study of the East, in particular the Middle East, was a developed, systemic scholastic prism through which the Orient is not only intellectually conceived and comprehended, but also, through the same process, the West is conversely defined as an oppositional binary to all that is perceived as the 'Orient'. He contends, 'the Orient that appears in Orientalism . . . is a system of representations framed by a whole set of forces that brought the orient into western learning, western consciousness, and later, western empire.'[3] This established power discourse on Islam and Muslims presents itself as a 'master narrative', or what Stuart Hall has termed as a 'regime of truth'.[4] Elizabeth Poole has examined the Foucaldian knowledge/power relationship in her research into how Muslims are portrayed in the contemporary British press. Her work refers to Hall's definition and employment of Foucault's discourse on power, stating,

> According to Foucault power is exercised over those who are 'known' through discourse. Those who produce discourse, therefore, have the power to enforce its validity so that it effectively becomes a 'regime of truth'.[5]

Essentially, as Said, Hall, Poole and others suggest, the epistemological 'othering' of Islam/Muslims that exists recognizably today as the discourse of Islamophobia, is merely a modality of what was formerly identified as Orientalism. And while the historical particularities, values and definitions developed within the two terms may differ, their primary function – how they operate in conjunction with each

---

[1] See M., Foucault, *The Archaeology of Knowledge* (London: Tavistock Publications Ltd, 1972).
[2] See E. Said, *Orientalism: Western Concepts of the Orient* (London: Penguin Books, 1991).
[3] Ibid., pp. 202–3.
[4] S. Hall cited in E. Poole, *Reporting Islam* (London: Routledge, 2002).
[5] Ibid., p. 101.

other in a hidden realm of unconscious cultural indicators and theological signi-
fiers – remains the same. Because Orientalism stressed difference, through it, 'the
West became more western and the East more eastern'.[6] The subsequent discourse
led to linguists labelling it a 'binary opposition' in which the West exerts its supposed intellectual dominance over the East, which is portrayed as the inferior,
silent 'other' managed, styled and restructured by Western authority over it. This
process is described by Said as the 'saturating hegemonic systems'.[7] Added to this
was a perpetuated self-generating Western discourse on the Orient which was self-
validated through the cross-referencing and interconnectedness of its texts and
representations.

In the current discourses of Islamophobia, the same methodology of repetition, cross-referencing and metonymy is employed in the negative framing and
representations of Islam and Muslims across the realms of politics and the media.
Reporting on the alarming rise in racism and anti-Muslim sentiment, the Open
Society Institute report on Muslims in the UK noted,

> There is evidence of severe discrimination and disadvantage experience by Muslim com-
> munities [in Britain] which operate as obstacles to those wanting to integrate. Tackling
> this disadvantage and discrimination is essential for integration, as is the cultivation
> among Muslims of a sense that they belong to wider society.[8]

While protection for British Muslims from racism and discrimination had historically been covered under the Race Relations Act, 1976, the Act had a very limited
application, particularly with regard to religious discrimination, which the Act had
never been intended to cover. In individual cases in which Muslims had applied
the law to address issues relating to specific anti-religious prejudice, rather than
racial discrimination, it had been limited to the employment context as the area in
which discrimination most often occurs.[9] However, the Act was eventually super-
seded by the European Convention of Human Rights and its subsequent domestic
application via the Human Rights Act 1998, which offered a limited extension
to cover religious discrimination. Further, the Employment Equality (Religion or
Belief) Regulations 2003, made it illegal to discriminate against people in employment or vocational training on the basis of their religion or beliefs. Later still, the
Equality Act 2006 further widened the scope to include the provision of goods,
facilities and services, education, the use and disposal of premises, and the exercise of public functions. However, despite the revised legislation designed to cover
loopholes in specific forms of religious discrimination, the compounding problem
in the current climate of anti-Muslim sentiment as a direct post-9/11 phenomenon

---

[6] Ibid., p. 9.

[7] Ibid., p. 47.

[8] See *Monitoring Minority Protection in the EU: The Situation of Muslims in the UK* (London:
The Open Society, 2002), p. 71.

[9] See *SI(1) (b) Race Relations Act 1979* (United Kingdom: Office of Public Sector Information,
1979).

is, when does Islamophobia replace xenophobia? This is a question that is currently being exploited by far-right movements like the British National Party and the English Defense League. Clearly, one form of discrimination does not exist at the 'expense' of the other, and the reality is that both forms of prejudice coexist and may even be interchangeable. Christopher Allen's research in to the rise of Islamophobia in Britain and Europe has extensively compared the correlations between racism and Islamophobia in the new trajectories of discrimination aimed at minority Muslim communities in the West. His work follows on from the original Runnymede Trust report (1997), and he says,

> One way of elaborating upon this [form of discrimination], if somewhat coarsely, is to consider the old British adage that 'all blacks *look* the same'. In the contemporary setting now emerging from the discourses and processes of this greater receptivity to Islamophobia, that the adage might be more appropriately reworded as: 'All Muslims are the same'.[10]

The Commission on British Muslims and Islamophobia report (2004) also agrees with Allen's findings that the negative stereotypes and remarks made by politicians and the media means that, generally, Muslims are represented in ways that, 'would not be acceptable if the reference were to Jewish people, for example, or to black people'.[11] But whether Islamophobia is merely a form of 'cultural racism' or a new type of xenophobia, manifest through religious discrimination, is difficult to assess. In any case, the academic arguments about whether 'Muslims are the *new* blacks' or 'does Islamophobia correspond with Anti-Semitism?' are perhaps lost in the everyday experiences of discrimination and prejudice suffered by many British and European Muslims. Further, for postcolonial Muslim settlers in the West, religious and racial differences are framed by previous imperial and colonial experiences still often expressed through outmoded colonial discourses: we are only a generation away from the 'no Irish, no blacks and no dogs' notices that were commonly displayed in hotels and guesthouses throughout Britain in the 1950s and 1960s.

Historically, western Christendom has theologized Islam in specific terms of negation, heresy and exclusion. I use the term 'Christendom' in this particular context as defined by Samuel Chew who says, 'the word "Christendom" is generally used to embrace the Catholic and Protestant states of Western Europe but it is occasionally used in a wider sense.'[12] As early as the medieval period, when European crusader Christians attempted to liberate the Holy Land from the clutches of conquering 'Saracens', Muslims were already theologically 'explained'

---

[10] C. Allen, 2004, 'Justifying Islamophobia: A Post-9/11 Consideration of the European Union and British Contexts', in *American Journal of Islamic Social Sciences*, 21:3 (Summer, 2004), pp. 1–25 (6).

[11] R. Richardson (ed.), *Islamophobia, issues, challenges and action* (Stoke on Trent and Sterling: Trentham Books, 2004), p. 7.

[12] S. C. Chew, *The Crescent and the Rose: Islam and England during the Renaissance* (New York: Oxford University Press, 1937), p. viii.

has a heterodox sect sent to scourge Christendom of its religious infidelities and heresies. A particular example is the eschatological understanding of Islam first developed by the early medieval theologian St. John of Damascus (c. 676 CE).[13] Conversely, Muslims have generally excluded Christianity through the creation of a binary world view – *dar al-Islam* ('the abode of Islam') and *dar al-Harb* ('the abode of war').[14] Where Christians (and Jews) have traditionally lived within dominant Muslims spaces, they have been regarded with a degree of suspicion and liable to pay the *jizyah*.[15] The impact of such 'theologies of exclusion' has historically meant a religious and cultural distancing between both faith traditions by which neither needed to consider the later realities of an intimate geocultural proximity. The developed distancing of both traditions was rapidly evaporated as a direct result of imperial conquest and postcolonial migration, respectively. Yet, as historical and political events unfolded rather succinctly within a few hundred years, both traditions advanced little, theologically, to engage with the reality of a reparticularized engagement with the other that would become both spatially and geopolitically intertwined. Paradoxically, where Islam and Christianity had in pre-modern times defined themselves in counterdistinction with the other, the advent of modernity imposed an environment in which the religious other eventually came to occupy both the real and virtual spaces of a globalized world. In the new modern engagement with the other, where previously Christianity had provided a theological justification for imperial conquest, while Islam was manifest as a khalifate imperial hegemony, the world could no longer be interpreted in terms of 'us' and 'them'. Although, while in the modern period Islamic ascendancy has given way to Western hegemony, the reassertion of an imagined, 'clash of civilizations' between all things Western (Christendom) and everything Muslim (the Islamic east), has created new intellectual and philosophical boundaries that replace any previous geocultural divisions that were compromised, if not eroded, by globalization. While Islam now occupies a place of increased proximity via postcolonial migration and settlement of Muslims in the West, the need to understand Islam now appears to be located within the discourses of sociology and psychology, rather than theology. As the outmoded and imagined boundaries between both religious civilizations were turbulently evaporated through the eventual processes of colonial capture and later postcolonial liberation, the historical coupling of both civilizations resulted in a complex socio-economic interdependence of mutual occupancy – the neo-imperialist management of, and investment in, burgeoning independent Muslim states, and postcolonial migration of much-needed labour forces to the former imperial metropolis. As a result, the pervading new social realities, particularly in the British context, raise two important questions;

---

[13] See N. Daniel, *Islam and the West* (Oxford: Oneworld Publications,1993), pp. 13–15.
[14] See T. Ramadan, *To be a European Muslim* (Leicester: The Islamic Foundation, 1999), p. 42.
[15] *Jizyah* – the exemption tax paid by religious minorities under Muslim rule.

can Christianity make a 'theological space' to include the Muslim other? And, can Islam legitimize Muslims as minorities in a predominantly Christian society?

Perpetuated Otherness

The contemporary (mis)placing of the 'problematic Muslim' within Britain and the West, as we have suggested, is not simply the result of acute Muslim 'anti-Westernism'. An anti-Occidentalism is seen as a consequence of past colonization by Britain of Muslim territories that has become manifest as a 'civilizational clash' perpetrated by a global network of al-Qaida, 'Islamic terrorism'. Nor is it limited to the anachronistic xenophobia of 'little Englander' narrow-mindedness towards the settlement of visibly different 'new Britons'. The placing of Muslims in the British context has perhaps more to do with the way in which Britons imagine Britain and Britishness – as a historical construction that is rooted within collective national consciousness. This is a Britishness that is the product of both historical revisionism and romantic imperialism that are both locked into a past Britain previously prefixed by the word 'Great'. It is a particular view of Britain in which the notions of 'greatness' are exclusively bounded by a narrow construction of national identity that is implicitly understood as 'white and Christian', if not Anglican Protestant. While the terms of reference for Britishness remain confined to a restricted understanding of who *we* are, 'who we are' requires a perpetuated notion of 'who we are *not*'. It is here where the Muslim other has much currency, in supplying *us* with a clear, ready-made definition of what we are *not* that is articulated through the complex historical, theological, political, social, geographical and cultural interactions between the Christian West and Islamic East. Leela Gandhi has described this form of polemical 'placing' and misrepresentation as, 'procedures whereby the convenient Othering and exoticisation of ethnicity merely confirms and stabilizes the hegemonic [and exclusive] notion of "Englishness" '.[16] Given the difficulties in extending the inclusivity into developed notions of Englishness as *the* hegemonic identity that both shapes and forms wider notions of Britishness, we will, therefore, briefly explore the history of our national identity as a means of resolving questions relating to Muslim inclusivity.

After the Reformation, the hybridization of English Christianity in the form of Protestantism expedited a localized theocracy that synthesized both spiritual sovereign and secular ruler in a single monarchy. The impact was a dominating sense of Protestant 'chosenness' in which all others were theologically excluded, even demonized. This reality is most chillingly realized in Luther's statement, 'May our dear lord Jesus Christ, help and come down from heaven with the last judgment,

---

[16] L. Gandhi, *Postcolonial Theory: A Critical Introduction* (Edinburgh: Edinburgh University Press, 1998), p. 126.

and smite both Turk [Muslims] and Pope [Catholics] to the earth'.[17] In an attempt
to theologically purify Britain's sceptred isle, Elizabeth I ordered the ethnic and
religious cleansing of her minions, and in January 1601, she issued a proclamation
to deport all 'Negroes [Africans] and Blackamoores [Muslims]' from England.[18]
From Elizabeth's reign onwards, English Protestantism helped to provide a new
religio-cultural framework for Britain, by which all others were evaluated. In
the process, asserted Protestant pietism and self-appointed chosenness not only
began an intolerant encounter with the other, it also provided new opportunities
in colonizing and empire building. In the subsequent developed imperial mind-
set, civilizing and Christianizing the heathen other was presented as a theological
justification for colonial conquest, and the racializing and demonizing of the
colonized other, through erroneous definitions and misleading stereotypes, provided a monolithic, yet seemingly plausible, representation of the demonic and
barbaric Muslim other. Conversely, the previously unconquerable Islamic lands
continued to be equated with the mysterious and impenetrable, yet albeit imagined, Muslim harems. Hence, the unobtainable Muslim Orient, like the women of
its harems, captured the imagination of its would-be conquerors. As ancient biblical narratives became an increasing source of inspiration in Renaissance art and
iconography, Protestantism established a religious conservatism that, while facilitating theological liberalism, imposed strict moral sobriety and sexual repression.
However, unveiling the Muslim other through erotic and sensual painted representations was an acceptable art that merely evidenced and exoticized Muslim
heathenism. If the early period of English colonizing had paved the way for a
tempestuous obsession – if not fetish – with the oriental other, the emergence
of scholarly Orientalism, as an ideological tool of imperialism and colonial conquest, reached its zenith during the British (and French) territorial expansionism
of the nineteenth century. The development of Orientalism provided both hegemonic and essentializing misrepresentations of the East (and thus, by implication,
Islam and Muslims) by the West. This phenomenon has been eruditely explored
by scholars such as Edward Said and Bryan S. Turner. In practical terms, the physical conquest of large parts of the Muslim world by Britain eventually witnessed
the advent of modern, secular liberalism as a direct imposition of colonialism.
The apparent mass unveiling of Muslim women, spearheaded by a middle-class,
Western-educated elite, became symbolic of the eventual conquest of Islam. It
might be argued that unveiling Muslim women is still considered a measure of
the conquest of Islam, as witnessed by the burqa-free women on the streets of
Afghanistan and Iraq. Further, the internalization of Western feminism, which
was particularly rooted in Christian theology and misogyny, by a few female
intellectuals in Muslim countries, has offered a misplaced encouragement for any

[17] Cited in N. Matar, *Islam in Britain 1558–1685* (Cambridge: Cambridge University Press,
1998), p. 154.
[18] P. Fryer, *Staying Power: A History of Black People in Britain* (London: Pluto Books,
1984), p. 12.

perceived de-Islamization project of Muslim lands. An unveiled Muslim woman has often been misinterpreted as someone who is ultimately 'secular, liberal, enlightened and liberated'. These simplistic and superficial interpretations are at best purely aspirational, and at worst a clear reflection of the British and European preoccupation with conquering the Muslim other.

The western European concept of a 'national identity', developed through both theological and political constructs, is the creation of the modern nation state with its own particular defined laws, boundaries, language and, ultimately, race. Many scholars claim the foundations of the modern nation state are located in the Reformation. Ismail Raji al-Faruqi has correlated the advent of denominational Christianity and the emergence of nationalist movements formulated from religious and ethnic identities.[19] Brian S. Turner has also noted that, 'Whatever the contradictory relationships between a capitalist economy and organised religion, Christianity came to provide a crucial basis of legitimacy for emerging nation-states'.[20] Within the process of modern nation building constructed around state government and state religion, social entities outside this nation-state framework would naturally be seen as others.[21] In contemporary usage, the term 'nation' has become a synonym for the state or citizens: for example, reference to the British nation also means British citizens. Whereas formally the term 'nation' was applied to a group of people who share a common descent, religion, culture, history and language, today the definitions of nation and nationality have distinctly political implications.[22] In this particular context, nationality has become equated with citizenship and civic society, in which anyone loyal to the state or residing in it is part of that nation state. Conversely, a traditionally nationalist interpretation argues that the 'nation' is a distinct community of people with a common ancestry, religion, culture, history and language. Nationalists, therefore, insist that nations exist independently of the state. This particular exclusive concept of the nation is based entirely on ethnicity, and it implies that religious, cultural, historical and linguistic identification with a specific ethnic group determines nationality. However, when exclusive definitions of what it means to be British and English put minorities at the periphery of society, forging an identity in the national context for many Muslims actually has more to do with how British they feel (or are *allowed* to feel), which in turn is relative to their own personal experiences and sense of their own place in the wider society. The negotiated forms of British/English identity manifest among a majority of second-generation British-born Muslims are also shaped by both the wider historical background and present

[19] I. R. Al-Faruqi, 'Common bases between the two religions', in A. Siddiqui (ed.), *Ismail Raji al-Faruqi: Islam and Other Faiths* (Leicester: The Islamic Foundation and The International Institute of Islamic Thought, 1998), p. 231.
[20] B. S. Turner, *Max Weber: From History to Modernity* (London: Routledge, 1992), p. 105.
[21] M. Seddon, D. Hussain and N. Malik, *British Muslims Between Assimilation and Segregation* (Markfield: The Islamic Foundation, 2004), p. 134.
[22] A. Philips, 'The Resurrection of England', in T. Linsell (ed.), *Our Englishness* (Norfolk: Anglo-Saxon Books, 2000), p. 49.

situation of minority communities in Britain, which suggests that such hybrid and fluid identities are a particularly evident process within minority populations.[23] However, the impacts of Islamophobia which explicitly suggest Muslimness as a form of self-perpetuated otherness, inhibit any meaningful engagement with Britishness/British identity from the majority British Muslim perspective.

The Postcolonial Predicament

When Muhammad's message of Islam was first declared in Makkah at the end of the sixth century, its principle tenet of monotheism and divine prophecy specifically identified it with Judaism and Christianity.[24] Islam's theological proximity to the pre-existing monotheistic traditions allowed a greater degree of religious and cultural pluralism within the newly emerging Muslim societies in Arabia and beyond. Diversity in cultural and theological expression has been a continuous feature of developing Muslim civilizations, and ideas relating to difference were traditionally seen as a cause for celebration, rather than tension. Muhammad's nascent community of believers in Makkah not only challenged the static and exclusive social hierarchies of polytheistic tribal Arabia, but positively integrated ethnic and racial others into their faith. Early important Muslims included Bilal the Abyssinian, Sohail the Roman and Salman the Persian, who were all extremely closely associated with the Prophet. As Islam spread over the continents of Arabia, Africa, Asia and Europe, 'Muslimness' evolved into multifarious geocultural and sociopolitical manifestations. In South Asia, sub-Saharan Africa and Eastern Europe particularly, Muslims have continuously existed as religious minorities, regardless of their often-shifting political status. In the premodern age, Muslim political identity was generally shaped by a sense of regional belonging and tribal/clan loyalty. Here, the Islamic world was a binary perception of two distinct spaces, Muslim (*dar al-Islam*) and non-Muslim (*dar al-harb*). However, after the imposition of western colonialism, Muslim cultures were reshaped into definite nation-state identities in which difference became an important tool in the reconfigurations of self-identity, also forcing a rethinking of how the world was/is divided within traditional Islamic theology. Further, two distinct features of colonial rule – the imposition of secular government and state institutions, and the large migration of colonized Muslim subjects into the imperial metropolises – presented particular challenges to contemporary Muslim societies and Islamic theology. The first feature has been the reordering of political authority and religious orthodoxy in traditional Muslim spaces as a direct result of colonial rule. The most observable impacts of colonization are a serious undermining

---

[23] J. Jacobson, *Islam in Transition: Religion and identity among British Pakistani youth* (London: Routledge, 1998), pp. 22–3.

[24] I. R. Al-Faruqi and A. Siddiqui (eds), *Ismail Raji al-Faruqi: Islam and Other Faiths* (Leicester: The Islamic Foundation and The International Institute of Islamic Thought, 1998), p. 147

of all traditional social institutions, a disturbing fragmentation of cultural conventions and an increasing secularization of religious life. The second feature, the migration and settlement of Muslims into Western non-Muslim spaces, has raised important questions regarding their cultural belongingness, the legitimacy of minority-status Muslims within Islamic jurisprudence and concerns regarding the potential 'Islamic threat' from existing diasporic Muslim minorities. The question for contemporary minority Muslims in Britain and the West is, 'is there a means of developing a new way of understanding Islamic jurisprudence in different contexts which informs both community cohesion and social integration in contemporary Britain?'

The rise in Muslim fundamentalism, often expressed through the militant (*jhadi*) and political (*jamaa'ati*) strands of modern Islamist thought, can be traced to the nineteenth- and twentieth-century independence struggles of former colonized Muslim lands by imperial powers like Britain. Throughout the period, neoconservative religious movements ran parallel, if not oppositional, to developing nationalist organizations as ideological reconfigurations for the rapidly decolonizing Muslim spaces. Both groups responded quite differently in proposing an alternative system of governance for their burgeoning independent countries. The nationalists generally adopted secular political ideologies, ranging from Marxism to National Socialism, as a means of facilitating a new nation-state identity that would be devoid of cultural divisions and religious sectarianism. The political Islamic movements tried to re-establish Muslim supremacy over coexisting religious minorities (*dhimma*) by insisting on a reinstatement of *khulafaah* (pl. of 'khalifah', meaning, 'caliph') systems of governance similar to that instituted by the former Ottoman–Turkish Sultans or the Mogul–Indian Shanshahs. During the independence struggles, the nationalists and the Islamists buried their ideological differences for the sake of defeating colonial occupation. However, after independence, the divisions soon resurfaced, and while the nationalists appealed to politically heightened nation-state sentiments, the Islamists claimed that the nationalists were little more than colonial servants who perpetuated the division of a once united Muslim world through their insistence on separate Muslim nation states. But the Islamists' assertion of a pre-colonial, unified 'Islamic Empire' is largely the product of historical revisionism. This increasingly popular claim of Muslim political unity belies the reality that, beyond the stretched borders of the Ottoman Empire, there simultaneously existed a significant number of alternative khalifates, such as the Alawites of the Maghreb, the Saffavids of Persia and the Moguls of India. This historical actuality appears to frustrate the Islamist vision of a united, post-nation state, Muslim *ummah* ruled by a single *khalifah*. Further still, the localised geoculturally specific forms of 'Muslimness' seriously hinder any Islamist aspirations to impose an overarching theological orthodoxy beyond the central creed of monotheism (*tawhid*) and prescribed ritual observances ('*ibadaat*).

The second distinct feature, postcolonial and Commonwealth Muslim migration to non-Muslim lands, has demanded a rethinking of how the world was/is divided within traditional Islamic theology. This still largely unresolved problem is central to understanding the issues of 'Western' acculturation by Muslims who understand Islam only from within a dominant Islamic society and, therefore, cannot appreciate a functioning 'minority status' Islamic way of life. Centuries of the Islamic 'legacy' coupled with the recent Western colonization of Muslim lands have increased the polarization between Muslim and non-Muslim spaces. Yet, beyond the legacy, back to the foundations of the *sunnah*,[25] we find many instances of Muslims living not only in non-Muslim spaces, but also perhaps more importantly, under non-Muslim rule and legislation. A growing number of Muslim scholars cite the example of the Muslims exiled in Abyssinia as a paradigm for developed Muslim minority status that is politically, socially, culturally and religiously rooted to the place of migration and settlement. The traditional categories of *fiqh* that permit abode in a non-Muslim country are, according to academics such as Tariq Ramadan, purely situational. Ramadan asserts that, 'To apply them to contemporary reality as they were thought out ten centuries ago appears to be a methodological mistake.'[26] While he argues for a new legal interpretation for what might be described as 'minority status Islam', Imtiaz Hussain has explored the social and cultural implications of the Abyssinian model from the Prophetic era, considering how contemporary western Muslims might resolve their current marginal predicament in terms of their political loyalties and ideas related to their religious belonging.[27] The implications of the Abyssinian experience for the peaceful coexistence and active civil participation of present-day British Muslims may offer some serious considerations in helping both Christians and Muslims in Britain to negotiate a more tolerant theological and cultural space for the religious other.

Contested Spaces: Orientalism and Occidentalism

Migration is not a new human phenomenon, and one can argue that Adam, the father of humanity and the first Prophet (according to Islam), underwent a migration as a result of his expulsion from paradise. Other Prophets have also experienced migration; Nuh (Noah) and Lut (Lot), for example, migrated from the impending Divine punishments brought about by the persistent evil-doing of their respective peoples. Ibrahim, (Abraham), the father of monotheism and Patriarch of the three Abrahamic faiths – Judaism, Christianity and Islam – spent most of his life in a state of *hijrah* (migration). Moses led his believing people from the despotic clutches of Pharaoh via mass migration from Egypt to the Promised Land. Migration is also a natural phenomenon within the animal world, and

---

[25] *Sunnah* – lit., 'practice', but understood to mean the actions, sayings and life example of the Prophet Muhammad.

[26] Ramadan, *To be a European Muslim*, p. 126.

[27] I. A. Hussain, 'Migration and Settlement: A Historical Perspective of Loyalty and Belonging', in M. S. Seddon et al. (eds), *British Muslims: Loyalty and Belonging* (Leicester: The Islamic Foundation, 2003), pp. 23–34.

many different species of birds, mammals and fishes migrate as a consequence of their 'natural disposition', or *fitrah*. But the processes of migration may not necessarily have direct religious connotations, and human beings employ migration as a means of seeking greener pastures, avoiding a natural disaster or taking refuge from war and conflict. The expansion of Islam has, since its nascent period, seen Muslims migrating and travelling to new domains. Indeed, the processes of migration and its impacts are at the heart of understanding the establishment of the *ummah*. The Prophet's *hijrah* from Makkah to Madinah signified the turning point for the establishment of Islam, the early Muslim community and the Islamic citadel. So significant is the *hijrah* in Islamic history that the calendar begins at the year of the Prophet's migration – a migration that provides *the* paradigm for all Muslim migrations, both ancient and modern. The early Muslim society of Madinah was primarily identified as two distinct groups: the *Muhajiroon*, or 'emigrants', from Makkah, and the *Ansar*, or 'helpers', of Madinah. *Hijrah*, in its religious context then, became a line of demarcation between a life of religious persecution and suffering in Makkah to a new life of religious freedom in Madinah. But the Prophet expanded the meaning of *Muhajir*, or 'one who emigrates', to include a disassociation of oneself from something harmful by declaring that, 'A Muslim is a person who does not harm another Muslim with his tongue or hands and émigré (*Muhajir*) is one who leaves that which God has forbidden'.[28] Although the *hijrah* from Makkah to Madinah facilitated the creation of the Islamic citadel, which provides a model for modern ideas concerning the Islamic state, there are some conceptual problems when applying the Makkah to Madinah *hijrah* as the *imthal*, or paradigm, for modern post-colonial migrations of Muslims to Britain and the West. The theological implication of the Makkan migration is that Islam must be established by geographical occupation, social interaction and political domination. Hence, many traditional *taqlidi* jurists (religious scholars who follow a traditionalist approach, known as a '*muqalid*', of 'legal imitation', or '*taqlid*') have made all migration from what they describe as '*dar al-Islam*' to '*dar ul-kufr*' ('the abode of disbelief') conditional and specific; to avoid persecution, trade and learning or invitation, or *da'wah*, to Islam. This legal specificity has imbued Muslim settlers with a religious sense of 'unbelonging'. That is to say that their physical migration and settlement to so-called non-Muslim spaces is denied any religious or cultural validity through a developed psycho-spiritual sense of disassociation or non-attachment, inculcated by religious authority or legal ruling – *fiqh*. However, cross-generationally, this state of being becomes less tenable simply through greater realms of social interactivity, integration and acculturation. This social reality has been discussed by many Western-based Muslim scholars including Tariq Ramadan and Taha Jabir al-Alwani.[29]

---

[28] Cited in ibid., p. 24.
[29] See Ramadan, *To be a European Muslim*, and T. J. Al-Alawani, *Towards a Fiqh for Minorities: Some Basic Reflections* (London and Washington: The International Institute of Islamic Thought, 2003).

The insistence that Muslim identity must be located within the historically reified sociocultural norms of '*dar al-Islam*' is at the root of the identity problems experienced by many self-conscious Muslims born in Britain and the West. The tension created between the realities of a developed western Muslim identity and a perceived religious infidelity based on a bipolar interpretation of the world into Muslim and non-Muslim spaces, precipitates a crisis of identity that can either result in an outright rejection of religious belief and tradition or a pull towards religious radicalism and ultra-orthodoxy. When this unsettling identity experience is coupled with social exclusion, racial discrimination, Islamophobia and ill-conceived foreign policies that appear to be increasingly focused on and concerned with Muslims, a fracturing or bifurcation of such complex and delicate multilayered identities can result in extremely reactionary and negative responses. While I would urge Britain and the West to embrace its Muslim minorities by taking extra steps to address their impedance as fully integrated citizens, I would advise that integration should not be at the expense of any community's distinct religious beliefs and practices. Encouraging Muslims to detach themselves from Islam, by whatever means, is extremely counterproductive to any claims of being a liberal, tolerant and inclusive societies. Besides, what contribution could assimilated Muslims, as disassociated individuals from their faith, offer to European society and civilization beyond post-Enlightenment self-alienation? At the same time, the self-perpetuated otherness and unbelongingness of some Muslim minorities in the West produces a resistance and reticence to engage with their new sociocultural environments.[30] This self-imposed alienation is not only a missed opportunity to develop human civilization and the progress of humanity; it is a fundamental abdication of the Qur'anic responsibility to, 'invite to the way of your Lord with wisdom and a beautiful preaching' (Qur'an, 16:125).[31] From this particular minority Muslim 'Occidentalist' perspective, there is both a faulted theology and a cultural misinterpretation relating to *fiqh* (jurisprudence) and '*urf* (cultural traditions) denying any religious contextualization and civilizational interactivity with the west. The inability of this subgroup to understand their minority-Muslim status within their new abode occasionally produces an exaggerated or extreme reaction to the perceived predicament. But how does one separate religion from culture when the misguided belief is that to 'westernize' Islam is to commit a theological innovation and cultural aberration? Trapped into this particular way of thinking, this introspective minority are religiously, culturally and psycho-geographically bound elsewhere and are, therefore, in the West, but not of it. I would boldly suggest that the migration paradigm of Makkah to Madinah is an inappropriate one for Muslims in the West, and its application has produced both a defective *fiqh* and,

---

[30] See K. H. Ansari, 'Negotiating British Muslim Identity', in M. S. Bahmanpour and H. Bashir (eds), *Muslim Identity in the 21st Century: Challenges of Modernity* (London: Book Extra, 2000).

[31] A. Y. Ali, *The Holy Qur'an: Translation and Commentary* (Beirut: The Holy Qur'an Publishing House, 1985), p. 689.

more importantly, a complete cultural misinterpretation of Muslims as minorities. The appropriate paradigm is *not* the Makkah to Madinah migration of the Prophet but, rather, the earlier migration of Makkah to Abyssinia.

The *hijrah* to Abyssinia took place eight years before the Madinan *hijrah* and revisited the earlier migrations to Africa mentioned in the Qur'an undertaken by Prophets, including Abraham, Joseph and Jesus. The question is, why did the Prophet Muhammad allow more than a hundred of his companions to migrate to Abyssinia? Abyssinia was well-known to the pre-Islamic Arabs of Makkah as a trading centre connecting northern and southern Arabia to the African continent via the Red Sea at Jeddah. It was a sophisticated ancient Unitarian (*muwahidoon*) kingdom which included Nubia, present-day Ethiopia, Eritrea, Sudan and large parts of Somalia. It also had strong historical links with the Arabian peninsula, particularly the people of Makkah. It was a former imperial power in the region, as well as being the major route into Africa and, as a result, was a prosperous kingdom. Some Makkans had direct ancestral roots to Abyssinia, including Bilal and the mother of Usamah ibn Zayd. The relentless persecution of the early Muslims by the pagan Arabs had a major bearing on the decision of the Prophet to allow migration to Abyssinia. Muslims could not openly declare their faith or practice their religion, and a few early believers, including Sumayah bint Khubaat, had been tortured and killed in an effort to make Muslims renounce Islam. After witnessing such suffering, the Prophet announced,

> If you desire you may migrate to Abyssinia, you will find a king there under whom no one suffers wrong. It is a land of truthfulness.[32]

When the pagans became aware of the migration, they sent an embassy to Najashi, the Abyssinian king, with gifts and tokens, in an effort to secure the extradition of the Muslims back to Makkah. But the King was just and he considered the Muslims' case, and after considering their beliefs he concluded, 'What has been revealed to your Prophet and what Jesus taught came from the same source' and he allowed them refuge in the kingdom with permission to freely practice their religion.[33] One of the 100 or so migrants to Abyssinia was Ramlah bint Abu Sufyan and her husband, 'Ubaydah ibn Jahsh. 'Ubaydah later rejected Islam and instead became a Christian. However, the Prophet forbade Ramlah to divorce her husband, who some years after died as a result of his addiction to alcohol.[34] Ten years later, the Prophet sent a proposal of marriage to Ramlah via Najashi, proving that correspondence and relations between the Prophet and the Abyssinian king were extremely cordial. It is also important to note that the Prophet did not order the migrants back to Arabia after his own migration to Madinah and even at times of great need, like the battle of Badr of Uhud. Muslims lived peacefully, loyally and respectfully as a

---

[32] Cited in Hussain, 'Migration and Settlement', p. 25.
[33] Ibid., p. 27.
[34] M. Y. H. Siddiqui, *The Prophet Muhammad: A Role Model for Muslim Minorities* (Leicester: The Islamic Foundation, 2006), p. 67.

religious minority among the Christians of Abyssinia. Negus also sent a delegation to Madinah to observe the Prophet and study the Qur'an, and it is recorded that when they met him and heard the Qur'an they wept with humility and submitted to the faith. The Muslims of Abyssinia lived as protected and integrated citizens of the Christian state, accepting Najashi as their sovereign ruler without any tension or contradiction of their allegiance to the Prophet Muhammad and Islam.[35]

Conclusion

It could be argued that the diaspora Muslim community of Abyssinia had direct contact and guidance from the Prophet, unlike the minority Muslim communities in the West today, who rely on guidance largely from religious scholars who are either based in the countries of origin of particular diaspora Muslim communities, or are imported to the West from there. The result is a skewed interpretation of loyalty and belonging from a limited perspective based almost entirely on the Madinan model of migration. Closer scrutiny must be paid to the Abyssinian migration model, which has greater resonance and similarity to the social and political realities of the West's minority Muslim communities of the present. Equally, there needs to be a complete revision of how Islam is framed and understood in the West. Negative and highly Islamophobic remarks made against Islam and the Prophet Muhammad can only heighten misunderstanding and sensitivities between minority Muslim communities and wider Western society, and their impact on increasing hostilities between Christianity and Islam or the West and Muslims cannot be over emphasized. Further, to claim that such unfounded remarks are not intended to exaggerate the cultural divide and religious sectarianism is difficult to accept, given the current global political climate. If Muslims in Britain and the West are to define themselves within the dictates of their primary texts – the Qur'an and Prophetic teachings – a theology of minority-status Islam must be developed by Muslim scholars, while at the same time, pressure needs to be brought to bear by rulers and governments from Muslim countries around the world on how Britain, Europe and America's governments, institutions and wider societies represent Islam and Muslims.

I. Response to Mohammad Seddon

C. T. R. Hewer

The relationship between any religious group and the society or state within which it lives is, as Mohammad Seddon's chapter indicates, always complex and variable. If we think only of Western European Christianity historically, we have moved

---

[35] For a detailed exposition on the Abyssinian migration, see M. S. Seddon, 'Ancient and Modern Muslim minorities under Christian Rule: A comparative study of Islam in 7th-century Abyssinia and contemporary Britain', in *Crucible: The Christian Journal of Social Ethics* (July–September, 2008), pp. 41–54.

from a situation in which the Pope of Rome was regarded as being empowered to remove kings who did not rule, according to his judgement, in ways approved by God, to a system of laïcité, and indeed in parts of Europe formerly under the influence of the USSR, enforced outward atheism. We have experienced princes deciding the religion of their territories and see the results of State Churches (Denmark), various forms of privilege (Germany, England and Eire), and historic connections (France, Italy and Spain). The Muslim position is no less complex, with periods of one united Caliphate, times of concurrent geographically limited multiple Caliphates (e.g. Abbasid, Umayyad and Fatimid Caliphates), semi-autonomous regions (Egypt under the Ottomans) and a non-Muslim majority ruled by a Muslim minority (the Mughals in India). Around the world today we see more or less Muslim rule under the hereditary direction of kings, emirs, and so forth, modestly cloaked dictatorships and 'emerging democracies'. We see the changing role of Islam in secular Turkey and in Iran under its religious-political leadership. Even if we look at Great Britain, the place within the structures of society played by the established Church of England, the disestablished Church in Wales and the Presbyterian Church of Scotland is by no means equivalent. The situation in which one religious community is dominant over the others is as much evident in the history of the dissenting churches in England as it is for the Muslim communities as highlighted in this chapter.

The monumental sociological shift that has come over Western Europe in the last 50 years cannot be overemphasized. A city as cosmopolitan as London (in terms of culture, ethnicity and religion) has never before existed. This is being replicated in varying degrees throughout the major cities and towns of Western Europe. We need to subject this to theological scrutiny: is there a theological justification for territoriality, or is religion used as a bulwark for tribal land rights? What Christian or Muslim grounds exist to say that my DNA-bearers have more right to live on this land mass than those whose forefathers inhabited parts of Africa or Asia? With both faiths speaking of the human being as steward (*khalifa*) under God, is not the whole of creation to be shared for the benefit of the whole of humankind?

The same monumental shift applies when thinking of the construction of human society in this new situation. Islam and Christianity are not tribal religions, giving guidance exclusively for their members. Both would say that they are the bearers of revealed wisdom, lived out by communities for centuries, on how to live the human project so that people may flourish into what both would describe in their different ways as 'the fullness of humanity'. The Islamic Shari'a, for example, drawn from the Qur'an and customary practice of Muhammad, is not guidance for a group of people called Muslims, but must be seen as the exemplification of the *din al-fitra*, the natural way for human beings to live and flourish. This changes the discussion from one of 'making space for Muslims in British society' to one of Muslims contributing from their accumulated treasury of wisdom to the common task of building a truly human society in Britain or elsewhere. In this way, neither the Madinan nor the Abyssinian models, as indicated by Mohammad Seddon, are sufficient. We are not in a 'majority guidance'

(Madinan) society or a 'majority-hospitality' (Abyssinian) situation, but one in which British citizens draw from their treasuries of wisdom (religious, cultural and inherited) to apply insights and guidance for the benefit of all in this new situation. We are in the process of transformation into something new (integration) and not one of accommodation of newcomers/minorities. In this case, ideas of living in *dar al-kufr* or *dar al-harb* (the land of unbelief or of war) are inappropriate; we are all in this together. There may be a sense of a psycho-spiritual withdrawal from the standards of the society in which one lives, but this cannot equate to a parallel society alongside wider society; that way lies disaster.

In a sense, perhaps British society needs to become more secular, in the original Indian usage of that concept, not as 'anti-religious' but as 'neutral to any particular religion' and thus to open the forum for all religious communities and others to participate and bring to the discussion their views on what values, ethics and life-visions make for a society that promotes human flourishing. How critical this will be in the next three decades as we work through the consequences of the economic crises and other demographic and social changes! This is bound to require a renegotiation of the post-1945 social contract in Britain as we deal with an aging population, a crisis in housing, education and employment, pension and healthcare issues and an ever more apparent shortage of young people to make up the workforce. In this transformation debate we are entitled to ask: what earthly use are our great religious traditions?

In rethinking the theological questions, a key must be diversity. We have slowly learned to live with a diversity of Christian standpoints and have come to value this, but we need to see this in other communities, too. To take two relatively small religious communities in Britain, the Buddhists and the Jews, both have a wide range of ways of understanding their faiths (some of which can be mutually exclusive) and codes of practice, and yet have sufficient common ground to 'belong' to one another. The same is true within the wide family of Islam. Wider yet, however, as we have families of faith that need to make room for what unites them as well as the diversities that they contain, which can easily overlap religious boundaries. Whether we think of the Abrahamic or the Indic families, both of which are well represented in Britain, we are reminded that they are only two of the families of humankind and that all people have something to contribute to this transformation debate.

II. Response to Mohammad Seddon

Mahmood Chandia

Mohammad Seddon's chapter presents itself as a proposal that aligns to an Islamic Reformist position similar to the ideas discussed by Tariq Ramadan et al. It raises several important questions. The crucial questions surrounding this particular debate, as far as I can see, are, 'How exactly does this change/reformation happen?' 'To what extent should Muslims embrace secularisation in the minority contexts?'

'What is secularisation in the British context?' and 'What does progress and modernity mean in the Islamic debate context?' Beyond these social and cultural issues is a more nuanced debate regarding the status of *fiqh al-'aqaliyyah* ('the jurisprudence of Muslim minorities') and revisiting the traditional approaches/ understandings of *fiqh* for Muslims in a minority position. Consequently, the revisionist approach is particularly framed within the 'Islam in the West' discourse. Here, the considerations are about, first, a Christian understanding of Islam or, rather, how is Islam understood by Christianity and can theology answer the important questions asked? If Britain is understood to be largely a secular country, then one needs to ask, does the Christian (religious) viewpoint relating to Islam indeed matter?

From the Islamic perspective, the primary questions explored by Seddon are, 'How does Islam legitimize Muslims living in a Christian space?' 'To what extent is the Makkah to Madinah or Makkah to Abyssinia (i.e. the two migrations) an appropriate paradigm?' and 'What represents *bay'ah* ('allegiance' or, 'loyalty and belonging') in the seventh-century Abyssinian setting and in the modern globalized setting of Britain?' This discussion seeks to discover the important similarities and differences of both settings in relation to the presence of Muslims as minorities.

Perhaps due consideration should also be afforded to other questions that need to be asked regarding the developed understanding of the wider social and cultural settings that Muslims found living in Abyssinia and find living in Britain. I would suggest that a lack of understanding of the host culture in its widest definitions is largely missing in the contemporary setting. Understanding the cultural traditions and practices of British society is paramount to answering the important questions about where and how Muslims as minorities may place themselves.

To this end and with regards to the wider questions of migration, the Qur'anic injunctions allow free emigration of mankind in particular from places where Islam was being persecuted and suppressed. There are several verses in the Qur'an that discuss migration (2:218; 97:4; 4:100, etc.) and also shed light on the semantic field of the root form '*h-j-r*' from which the word '*hijrah*' comes. The question of the prohibition or permissibility of specific forms of migration have a greater nuance within the developed methodologies of Islamic jurisprudence (*fiqh*) and may even differ between various methodologies and from particular time and space contexts. As for the minority Muslim situation in the UK, where more than 50% of the Muslim population is now born in the UK, minority Muslim status may have more similarities to other, earlier, migrations of religious 'others', such as the Jews and Catholics. Understanding their historical migration experiences and narratives might offer some important insights for Muslims to consider. The previous experiences of religious migrants may also further help Muslims to shape/understand manifest aspects of their being and belonging within the specific British context.

Moreover, the question facing traditional Muslim scholars relates largely to ideas about the flexibility offered to Muslims within the framework of Islamic jurisprudence via the various *madhahib* (major legal schools). A combination of the theological and sociological explorations and experiences of the minority Muslim predicament forces the question, 'at what point do we become comfortable as Muslims in the UK?' This is a leading question that points towards a sense of the Muslim community 'maturing' and is perhaps a question easier asked through the process of organic growth, cross-generationally. By this I mean the increasing interactions between Muslims and wider society as a lived experience from one generation to another. In this natural process, the mutual terms of reference are fully developed within both communities – Muslims and the wider British society, feeling at ease with one another and avoiding the imposition or the perception of imposition of each other's beliefs and practices upon the other. This consideration of the 'organic development' of a community/ies can perhaps offer the 'two migrations paradigm', albeit useful, a more panoramic and richer perspective.

III. Concluding Comments

Mohammad S. Seddon

I am grateful to both Chris Hewer and Mahmood Chandia for their insightful and thought-provoking responses to my chapter. They have posed a number of pertinent questions for consideration. Picking up from some of the issues raised by Chris, I would concede that there is little to disagree with in his wider comparisons of the historical, political and theological developments within Christianity and Islam. However, I would make the distinction that while Western European 'Christendom' developed as a theological and political response that eventually disestablished Roman Catholicism as the overarching theocracy, an event that precipitated religious pluralism and national identity via sovereign independence, nation statism and post-Enlightenment anti-essentialism, any similar developments across the post-imperial, decolonized Muslim spaces in what was formerly theopolitically understood as *dar al-Islam* were not a matter of choice. This is because where theological scepticism and sovereign territorialism became a means of European self-empowerment, the imposition of hereditary tribal kingdoms and 'big brother' *ubernationalism* are the unfortunate residue of Christendom's colonization of *dar al-Islam*. I am also less optimistic of the possibility of 'emerging democracies', whether externally imposed or by the will of the people, flourishing across the much-fissured 'Muslim world'. A further irony that is the modern, secular nation state of Turkey – as a deterritorialized former pan-Islamic caliphate just less than three generation ago – is now grappling with what it means to be both European and Islamic, a perplexing question for modern Turks and their European neighbours, but one that would have been given little consideration in the Eastern European provinces during Ottoman rule. What Chris (and Mahmood) appears to be advocating in the absence of any inclusive theology in the British Muslim context is an ethical approach to religious and cultural pluralism based on mutual ideas of the 'common good'. This is to be commended, but seeking answers to real theological problems through Christian Ethics or *maqasid al-shari'ah* (principles of religious law) suggests an inventive stretching of theology, inclined towards a secular humanist position, aimed at solving religious difference. This overtly humanist approach offers a strange and uncomfortable bedfellow for the more religiously inclined from both traditions. Further, the mutual reciprocity implied leads me to accept that we are not, indeed, in 'a "majority guidance" (Madinan) society' as Chris rightly observes; however, I would strongly dispute the assertion that we are *not* in 'a "majority-hospitality" (Abyssinian) situation'. Any claims that Christianity, like Islam, is a 'minority faith' in Britain need to be measured against the empirical realities of the UK's Anglican Protestant constitution and vicarious notions of Christian belonging attested by at least 73% of Britain's population.[36] However, I do agree that moving beyond the post-colonial migration phenomenon of the late twentieth century, for both indigenous Britons and Muslim settlers, will be the litmus test for any developed practical theologies intent on healing religious and cultural discord. Further, If the future flowering of British society is to allude to a type of Andalusian idealism, then the currency of multiculturalism, presently framed both culturally and religiously within a distinctly Anglocentric Britishness, needs to be significantly reconsidered.

While Chris asks overarching questions that seek to explore what kind of inclusive society Britain might become, as a mutually inclusive process that is largely built on humanist principles correlating with Christian religious ethics and Islamic legal definitions, Mahmood focuses on asking specific questions of Muslims. In doing so, he poses a series of rhetorical questions that broadly ask, 'How do Muslims become minortorian, modern and secular?' Thereafter, he seeks an understanding of how minority Muslims are framed within the context of Christian theology and Western civilization. To address the first question, one needs to refer to the migration and settlement history of Muslim communities in the West, tracing their experiences in the realms of racism, discrimination and social exclusion before considering the many complex ways in which Muslims negotiate modernity and secularity as a central feature of their lives and engagement in the wider spheres of Western societies. I would suggest that the detailed studies of sociologists like Tariq Modood and Muhammad Anwar offer us a great deal of empirical evidence that measures the acculturation and integration processes and experiences of British Muslims. As for how we might understand the 'placing' of Muslims/Islam within a Christian theological and civilizational schema, the answer to this deeply complex and ever-changing historical narrative has also been explored in the seminal works of Edward Said, Rana Kabbani and Ziauddin Sardar, to name but a few.[37] Perhaps Mahmood's most pressing questions are those relating to how Muslims theologically justify not just a minority relationship to

---

[36] This statistic is taken from the 2001 Census.
[37] For an extended discussion on this subject, see M. S. Seddon, 'Locating the Perpetuation of "Otherness": Negating British Islam', in M. S. Seddon, D. Hussain and N. Malik, *British Muslims Between Assimilation and Segregation: Historical, Legal and Social Realities* (Markfield: The Islamic Foundation, 2004), pp. 119–44.

'majority-hospitality' Christianity, but also how they legitimize their broader attachment to and understanding of Western civilization. Here, the answer lies not only within the Prophetic examples of *hijrah* to Abyssinia or Madinah, including the semantic and jurisprudential possibilities; the discussion requires a developed engagement with the term *makkaniyyah* (lit., 'placement'). As a concept, the term implies the 'placing' or 'acculturating' of oneself, or community, within a specific sociocultural context, exactly as the Muslim migrants did in both Abyssinia and Madinah. Engaging with the idea of *makkaniyyah* both aids Muslims in answering their 'loyalty and belonging' predicaments, and conforms to the wider notions of migration from the Qur'anic paradigms. Further, the idea of minority Muslims becoming embedded or acculturated into wider society allows for an 'organic development' in terms of their aspects of 'being and belonging' within the specific British (and Western) contexts. At the same time, it addresses Mahmood's key question, 'at what point to we become comfortable as Muslims in the UK?' What is clear from our discussions relating to how the exclusive, historical particularities of Christian theology and Islamic *fiqh* find difficulty in accommodating religious pluralism and diversity, is that a degree of theological rethinking is needed within both religious traditions. Whether in the process of negotiating theological negation within both faith traditions the solutions are gleaned through an ethical application of theology or a reformist position that is aimed at revising limited jurisprudential interpretation, the end results appear to provide a more practical theology.

3 The Lord of All: Rediscovering the Christian Doctrine of Providence for the World

Tom Greggs

Systematic theology should be the most humble of all disciplines in the theological enterprise. Its role is to engage in second order statements about the Christian faith which might aid the reading of Scripture in the preparation of sermons which proclaim the good news of the Kingdom of God to the people of faith. And having listened to this proclamation, systematic theology must rethink its own propositions in light of the command of God in the word heard through the proclamation that arises from Scripture. The so-called system can never be static or completed, therefore, but must be dynamic and responsive to the call of God and to the endless depths of the Bible.

However, given its role within the hermeneutical cycle, informing the reading of Scripture and the sermons that arise from that reading, and then being informed by the sermons and led back to Scripture, systematic theology must recognize that its own speech has a determining role in informing the preaching of the church, and thereby in shaping the church and the society of which the church is a part. Systematic theology has, therefore, both a descriptive role, as it arises from within a tradition, and a prescriptive role, as it seeks to shape and form that tradition. In its prescriptive role, systematic theology must be alert to the effects it has on the church and society. Systematic theology should never exist, therefore, as if it were simply an intellectual game separated from its relationship to, and impact upon, the church and society; nor should it understand its relationship to the church as being singularly creative: it is in arising from its descriptive enterprise that its prescriptive work has a place, because the context of the prescription is in response to the preaching of the church, in light of the reading of Scripture. The prescriptive work of systematic theology is, while always provisional, directed towards the context from which the description has arisen, with the desire to make that description more true to Scripture.

At a time when the place of religion and the religions is very much on the national and international stage, there is a responsibility for theologians to consider how to understand the place of the religious other in their theological systems.[1] As a people who are called by Scripture to 'seek the peace of the city' (Jer. 29.7), systematic theologians must engage in their own way in protecting and creating peace in the complexly secular and religious societies in which the church exists.[2] Theology must attend to areas in Christian self-description which might offer the potential for hospitality and peace towards the religious other, through forming from Christian self-description the potential for future sermons which are true to that genuine Christian identity, and which offer a hospitable place for the other. In offering a light framework with which to read Scripture, systematic theology should seek to articulate the doctrinal and theological rationale for the potential of such hospitality.

No single chapter (or indeed volume) could hope to achieve this in and of itself. The present piece cannot be, therefore, a piece of regular dogmatics, in that there is not the space to engage in the various interconnections of individual doctrines in their relations to each other. This piece is instead a work of irregular dogmatics,[3] that seeks to identify and engage one major doctrine of the Christian church, that of providence, and to seek to identify from it what might be gained from attending carefully to it for the broader theme of exclusion and religion.[4]

The method of seeking to identify one central doctrine which is particularly and exclusively Christian and working on that doctrine might seem an odd one in terms of preventing exclusion. However, if systematic theology has a formative role in shaping communities through its simultaneously being informed by and informing of Christian preaching, and if systematic theology can identify areas of Christian proclamation that might help with the propagation of peace (or at least the prevention of exclusion), then it will have practical implications for the church and society by aiding the reading of Scripture for the preachers who are confronted regularly with congregations comprising members of society. That this discussion takes place singularly within the context of the Christian community does not undermine its desire to prevent wrong forms of exclusion. It is not the place of the Christian to

---

[1] See my 'Legitimizing and Necessitating Inter-faith Dialogue: The Dynamics of Inter-faith for Individual Faith Communities', *IJPT* 4 (2010); and 'Religionless Christianity and the Political Implications of Theological Speech: What Bonhoeffer's Theology Yields to a World of Fundamentalisms', *IJST* 11 (2009), pp. 293–308.

[2] The term 'complexly religious and secular' is borrowed from D. F. Ford, 'Gospel in Context: Among Many Faiths', paper presented at the Fulcrum Conference, Islington, Friday 28 April 2006.

[3] Cf. K. Barth, *Church Dogmatics* (Edinburgh: T & T Clark, 1956–1975), vol. I, pt. 1, pp. 275–8. Henceforth, *Church Dogmatics* is cited as volume/part, page (e.g. I/2, 3, etc.).

[4] This is a method which has been used in Christian theology in J. A. DiNoia, *The Diversity of Religions: A Christian Perspective* (Washington, DC: Catholic University of America Press, 1992).

offer dictates or even advice to the religious other. To do so is a version of inclusion that includes by doing violence to the otherness of the other: it includes by making the 'other' the 'same'. To limit with humility the focus of the discussion and potential implications is not an engagement in exclusion, but a recognition of the various exclusivisms in operation in theological speech. Limiting the remit of the piece determines that I can never be so arrogant as to presume to speak on behalf of, or to change, those who are members of other faiths or none, but only those who are members of my own community.[5] Indeed, the focus of this piece is even more narrow still, since it is articulated in the context of the author's own ecclesial setting, that of evangelical Protestantism. In concrete terms, therefore, this chapter seeks to influence the preaching of evangelical Christians in terms of the issue of the exclusion of the religious other, by attending to one motif of Christian theology that reminds the preacher of the universality of God's grace. It is in this way that, in addition to addressing theoretical questions about exclusion, this chapter seeks to have practical implications for the life of the church in the world.

Equally as strange may seem my choice of interlocutor for this essay. Karl Barth is popularly understood to be an antagonistic exclusivist with concern only for the Christian, and even then only really for the Calvinist. Within his discussions of providence, Barth even refers at one point (in a way which is unpalatable for our contemporary setting) to 'the semi-biblical religion of post-Christian Judaism and the paganised form of this religion, Islam'.[6] Barth's attitude to other religions is hardly progressive. This is problematic especially when one considers that Barth's magnum opus is often read scholastically and treated as a monolith either to be rejected or accepted *in toto*. However, to be true to Barth, it is necessary to treat him in the same manner that he thought it was necessary to treat Calvin: 'those who simply echo Calvin are not good Calvinists, that is, they are not really taught by Calvin. Being taught by Calvin means entering into dialogue with him, with Calvin as the teacher and ourselves as the students, he speaking, we doing our best to follow him and then – this is the crux of the matter – making our own response to what he says.'[7] It is such a dialogical approach towards Barth that this essay seeks to follow, as it desires, in dialogue with the great Basel professor, to articulate a theology of providence which can serve the church and world in this time of religious conflict,[8] a conflict often undergirded by separationist and exclusivist approaches to the religious other preached from pulpits of (among others) the evangelicals of my own ecclesial community.[9]

---

[5] For more on this, see my 'Legitimizing and Necessitating Inter-faith'.

[6] III/3, p. 28.

[7] K. Barth, *The Theology of John Calvin* (Grand Rapids, Eerdmanns, 1995), p. 4.

[8] For exegetical discussion of Barth on providence, see K. Tanner, 'Creation and providence', in J. Webster (ed.), *The Cambridge Companion to Karl Barth* (Cambridge, CUP, 2000), pp. 111–26; and G. Hunsinger, *How to Read Karl Barth* (Oxford: Oxford University Press, 1991), pp. 185–224.

[9] See my *Barth, Origen, and Universal Salvation: Restoring Particularity* (Oxford: OUP, 2009), pp. vii–xv.

A Strong Doctrine of Providence

For all of Barth's seeming religious exclusivity, his *Doctrine of Creation* presents a tremendously strong doctrine of providence. Indeed, it is necessary to remember that while Reformed theology has traditionally taught double predestination, the doctrine of election has always been articulated alongside a strong doctrine of the providential guiding of all of history by God. The sense of this providential preservation and guiding cannot be limited. For Barth, the depth of this is almost unfathomable:

> Everything was open and present to Him: everything in its own time and within its own limits; but everything open and present to Him. Similarly, everything that is, as well as everything that was, is open and present to Him, within its own limits. And everything that will be, as well as everything that was and is, will be open and present to Him, within its own limits. And one day – to speak in temporal terms – when the totality of everything that was and is and will be will only have been, then in the totality of its temporal duration it will still be open and present to Him, and therefore preserved: eternally preserved; revealed in all its greatness and littleness; judged according to its rightness or wrongness, its value or lack of value; but revealed in its participation in the love which He Himself has directed towards it. Therefore nothing will escape Him: no aspect of the great game of creation; no moment of human life; no thinking thought; no word spoken; no secret or insignificant enterprise or deed or omission with all its interaction and effects; no suffering or joy; no sincerity or lie; no secret event in heaven or too well-known event on earth; no ray of sunlight; no note which has ever sounded; no colour which has ever been revealed, possibly in the darkness of oceanic depths where the eye of man has never perceived it; no wing-beat of the day-fly in far-flung epochs of geological time.[10]

God's involvement in every aspect of creation is a reality that can neither be suspended nor removed, as it is grounded in the very ontology of God in the second mode of His Being: 'in Jesus Christ God gave to the creature far too high a dignity, and God bound Himself to the creature far too seriously and unreservedly, for Him to be able to repent and to desire to be in isolation and apart from the creature.'[11] Clearly, all things are not held to be equal by God: everything will need to be judged, 'judged according to its rightness or wrongness, its value or lack of value'.[12] But God's involvement in His creation, His guiding and preservation, is universal and eternal for creation.

This strong doctrine of providence does not determine, however, that God can be confused with world events. Barth is emphatic that the God who providentially

---

[10] III/3, pp. 89–90.

[11] III/3, 89. Cf. on election, my *Barth, Origen, and Universal Salvation*, ch. 2; and P. Nimmo, 'Election and Evangelical Thinking: Challenges to our Way of Conceiving the Doctrine of God', in T. Greggs (ed.), *New Perspectives for Evangelical Theology: Engaging God, Scripture and the World* (London: Routledge, 2009), pp. 29–43.

[12] III/3, p. 89.

guides the world is the King of Israel.[13] However, Barth posits a connection between the events of Scripture and the belief in God as being the ruler of the world. On the one hand, the basis of this is in Scripture:

> To apprehend and affirm the idea we have to think of definite periods in human history as this name leads us. And we have to think of definite places – the land of Canaan, Egypt, the wilderness of Sinai, Canaan again, the land on the two sides of Jordan, Jerusalem, Samaria, the towns and villages of Judaea and Galilee, the various places beyond in Syria, Asia Minor and Greece, and finally Rome. We have to think of definite events and series of events which according to the witness of the Old and New Testaments actually took place at these periods and in these places, relating them always to the spoken and actualised 'I am.' And then necessarily we have to think of the concrete Scripture which bears witness to these events, the text of the Old and New Testaments.[14]

But, on the other hand, the Scriptures teach a God who is Lord of *all* things: 'For the Subject who speaks and actualises the "I am" in these events, the King of Israel, *is the God who rules the world*.'[15] Put otherwise, Barth posits a total salvation which includes all things in the victory of Christ:

> He is not only the way and the truth; He is also the life, the resurrection and the life. If He were not the Saviour in this total sense, He would not be the Saviour at all in the New Testament sense. It is a serious matter that all the Western as opposed to the Eastern Church has invariably succeeded in minimising and devaluating, and still does so to-day, this New Testament emphasis. And Protestantism especially has always been far too moralistic and spiritualistic, and has thus been blind to this aspect of the Gospel. In this respect we have every cause to pay more attention rather than less. We certainly cannot afford to make arbitrary demarcations, and therefore not to see, or not to want to see, the total Saviour of the New Testament.[16]

The breadth of the providential sustenance of God is difficult to limit for Barth.

Clearly, there are things in creation which are contrary to God's will and providential guidance; Barth discusses these things in the very same volume as his doctrine of providence, under the title 'Nothingness'.[17] However, it is clear that God's involvement in every tiny detail of creation and history includes, to some degree, the existence of other religions: they do not count simply as 'Nothingness'. Barth expounds this through a discussion of 1 Corinthians 13.12, about which he writes,

> What does it mean for an understanding of creaturely occurrence that it takes place in this co-ordination under the divine rule? We venture to answer, as we may well do in the

---

[13] See, for example, III/3, p. 176.
[14] III/3, p. 177.
[15] Ibid., emphasis added.
[16] III/3, p. 311.
[17] III/3, §50.

light of 1 Corinthians 13.12, that creaturely occurrence acquires in this co-ordination the character of a mirror. The distinction and inter-connexion of the two historical sequences are both brought out in this comparison. The original, God's primary working, is the divinely ruled history of the covenant. The mirror has nothing to add to this. In it the history of the creature as such cannot play any role. The mirror can confront it only as a reflector. It cannot repeat it, or imitate its occurrence. It can only reflect it. And as it does so it reverses it, the right being shown as the left and *vice versa*. Yet the fact remains that it gives us a correspondence and likeness.[18]

However, applying these themes to religion does not determine that there is an easy liberal notion of the historical relativity of all religions as reflections of the real thing, but not the real thing itself. Barth questions the existence of other religions through a discussion under this theme of Israel:

> How strange it is that there is still a people Israel, and that this people is so brightly spotlighted in our own day! Nor is there lacking the phenomenon of gods and their worship, of sacrifices, prayers and the like, of religious history. We must be careful not to identify the reflection with the original, the history of the creature with the true history of salvation. For reasons which have nothing to do with its creatureliness, the former is one long history of the very opposite of salvation, as emerges even more clearly in religious history, and in what is known as 'Israel' in world history. But we cannot overlook or deny the fact that creaturely history is still similar in every respect to the history of salvation, as a reflection resembles the original.[19]

While the assessment here of the typological category of 'Israel' seems on first reading to be rather negative – not confusing the continued existence of the religious creature with the *Heilsgeschichte* – there is, nonetheless, a sense in which there is genuine reflection of the history of salvation in these others: 'its occurrence is calculated to reflect and illustrate and echo these acts of God'.[20]

Differentiated Exclusivisms

It is necessary now to be a little clearer in terms of what Barth is doing with regard to the providential work of God and its relationship to other religions. As we have seen already, all that Barth states about providence arises out of specifically Christian speech and the basis of the Christian tradition, grounded supremely in Scripture. For Barth, the subject of providence must be discussed and undertaken 'from a Christian standpoint and with Christian material',[21] but its subject is the universal Lordship of God. In this, Barth is radically inclusive of all creation, but radically exclusive in terms of the basis for the claims he makes. It is as the result

[18] III/3, p. 49.
[19] III/3, p. 50.
[20] Ibid.
[21] III/3, p. 33.

of the special history of God with His particular people that one may know the
providential power of God in general world-occurrence. Only the radical exclusivity of the former can be the basis for any speech about the latter:

> That world history in its totality is the history in which God executes His will of grace
> must thus be taken to mean that in its totality it belongs to this special history; that its
> lines can have no other starting-point or goal than the one divine will of grace; that they
> must converge on this one thin line and finally run in its direction. This is the theme of
> the doctrine of providence. It has to do with the history of the covenant, with the one
> thin line as such. Or rather, it has to do with it only to the extent that it for its part is
> undoubtedly one among the many other lines of general world-occurrence, and that
> these many other lines of general world-occurrence have their ontic and noetic basis
> in the fact that the God from whom they come and to whom they return pursues on
> this one line the special work which the creature must serve on these other lines. The
> doctrine of providence must not level down the special history of the covenant, grace
> and salvation; it must not reduce it to the common denominator of a doctrine of general
> world occurrence. In so doing it would lose sight of the starting-point and therefore of
> its concept of the subject. And then it would no longer be speaking of the world domin-
> ion of God revealed in His Word. This God is the Father of Jesus Christ, the God of
> Abraham, Isaac and Jacob, the God of the prophets and apostles, the God who pursues
> His special work on this special line of world-occurrence. The doctrine of providence
> presupposes that this special history is exalted above all other history.[22]

This is no doubt a part of the radical inclusivity and exclusivity that is required of
monotheism: there (exclusively) is only one God, who is (inclusively) the God of
all the world. Barth puts it thus: 'There is no other meaning or purpose in history.
For there is no other God.'[23] While knowledge of God and God's special work is
known only through the salvation history of the Judaeo-Christian tradition, that
exclusivity does not mean that God is not the God who in His providence guides
all the world as well: 'There is only one God – the God of Jesus Christ – and God
is *that* God in all God's dealings with creatures.'[24]

I want to refer to this theological manoeuvre as a move of 'differentiated exclusivisms'. By this is meant that the exclusive knowledge of providence arises from
the special revelation of God to His people in Israel and the church (exclusively),
that it is (exclusively) the Christian God who is the ruler of all creation, *but* that
this God is (in a radically inclusive way) the God of all the world.

To understand this divine governance, one must understand the twofold rule of
divine governance. First, it is necessary to look at world events in general outwards,
from the particular (and exclusive) events attested in the Bible and the covenant of
grace executed in Israel and the community of Jesus.[25] Second, one must look back
from world events of nature and history to events attested in the Bible, from the

---

[22] III/3. pp. 36–7.
[23] III/3, p. 36; cf. p. 176.
[24] Tanner, 'Creation and providence', p. 114.
[25] III/3, p. 183.

promise which initiated it to the final fulfilment.[26] For Barth, it is true that 'general events have their meaning in the particular'.[27] Without this relationship to the particularity of the Judaeo-Christian tradition, the providential sustaining of the world would become little more than the 'activity of a chief Monad'.[28] In this way, Barth differentiates the God of Christian theology from other expressions of the divine:

> In most religious and philosophical systems there is some conception of a relationship between a higher and lower principle, an absolute, infinite, unconditioned or heavenly being and an earthly, spirit and matter, nature and reason, and of the superiority and even dominion in this relationship of the first and higher element over the second . . . But the relationship between Creator and creature with which we have to do in the Christian belief in providence stands outside this debate. The question whether there is in this relationship a Lord, and who this Lord is, is settled before it is asked. This alone shows us that the belief does not belong to the same category as religious and philosophical systems.[29]

Barth is conscious here of the danger of deducing God from or confusing God with history.[30] The key aspect for providence is that the Christian sees God *first*, the God who then illuminates this history for the Christian. This helps humans to see in the creation, in all of its multiplicity and confusion, a divine 'Nevertheless'. Crucially, this is only possible in *first* knowing God's providence. The Nevertheless 'is grounded in a supremely illuminating Therefore'.[31] Christian faith enables the Christian to see the world in a different way, identifying (albeit without transparency) the providential guidance of God in the world.

However, this providence is grounded in the person of God, and cannot be confused with a *principle* of providence. Not only is this the case for panentheism and pantheism, but it is also true for Barth of Christianity's brother religions of Islam and Judaism. He writes,

> Its [Rabbinic Judaism's] God and Ruler of the world has necessarily a strangely obscure and hidden character. The devout Jew is never wholly clear as to His love or wrath, His grace or judgment. And His obscure character is projected into His government of the world, which the devout Jew follows, but only with anxious and hypercritical concern to justify it, and not with the childlike confidence of the clear presupposition that He the Lord will always be in the right. Where it is not known that God has already done the right in a fulfilled history of salvation, it is impossible to attain to this presupposition in respect of His rule of the world. And in Islam this obscurity of God and His rule has been made a principle and therefore a caricature.[32]

---

[26] III/3, pp. 183–4.
[27] III/3, p. 184.
[28] III/3, p. 191.
[29] III/3, p. 27.
[30] Cf. III/3, pp. 123–4.
[31] III/3, p. 44.
[32] III/3, p. 28.

This is a deeply painful and difficult claim on Barth's part, and no doubt we would not wish to express these matters thus today. However, it is worth noting that the primary distinction here between the Christians and their Abrahamic brethren is exclusive *knowledge* of this reality: for Barth, the Jewish person is never 'wholly clear as to His [God's] love or wrath, His grace or judgement', and the concern with Islam is the making into a principle of God's obscurity and rule. Barth never, it is worth noting, considers that this is not God (in the sense of the proper noun); rather, his concern is the *perception* and degree of *knowledge* of the One God. Here, we may see a further level of differentiated exclusivisms: Judaism is differentiated as closer to Christianity than Islam, which is in turn – as the passage above unfolds – differentiated from pantheism and polytheism.[33] The revelation of God, even in His hiddenness, is the basis for the Christian doctrine of providence, not the general history itself. In this way, the Christian doctrine of providence is differentiated from all other expressions of providence. However, this does not limit God's providential guidance only to that which is Christian. The Christian is called in recognition of the providential power of God to recognize 'the revealed God in His hiddenness' and, as a child of the Father, to 'find his way about the House of the Father'.[34] Through the doctrine of providence, the Christian is called in exclusivity to recognize the universal lordship of God: from the particular expression of her faith, she is led to the universal of God's providential reach.

Differentiated Participation

These differentiated exclusivisms do not end simply with issues of epistemology (at least in terms of modernist understandings of 'knowledge'). The exclusive capacity of Christian doctrine to offer a true recognition of the universal lordship of God also determines a differentiated participation in history and providence for the Christian in contradistinction to all others. This does not determine that those outside of the Christian faith are not part of God's providential purpose; rather, it determines that the response to providence will be distinctive. We might identify this distinctive participation in God's providence in terms of the active participation of the Christian compared to the passive participation of the non-Christian.[35]

Barth arrestingly puts this as follows: 'Of all creatures the Christian is the one which not merely is a creature, but actually says Yes to being a creature.'[36] This is

---

[33] III/3, p. 28.

[34] III/3, p. 251.

[35] See J. M. Graham, *Representation and Substitution in the Atonement Theologies of Dorothee Sölle, John Macquarrie and Karl Barth* (New York: Peter Lang, 2005), pp. 318–20 & 396; cf. G. Hunsinger, 'A Tale of Two Simultaneities: Justification and Sanctification in Calvin and Barth', in J. C. McDowell and M. Higton (eds), *Conversing with Barth*, (Aldershot: Ashgate, 2004), pp. 76–9.

[36] III/3, p. 240.

because the Christian recognizes in her existence, alongside all others, the genuine universal Lordship of God in history. As Barth puts it with regards to the Christian,

> in virtue of what he (and only he) can see, the Christian is the one who has a true knowledge in this matter of the providence and universal lordship of God. This providence and lordship affect him as they do all other creatures, but he participates in them differently from all other creatures. He participates in them from within. Of all creatures he is the one who while he simply experiences the providence and lordship of God also consents to it, having a kind of 'understanding' – if we may put it in this way – with the overruling God and Creator.[37]

This does not mean, however, that the Christian has insight into the mysteries of existence; rather she is the only one 'who knows that there is no value in any of the master-keys which man has thought to discover and possess.'[38] This closing down also involves, therefore, an opening up, grounded in the very mystery of God, because the active participation that the Christian has in providence is in the *universal* lordship of God. Providence and the universal lordship of God are 'actual to the Christian in faith, in obedience, and in prayer'.[39] It is these which are the forms of the Christian attitude, notably an attitude which is marked by dynamism.[40] Faith, therefore, does not lead the Christian simply inwards – into the community or even the religious self. Instead, writes Barth: 'It is as he participates in Jesus Christ in faith that the Christian participates in the divine providence and universal lordship. The same Holy Spirit who first led him into the narrower and central sphere now leads him out over its periphery into the wider circle.'[41] Participation in the universal lordship of Christ determines an outwards and open perspective on creation. In obedience and by the power of the Spirit, the Christian is called to participate in the more general sphere of God's providence. In this the church is obedient to its calling. This calling is the calling 'obediently to participate in the lordship of God in this more general sphere, and therefore – and this is the real problem of obedience – to participate in it actively, justifying by his conduct that which God Himself is doing in this sphere'.[42] To be a Christian is, therefore, to be obedient to God's purposes *in the world* and not to form an isolated community separated from world-occurrence. Furthermore, it is in this way that one is to understand Christian prayer: 'the asking community stands together with its Lord before God on behalf of all creation.'[43] The service of prayer in the church community is not for religious self-preservation, but for the world more broadly.

[37] III/3, p. 242.
[38] Ibid.
[39] III/3, p. 245.
[40] Ibid.
[41] III/3, p. 248.
[42] III/3, p. 257.
[43] III/3, p. 279.

Thus for Barth, while God's providence rules all people, and we should not see other religions simply as 'Nothing', there is a differentiated level of participation for the Christian in comparison to that for the rest of humanity:

> His sovereignty is so great that it embraces both the possibility, and, as it is exercised, the actuality, that the creature can actively be present and co-operate in His overruling. There is no creaturely freedom which can limit or compete with the sole sovereignty and efficacy of God. But permitted by God, and indeed willed and created by Him, there is the freedom of the friends of God concerning whom He has determined that without abandoning the helm for one moment He will still allow Himself to be determined by them.[44]

The active participation of the believer in Christ in providence is such that, while God's sovereignty cannot be limited, the Christian is able to participate actively, while the others participate only passively. What one can see here, therefore, is not a distinction based on any limits of God's providential guidance, but instead a distinction based upon the response to providence. God's providential hand reaches to all people; but by the power of the Holy Spirit, the Christian is able to respond to this providence by actively participating in it.

What Does this Mean for Exclusion? Some Extensions of Barth for Other Religions

This all too brief tour of Barth has attempted to suggest various ways in which his doctrine of providence might be related to the existence of other religions. The purpose of this section of the chapter is to seek to draw some analytical comments from the foregoing discussion, and then to seek to think with Barth and, perhaps, point beyond him. In doing this, it is hoped that the theological themes tackled might be useful ones for the preacher to take back to Scripture in order to aid him or her in preaching in today's age and generation in which conflict between the religions is such a dominant discourse.

Firstly, the strength and weight of Barth's doctrine of providence determines that we must all recognize the very breadth and distance of God's reach. It is all too easy for Christian systematic theology to engage in various dualisms or binaries, seeking to identify where God is or is not present. Due attention to providence determines that one cannot think simply of God as present in some places and not in others. The God of the Christian faith is the God of all the world: there is no other god but the omnipresent Lord. Despite human, sinful rebellion, all of history is guided by Him, and the Christian is called to recognize the presence of God's will in all things – even when that will seems profoundly confusing and mysterious. To recognize the need to look outwards to the work of God in all the world from within the perspective of Christian faith is a healthy remedy to idolatrous propensities of identifying spaces in which God may be considered to be present and providentially guiding, and places in which God may be understood

---

[44] III/3, p. 285.

to be absent. Understanding the tremendous, detailed engagement of God with all creation forces the Christian to be more positive in her assessment of the world, seeing it as a place in which she is called to see God's action not simply within her community, but beyond the community as well. In an age of strife between the religions, rather than locating the idolatry of the religious other, the Christian is called away from the localizing of God (innate to idolatry) and towards true monotheism, which affirms that there is only one God.

This monotheism is, secondly, deeply Trinitarian for the Christian theologian. This Trinitarian dynamism leads to the need to articulate the differentiated exclusivisms and differentiated participation pointed to above. Through knowledge of Christ, the Christian is in the exclusive place from which to know the presence of God in all the world. Moreover, she is able to participate in this differently from all other peoples – actively participating in providence. Her faith, obedience and prayer, in the power of the Spirit, become an active participation in the providential workings of God. This does not determine that God is not present among non-Christians, or that His providential power is somehow rendered impotent; simply that the Christian engages differently in God's providence than the non-Christian. There is a reason, still, to be Christian, rather than a member of any other faith: particularity is retained.

Barth also, thirdly, points to a manner in which there might be deeper levels of differentiation between faiths. Barth is clear that providence is based on faith in Christ, and in that way the other Abrahamic faiths cannot know it in the same way as Christians, and he is clear that the Holy Spirit is the operation of God, who allows for active participation in providence. However, Barth does point to Rabbinic Judaism and Islam in their articulations of providence. While he does caricature (unhelpfully) the versions of providence that these faiths articulate, he still recognizes the distinction between their expressions of providence, and between their expressions of providence and those of pantheism, panentheism and polythesism. There are clear levels of exclusivity in operation here, and the other monotheistic faiths, since they affirm there is only one God, will inevitably share some of the Christian's concerns with regard to providence. They will not share these, nor the Christian's fuller knowledge and active participation, in the same way as the Christian, but nor will they share these in the same way as the pantheist and polytheist.

Thus, the Christian doctrine of providence is multiply differentiated: ontologically, God is Lord of all of the earth, but the reality of this is known only and exclusively in Christ, and this is known therefore by Christians most fully, who may – exclusively – by the power of the Spirit, participate actively in this providence. However, this participation in providence presses beyond the closed confines of the church and back into the world of which God is Lord. Certainly, Barth's doctrine of providence enables the Christian to seek to live faithfully as a Christian in a world which is marked by pluralism and competing exclusivisms, without retreating to a sense of the exclusive operation of God as simply within the Christian community. For Barth, this is all held together in ultimate eschatological hope:

> God created the conditions and pre-conditions and pre-pre-conditions of all creaturely working. God gave them to the creature. All the preliminaries of creaturely activity were

the effect of God's activity, of His friendly activity in the sense and to the end revealed and active in Jesus Christ, and in the history of the covenant of grace, of His activity as it was determined and controlled by His saving will. From the very first the purpose of God was to save and glorify the creature.[45]

From first to last, for Barth, God's plan for all creatures is their glorification; this is a plan not only for those who share in the special history of God with his church, but also for all creation, over which Christ is *pantokrator*.

There are, however, places in which one may wish to press beyond Barth. The differentiated exclusivisms which underlie his work could helpfully be discussed in terms of the differentiated covenants of God with creation. While for the Christian these might all be a varied participation in God's covenant with humanity in the person of Jesus Christ, Scripture is filled with varied covenants, and with God's differing relationships to creation. The Noahide covenant, for example, belongs specifically to the general sphere of God's covenant with all creation, and the promise of his preservation.[46] Furthermore, God's special history of salvation does not seem to be singularly focused on the people of Israel. Promises (or covenants) are made between God and Ishmael. In Genesis 16 and 21, one can see the promise of God to the descendants of Abraham through Hagar: there is a special purpose (more particular than the general purpose) present with these people. Differentiated exclusivism and participation require further development beyond the simple binary of God's special and general operations in providence. There is a special relationship of God with the children of Ishmael, just as there is with the children of Isaac, who do not enter the new covenant. Barth hints at this theme, but for those living today, there is perhaps the desire to develop his assertion:

> That world history in its totality is the history in which God executes His will of grace must thus be taken to mean that in its totality it belongs to this special history; that its lines can have no other starting-point or goal than the one divine will of grace; that they must converge on this one thin line and finally run in its direction. This is the theme of the doctrine of providence. It has to do with the history of the covenant, with the one thin line as such. Or rather, it has to do with it only to the extent that it for its part is undoubtedly one among the many other lines of general world-occurrence, and that these many other lines of general world-occurrence have their ontic and noetic basis in the fact that the God from whom they come and to whom they return pursues on this one line the special work which the creature must serve on these other lines.[47]

Recognizing God's ways with His other people is part of recognizing the covenant of grace uniquely revealed to the Christian. It recognizes that God is not only the God who is 'the Father of Jesus Christ, the God of Abraham, Isaac and Jacob, the

---

[45] III/3, p. 119.
[46] See G. O'Collins, SJ, *Salvation for All: God's Other Peoples* (Oxford: OUP, 2008), pp. 7–12.
[47] III/3, pp. 36–7.

God of the prophets and apostles',[48] but also the God of Ishmael, of Melchizadek, of Rahab, of Jethro and even of the pagan centurions. Systematic theology must take seriously the reality that the church's Lord is the Lord of all, and should recognize that in breaking down boundaries, we are likely to find God on the other side, there already. It is this message which systematic theology must make clear to a generation of preachers facing the complexities of a pluralist world.

I. Response to Tom Greggs

David Clough

To be an elector in the northwest of England on the 8 June 2009 was an uncomfortable experience: it was the day we learned that one of our eight representatives of the region in the European Parliament would be Nick Griffin, the leader of the British National Party (BNP), which advocates racist policies on immigration and other issues. To be a Christian elector was still more uncomfortable: the BNP often links Christian and racial identity in ways reminiscent of Nazi ideology and proposes expelling other religions from the United Kingdom. Tom Greggs accepts in this chapter the responsibility of theologians to attend to such political realities, noting that 'systematic theology must be alert to the effects it has on the church and society' (p. 44). Some of the theological tasks in this context are clear: theologians must anathematize the blasphemy of linking racial and religious identity in this way and reject the attempt to promote bigotry in the name of Christian faith. Other theological tasks, however, are less clear and more challenging. We should ask whether, for example, Christian preaching and witness in relation to members of other religions has contributed to attitudes that can be exploited by racist organizations, just as Christian anti-Semitism contributed to a political and social environment that made possible the acceptance of Nazi genocidal policies towards the Jews. If systematic theology should attend to the effects it has on the church and society, then theologians should be committed to being alert to the impact of Christian attitudes towards the religious other and, where this impact seems problematic, engage in the task of reconsidering whether our theological formulations are an adequate interpretation of Christian scripture and tradition in the context in which we find ourselves. This is the ongoing and always new task of theology: to discover how to express and communicate the truth of God and God's relations with creation in a new context that demands answers to new questions and responses to new challenges.

In this chapter, Tom takes up the challenge of rethinking a theology of the religious other in order to reform Christian preaching on the topic. His intended audience of evangelical Protestants is a tough crowd to win over on this issue, where Jesus's words 'no one comes to the Father except by me' (Jn 14.6b) have often been

---

[48] III/3, p. 37.

interpreted to mean damnation for those not confessing Jesus Christ in a particular way. Tom has the potential to win hearers for a wider view of God's purposes, even in this constituency, however, because he is advocating not a sloppy religious pluralism, but a particularist Christian interpretation of providence that remains guided by biblical and doctrinal norms. Choosing Barth as an interlocutor is an obvious additional asset: despite the uncomfortable Barthian texts concerning Jews and Muslims that Tom does not attempt to pass over, Barth's breathtaking vision of the boundless graciousness of God is that of a theologian intoxicated by the grace of God in Jesus Christ. To begin an argument for openness to the religious other at this point ensures that it will be seen to be the fullest expression of embracing a Christian vision of God, rather than the marginalization of central Christian insights in the context of a misguided interfaith project. The idea with which Tom concludes, of multiple covenants as a way towards expressing the authentic and particular relationship with God of Jews and Muslims, is particularly suggestive and fruitful, and deserves further exploration.

It should already be clear from the above that I am enthusiastic about this project of thinking with and beyond Barth to affirm God's providential care for all creation and therefore particular religious others. The long passage Tom cites from Barth concerning the universality of God's providential care (p. 47) cannot leave us comfortable with the exclusion of other creatures from a place in God's purposes on religious or other grounds. I share the view that it is precisely a commitment to be faithful to the Bible and Christian doctrine that drives us to reject exclusionary underestimates of God's creative and redemptive purposes. If I am to join the project of attempting to reshape Christian preaching on this issue, however, I would wish to do so in relation to three questions provoked by this chapter.

In the first place, I wonder whether the Barthian contrast of *active* Christian participation in lordship of God with non-Christian *passive* participation deserves to be taken up as uncritically as Tom seems to here (pp. 54). Of course it is necessary in the context of affirming the universality of God's purposes to make clear what the particular attributes of Christian believers are. Barth's characterization of this difference as 'the Christian is the one who has a true knowledge in this matter of the providence and universal lordship of God', quoted by Tom (p. 53) seems to me a good statement of this.[49] What I am not clear about is why it is necessary to follow Barth in making the transition from this distinction of Christians based on knowledge and belief to the active/passive distinction based on practice. One reason for resisting this move is a simple one of accuracy. When, after the plagues God brought on Egypt, the Egyptians encouraged the Israelites to leave, giving them silver and gold jewellery and clothing, the Egyptians were instruments of God's providential care of Israel. They participated in God's lordship unconsciously, but

---

[49] Such a particularist claim will seem offensive to those seeking to affirm, pluralistically, the equally valid insights of all religious traditions, but it seems to me that to take this latter view is to deny any reason for being a Christian at all, as well as to make the 'other' the 'same', as Tom notes (p. 46).

not passively: they were active in providing for Israel's departure. In an analogous way, Christians should consider those without Christian faith who provided relief supplies to those affected by the recent disaster in Haiti as unconscious but active participants in God's providential care for those in need. Many non-Christians are active in this way about God's work, though they would not characterize their activity in this way. To call such action passivity seems a mistake. Beyond a concern about accuracy, the active/passive distinction is in danger of suggesting that Christians are the only ones who actively care for others, with others merely being passively manipulated in order to bring about the outcomes God seeks. This could be interpreted to suggest that non-Christian acts of goodness are not properly human acts at all. It does not seem to me that we can say this without disrespecting the other. Instead, we should affirm that the universal lordship and providence of God means that, even among those who do not confess Jesus Christ as Lord, God is able to work to realize God's purposes through their active, but unconscious, participation.

The second point I wonder about is what the consequences of this line of theological development are beyond relations with Jews and Muslims. The differentiated covenants explored at the end of the essay are readily applicable to these two faith traditions, but what are Christians to make of other religious others? The strong affirmations of the universal characteristics of God's providence mean that no creature is outside God's providential purposes, but this chapter makes clear its aim of being particular, rather than generalizing. Religious others beyond the Abrahamic faiths must find their own particular place in God's providence, then. They are not heirs to the covenants enacted with the descendants of Abraham: does this mean they are among the many bound up in the Noahide covenant, together with the non-religious others also embraced by God's providence? As my chapter in this volume makes clear, I am also interested in the creatures who participate in this Noahide covenant who are beyond the boundary of the human, but that may be for another time. In any case, it seems we are stuck with a large general category in the Noahide covenant made up of non-Christian and non-human creatures. Is there something more particular we should be saying about other religious others, perhaps through some other language than that of covenant?

The third question this discussion raises concerns the consequences for an understanding of Christian mission, which seems a particularly important issue given the evangelical audience explicitly addressed by this chapter. If we believe that those outside a particular Christian group will be damned unless they confess Jesus Christ as Lord, the consequences for a theology of mission are straightforward: there is an imperative grounded in love of neighbour to evangelize in order to save as many as possible from damnation. What, then, are the consequences of this particularist and differentiated account of the religious other for Christian mission? If we retain a belief that Christianity understands most fully the truth of God's lordship and providence, as I agree we should, then we will be glad when those who have not previously recognized God in Christ come to this belief and knowledge of God. If, however, we acknowledge a providential purpose in God's covenant with Abraham's descendants through Hagar and Sarah, does this mean we should not seek urgently to lead them away from their own religious traditions to the Church? And again, what would be the result of asking the same question in relation to other religious others? The answer I am inclined to give is that the further our neighbours seem from recognizing the truth about God witnessed to by Christians, the more urgent the need to seek to bring the gospel good news to them. This need would seem least acute in relation to Jews and Muslims who are co-heirs with Christians to the promises made to Abraham, and most acute for those in desperate need of escape from nihilistic and destructive despair. I am aware, however, that this would not be the only option for interpreting the implications of this account of providence for Christian mission.

In conclusion, I am grateful for this instance of creative and faithful theological thinking in response to the demands of a new social and political context, and trust that it will precipitate new reflection by evangelicals and other Christians about the place of the religious other. Through such reflection and by other means, let us hope that it becomes increasingly apparent to the population at large that Christian doctrines are not available for co-option as props for racial or religious exclusion, and that a Christian view of God's universal providential care excludes only views that underestimate its boundless graciousness.

II. Concluding Comments

Tom Greggs

I am grateful to Professor David Clough for his thoughtful and provocative engagement with my chapter in this book. I am especially glad that he has highlighted the contextual concerns which have led to the piece, and for his comments on the political situation of our time. The response raises three helpful issues, and it seems most wise if I simply offer some brief thoughts about each of these.

The issue of passive/active engagement is an important one to be raised. The suggestion of a conscious engagement in God's providential purposes for Christians compared to unconscious engagement for non-Christians is, however, wrought with difficulties in my mind. Principal among these is that Christianity becomes simply some secret *gnosis*, with faith simply amounting to knowledge of a reality which is unaltered by faith. Certainly, God's providence is so strong and far reaching that people clearly will engage in performing His will and purposes even outside of faith: the example of Haiti pointed to is one case among millions. But the reality of faith as knowledge, acknowledgement *and* recognition determines that in knowing God's providential rule over the world, the Christian will seek to actively perform acts that correspond to God's will. The prayer 'Thy will be done on earth as it is in heaven' is one in which the Christian seeks a life of *active* correspondence to God's will, rather than passively being engaged in His sovereign rule; this prayer is the key. The Egyptians pointed to in the response had not been *actively* seeking God's will, but were alerted to God's universal sovereign rule and became aware that they were subject to His will (by virtue of the deaths of all of the first born), becoming passively submissive to His call of 'Let my people go'. In more positive instances alluded to by David there is, conversely, no active engagement in *God's will*.

Secondly, I am immensely glad that the matter of non-Abrahamic religions has been raised; this is helpful. There is certainly a need for much further exploration of these themes, and were there space, it would be good to consider these. However, two comments might be of use here. First, suffice it to say now, that I am convinced of the need for a plurality of engagement with different faith traditions, rather than one substantialized and universal approach: engagements with other faiths should always be specific and dynamic. With regards, therefore, to non-Abrahamic faiths, the dialogue concerning providence will be significantly different from faith to faith. In that way, the discussion of Islam and Judaism contained in this chapter should be thought of as indicative of an approach to engagement with other faiths which will need to be variously reconfigured from religion to religion. As Lindbeck puts it, 'different religions are likely to have different warrants for interreligious conversation and cooperation.'[50] What is offered in my chapter is just one attempt within just one religion to find a place for a more positive view of the religious other in a context in which relationships between Abrahamic faiths are strained. A dynamic engagement with other faiths determines that there is space for a plurality of approaches, of which this is just one. The ways of thinking about non-Abrahamic others might concern Jesus's engagement with gentiles, or God's use of the surrounding nations, or rules about hospitality to the stranger, and so on. Secondly, in terms of my thinking about multiple covenants, I now wonder whether the Noahide covenant is more meaningful for those who believe they stand under God's sovereignty, and should thereby be thought of by Christians as an expression of God's covenantal relationship with members of other faiths. Perhaps the broader and more universal category might be found in the covenant of creation and in the Adamic covenant? I am glad to be asked to engage further with this area, and it is perhaps in this direction that my future work might develop.

Thirdly, the response raises the issue of mission and the urgency of the gospel. This is a significant issue for anyone who considers the work of God outwith the walls of the church. In some ways, it relates to my first point: there is a need for a reason to be Christian, found in the present, active life of faith. This is a theme I have dealt with in detail before,[51] and I think the missional drive of the church is grounded in bringing the intensity of God's Spirit into situations, relating Christ's eternal work to the present. The missional activity of the church is, therefore, one primarily of witness and realization. Barth writes,

the Christian is a witness, a witness of the living Jesus Christ as the Word of God and therefore a witness to the whole world and to all men of the divine act of grace which

---

[50] G. A. Lindbeck, *The Nature of Doctrine: Religion and Theology in a Postliberal Age* (London: SPCK, 1984), p. 55.
[51] See T. Greggs, *Barth, Origen, and Universal Salvation*, esp. ch. 7.

has taken place for all men. Thus in what makes him a Christian the first concern is not with his own person. He is referred, not to himself, but to God who points him to his neighbour, and to his neighbour who points him to God. He does not look into himself, but in the most pregnant sense outwards.[52]

Christian engagement in mission should be reorientated towards engaging in witnessing to the reality and Lordship of Jesus Christ. This involves a preoccupation not with the Christian self (and perhaps not even with making the other a repetition of that self), but with the other who, as a neighbour, leads us to God.

All of these points are expressed far too telegrammatically, given the depth of insight that is offered in the response to my chapter. However, I hope that the above discussion may suggest the direction in which my thinking is led through David Clough's perceptive comments.

---

[52] IV/3, p. 652.

4 Does Sustainable Development Have a Future?

Celia Deane-Drummond

Climate change is the greatest humanitarian challenge facing humankind today. And it is a challenge that has a grave injustice at its heart.

Kofi Annan[1]

Development: A Question of Multiple Exclusions?

The very term 'development' is one that is politically loaded for those in the poorest communities of the world, for it implies joining onto a path of social and economic change that imitates the kind of development experienced in the richer nations of the world that are offering so-called 'development' packages. This model of development is based on a growth economy, where development is measured in terms of economic growth. The dominant model of development, in other words, excludes from discussion those who are on the receiving end of the resources offered and presses for growth of means to produce those goods to be consumed in the global market. But development that is driven by the global market economy also excludes in another way, in as much as it seems to encourage particular economic and social goals that originate in the liberal traditions of the richer nations of the Northern hemisphere. As such, it may be perceived as yet another form of colonization, an imposition on highly vulnerable communities of a particular way of life and social economy.

The climate change debates of recent years have highlighted both the complexity of this issue, and also the social exclusion and protectionism of different nation states – it seems almost impossible to reach genuinely shared goals that are internationally recognized and accepted. Yet those on the receiving end of the worst of

[1] Cited in GBM (2009), The Green Belt Movement Approach, Responding to Climate Change from the Grassroots (London/Washington: GBM International, 2009), p. 4.

climate impacts are, by any analysis, the most vulnerable and poorest members of the global community. Although some climate change happens anyway without human activity, the consensus of opinion is that activities that are human in origin are the main contributors to the global climate changes experienced in recent decades. There are also some who argue that we are close to what might be termed a tipping point, when climate impacts will be irreversible, and then get progressively worse.[2]

At the United Nations (UN) Climate Change Summit in Copenhagen in December 2009, the failure of richer nations to offer additional funds specifically related to climate change for those in the so-called developing world, over and above existing commitments, showed the difficulty of gaining a genuinely inclusive position when national or clustered national vested interests hold sway. The Danish text that appeared in the first week of negotiations at COP 15 seemed to serve European interests, but this was followed by another from South Africa, China and India, and two other texts, one from the rest of African nation states and one from the Pacific Island Communities. It was therefore hardly surprising that no legally binding agreement was reached at the end of the two-week period, but only a last minute political accord that could at best act as a holding exercise before other agreements are set up. While there are good arguments for legally and politically binding agreements in negotiations over climate change, I will suggest in this chapter that there is a strong need for *morally* binding agreements as well, based on transforming the typical Westernized view of social justice. Until the Western world faces the moral urgency of this problem, I have my doubts that there will be the political resolve to set up legally or politically binding international agreements.

Stories from the South

Although those in the South may not have heard of the term climate change, and may not know the theoretical reasons why sustainability is important, the stories of those who are experiencing the worst impacts of climate change make present its sobering reality. Hearing such stories is particularly important for those in Western democracies who are shielded from the worst effects of climate change through either accidents of geography or access to resources. Although the media has played its part in raising awareness of climate change, the number of citizens actively involved in political debate remains comparatively small. Yet a strong movement from the grass roots is perhaps the only way in which the political will to make changes will become energized and, eventually, national and international agreement reached.

In Cambodia, for example, the combination of drought, floods and typhoons undermines the very possibility of subsistence existence for peasant farmers. Mr Vanna, a volunteer vet with Development Partnership in Action in the Chum

---

[2] For a discussion, see M. Northcott, A Moral Climate (London: DLT, 2007).

Kiri district of Southern Cambodia, points out the cruel implications of climate change. He says, 'Our community is really concerned about increasing frequency of drought. If drought happens every year, it will continue to cause infectious diseases in our community and also in our livestock. And we depend on our livestock for income generation and to help us with our labour.'[3] Alongside this are problems related to access to clean water and health problems such as diarrhoea and dehydration, failed crops and an increase in pests. The community as a whole is suffering – including people, crops and animals. Those working to try and counter extreme poverty are seeing the fruit of years of hard work literally washed away. This is compounded by the collapse in global financial markets that showed up the vulnerability of high-risk investments. Ironically, perhaps, the work of charitable development agencies is boosted by a booming market economy that itself is part of the underlying problem that they seek to address.

Areas such as Niger and parts of Kenya, as well as other regions in Africa, are suffering drought that has increased in intensity. The way of life of those living in the Sahel desert region of Africa is under threat, as is that of the cattle-herding communities in Kenya. Chiri Bule, a farmer from Kenya, explains, 'The drought is often these days. It keeps coming back. Before we used to receive rain twice a year, but now it is sometimes only once, sometimes not at all.'[4]

Pacific island communities like the Kingdom of Tonga are likely to disappear altogether, erased with the next large tidal wave. Sr Senolita Vakata of Caritas International makes the following comment: 'We are lucky if a year goes past without a cyclone or hurricane hitting our country.'[5] Access to shallow fishing is completely disrupted due to coastal erosion and rising sea levels. Other low-lying regions, such as Bangladesh, face the prospect of extreme flooding and the eventual disappearance of low-lying areas through rising sea levels. It is hardly surprising, therefore, that at the 2009 UN Copenhagen Climate Summit, those representing the Pacific Island communities became angry when their call for a cap on overall target global temperature rise to 1.5 degrees Celsius was pushed to one side.

Failing harvests are common to Africa and South America alike. Maria Ferreira, from a village community in Brazil, comments, 'We need yams for porridge for breakfast but we don't have enough. Before we planted yams in the shade or sun and they all grew well. When the sun is so hot it's not good for the earth. Before the grass was always green. The football pitch is now yellow. It's so dry.'[6] Such examples represent only the tip of the iceberg – literally millions of people are now thought to be under threat from climate change, and the likely social disruption and human misery caused by environmental migrants is difficult to appreciate.

[3] C. Deane-Drummond, Seeds of Hope: Facing the Challenge of Climate Justice (London: CAFOD, 2009), p. 15.
[4] Ibid., p. 13
[5] Caritas Internationalis, Climate Justice: Seeking a Global Ethic (Vatican City State: Caritas Internationalis, 2009), p. 7
[6] Caritas Internationalis, Climate Justice, p. 9.

Defining Sustainable Development: A Western View

The term sustainable development started to be used over 20 years ago, in 1987, when the Brundtland Report defined sustainable development in the following way: 'Sustainable development is development which meets the needs of the present without compromising the ability of future generations to meet their own needs.'[7]

But given the stories of climate change from the South, what might sustainability actually mean? For even the survival needs of the present are definitively not being met for poor people in many parts of the world, and the prospect for future generations looks bleak – for some there is no future, where homelands are literally disappearing through rising sea levels or drought. The original Brundtland report perceived the loss of species diversity as a problem related to specifically human needs in the future, so that their loss compromised the ability of future human generations to meet their needs. But the study of climate change has shown how this assessment is oversimplified, since other species contribute to climate stability. Rainforests, for example, act like lungs for the planet, absorbing large quantities of carbon dioxide. This is one reason why destruction of the rainforest is so problematic, for it is meeting short-term human demands at the expense of long-term flourishing. In some cases, such as forest clearance for cattle ranging to prop up the hamburger market in the West, it is unnecessary for basic human needs.

The UK government has regularly spoken of sustainable development as a simple balance between present and future needs, baldly naming it as securing the future. Yet can development, which implies growth, be compatible with sustainability, which, in the context of climate change, implies a restriction on that growth in order to secure any possible future? The Report entitled 'Sustainable Development in a Changing Climate', released on 20 May 2008 by the House of Commons Development Committee, recognized that a separation of government strategy on climate change from that on sustainable development was mistaken. However, climate change still seems to be added onto the agenda as another issue to be considered within the framework of a market economic model of sustainable development, rather than challenging the overall validity of that model. This resulted in oxymoronic phrases such as 'progress towards sustainable development took account of climate change'.[8]

The White Paper published by the Department for International Development (DfID) in July 2009 takes up this theme in *Building Our Common Future*. However, the framework for that White Paper seems to be one in which environmental impacts are reduced to carbon emissions, which in turn are simply added to a specified economic model of development. CAFOD's Response to DfID's White

---

[7] World Commission on Environment and Development (1987) The Brundtland Report, Our Common Future (Oxford: Oxford University Press), p. 1.
[8] House of Commons Development Committee, 'Sustainable Development in a Changing Climate' (London: DfID, 2008), p. 9.

Paper Consultation is correct to criticize the White Paper's failure to adequately recognize that environmental impacts relate to specific lifestyle choices; for example, water shortages in impoverished regions owe as much to the production of water-intensive food sold to the Western world as to climate impacts. They also challenge the assumption that economic growth will automatically benefit the poorest members of society through some sort of trickle-down effect.

On the other hand, those who press for greater recognition of the importance of the well-being of all creaturely life in sustainable development argue that *all life* needs to be sustained, not just human life. The interconnectedness of all living systems in climate change discourse has heightened the need for a broader definition of sustainability that is inclusive of peoples and other creatures, rather than exclusive. Lesley Anne Knight, General Secretary of Caritas Internationalis comments, 'The answer to the climate change crisis lies in the hands of humanity – in a revived sense of solidarity and a realisation that we all have a duty to work towards the common good. . . . Like the global financial crisis the climate change crisis can be seen in terms of excessive borrowing: we have borrowed from the atmosphere and biodiversity of the future.'[9]

However, addressing climate change as such does not necessarily go far enough in protecting the diversity of different life forms, for climate action is concerned only about those species that, according to present knowledge, contribute in some way to climate stability. It is therefore a somewhat fragile basis for ecological conservation. It is here that tensions between sustainability and development arise; for the so-called poorer nations of the world, what shape of that development does justice demand? What might that justice mean?

What Justice? Whose Justice?

Social theories of justice making in the Western world have more often than not relied on various theoretical forms of social contract theory, pioneered by the work of philosopher John Rawls. It is important to spell this theory out in order to take account of the way justice and development is perceived in the West. John Rawls's difference principle states that where economic and social inequalities exist, they must be conditional on being of greatest economic benefit to the least advantaged in society.[10] Importantly, Rawls uses income and wealth as a measure of advantage. He also assumes that the contracts drawn up will be those between social equals.

This procedural theory of justice relies on an economic model of development in terms of Gross National Product (GNP) that is only really relevant in affluent liberal Western democratic societies. It represents a theoretical basis for justice making that largely fails to engage with the problems of gross global injustice and the

---

[9] Caritas Internationalis, Climate Justice, p. 4.
[10] J. Rawls, Theory of Justice, 2nd edn (Oxford: Oxford University Press, 1999), p. 53.

needs of those in the poorest regions of the world. Such problems include the fact that gross inequalities between rich and poor are widening even further for 80% of the world population. Somewhat shocking statistics include facts such as that 80% of the world population lives on less than $10 a day, more than 385 million live on less than $1 per day, and one in two children live below the poverty line.[11]

Alastair MacIntyre challenges the notion that we can arrive at grand theoretical schemes for justice making, believing that how we conceive of justice and rationality are wedded to particular cultural traditions and histories.[12] Amartya Sen, an Indian economist presently at Harvard University, implicitly follows this lead, and was one of the pioneers of an alternative way of conceiving development (and therefore what is just) as grounded in that which enables persons to flourish, rather than starting from the premise that development could be framed simply in terms of GNP.[13] Sen argued that we start with envisaging *capability* of agents in order to decide what justice entails.

Overall, Sen suggested that development should be thought of as *freedom* to perform certain goals, and that freedom required a degree of prior social stability and security. The actual goals pursued would vary and would have to be worked out by local deliberative democracy. Yet how far might this approach be somewhat contradictory, on the basis that deliberative democracy and associated freedoms are still assumed to be normative? Further, what particular challenges might this approach offer to global injustices where the market economy is given free reign? One of the reasons that his work has become so influential is that it seems to leave existing market economic systems in the Western world intact. His capability approach seeks to widen what development might entail, so that simply meeting economic needs is not sufficient; rather, it seeks to enable people to meet their particular aspirations. It is therefore understandably attractive to Western audiences influenced by liberal ideals of freedom and aspiration.

Martha Nussbaum succeeds, in my view, in adapting the capability approach of Amartya Sen, but rooting it more firmly in a theoretical framework of a specified list of goods. She does not press for a specific, detailed vision of the common good, but still arrives at a generalized list of goods that can then be adapted to different cultural contexts.[14] She believes, like other scholars influenced by natural law, that there are some goods that promote human flourishing that are universal in applicability. This both allows for some local community flexibility in interpretation of what the good might entail, and is tailored according to a list of capabilities that are desirable for human individuals. Examples of flourishing for humans include

---

[11] Poverty Facts and Stats, http:www.globalissues.org/article/26/poverty-facts-and-stats, accessed on 24 July 2009.

[12] A. MacIntyre, Whose Justice? Which Rationality? (London: Duckworth, 1988).

[13] A. Sen, Development as Freedom (Oxford: Oxford University Press, 1999); A. Sen, The Idea of Justice (London: Penguin, 2009).

[14] M. Nussbaum, Frontiers of Justice: Disability, Nationality, Species Membership (Cambridge: Harvard University Press/Belknap, 2006).

life, health, political affiliation, control over one's environment and relationships with other species, to name a few.

Like Amartya Sen's capability theory, it moves away from narrow conceptions of what is required according to crude estimates of GNP; rather, it seeks to set the bare minimum of basic human entitlements required for flourishing and, therefore, is in concert with the universal notion of human rights. She situates what makes for human flourishing as that in *relationship* with others, including the others of the non-human community. Instead of the independent actors proposed by Rawls, where each stand to gain from the social contract, Nussbaum's approach allows for the possibility of an unequal gain by one party, so that *fellowship*, not just mutual advantage, should be the goal in any transaction. There are some risks in this strategy, such as, How far can others be fairly represented in drawing up a list of goods? Is there a danger that universalism, even if well intentioned, will not sufficiently protect the different norms from diverse cultures and traditions, including religious traditions? Who is responsible, in other words, for drawing up the list of goods that are supposedly self-evident? Sen's approach, which puts more emphasis on goods arrived at through processes of local deliberative democracy, has its advantages in that it may allow for more local variation. The difficulty of Sen's approach to capability relates to a similar one of Rawls's theory, namely, how can legally binding agreements be reached across national boundaries? In other words, can attention to locally binding agreements be compromised on occasions in the name of a broader transnational notion of the common good, from which all will receive benefit?

Exclusive or Inclusive Justice Making?

Secular Western philosophy has engaged in a heated debate about who or what might legitimately be included in theories of social justice. In order to arrive at a reasoned position, it is important to distinguish between *distributors* of justice and *recipients* of justice. While those adopting a purely contractual theory of justice would, in general, argue for the exclusion of other animals (or future humans) in theories about justice, such theories generally fail to acknowledge that some entities may be recipients, rather than agents, of justice.[15] This allows for a reasoned inclusion of other animal species as those that are also recipients of distributive justice.

But this does not, in my opinion, go far enough, for other creatures on the receiving end of distributive justice will always and inevitably be at a disadvantage compared with the demands of the human community. Kantian methods of social contract theory fail in as much as they assume obligations of justice between equals, so that obligations to non-humans are always ones of *charity*, rather than

---

[15] A. Dobson, *Justice and the Environment: Conceptions of Environmental Sustainability and Dimensions of Social Justice* (Oxford: Oxford University Press, 1998), pp. 64–9.

strictly that of *justice*. Much the same critique applies to those who are disabled or in situations of extreme poverty – they are, in effect, excluded from the structure of justice making. In other words, if other creatures and other groups outside social contracts can only be recipients of justice, is this not equivalent to charitable action, rather than strictly one that justice requires? For developing nations, becoming recipients of justice only is likely to seem condescending and patronizing, in as much as while they may receive certain advantages through such an approach, it fails to acknowledge their place in decisions about what justice requires.

The advantage of Nussbaum's approach is that it provides some clear guidance as to what might be appropriate entitlements for different global communities and different animal species where such entitlements may come into conflict. In this scheme, duties are indirect, rather than direct, obligations. Nussbaum challenges, first, the idea of equality as a prerequisite for *subjects* of justice. There are, however, some drawbacks to her theory in the present discussion of sustainability. While Nussbaum recognizes that compassion is important in alerting us to the suffering of other animals, and presumably other peoples, her approach does not properly distinguish where the injury has come from. She also fails to consider the import-ance of ecological justice, that is, wider notions of justice making that are relevant to the flourishing of species other than animal kinds. While a degree of focus on other animals is reasonable, given their kinship with humankind, questions of sustainability open up larger issues on the flourishing of creatures in general and ecological welfare, as well as that of individual animals. It therefore implies eco-justice, rather than justice constricted to human societies. The difficulty, of course, is how to adjudicate when interests between people and other species come into conflict. Climate change may be of assistance here, in as much as it shows that any assumption that development and conservation will always work against one another is deeply misguided. Rather, the good for the whole community needs to be sought in a way that is inclusive of the flourishing of people and planet. If, in dire humanitarian emergencies, consideration of planetary needs or that of other animals becomes strained, such action has to take into account the emergency, short-term nature of such measures, for in the long term it works against the needs of human communities, as well.

Can There Ever Be Just Global Structures?

If we understand sustainable development to mean more than that relevant to local national interests, then it maps onto discussions about global inequalities and glo-bal justice making. This is crucially important for the so-called developing nations. Environmental justice is about the specific area of justice making connected with environmental goods. Michael Northcott is appreciative of Nussbaum's critical stance towards the liberal notion of the autonomy of nations that neglects pro-found inequality between them. He also comments on the classical idea of the 'law of nations' as a natural law basis for agreement between nations in international treaties sharing the global commons, arguing that Nussbaum's Grotian approach fosters a law 'analogous to a global law of love'.[16] Unfortunately the difficulty of putting such a global 'law of love' into practice became all too evident at the UN Summit Conference on Climate Change, where early tensions between different subtext agreements undermined the trust needed between nations as a basic starting point for negotiations.

Northcott believes, however, that Nussbaum fails to explain *why* duties are owed across boundaries, and how citizens might embrace and own such duties and make such sacrifices. This is particularly relevant in the context of discussions about international development. I believe there is some substance to this criticism, in that Nussbaum fails to provide adequate reasons *why* her approach should be adopted by different nations or individuals, other than a reference to sharing common ground with human rights approaches that she seems to believe are self-evidently justified.

Those aspects of Rawls's theory that Nussbaum is keen to promote concern human rights, human dignity, human equality and fair terms of cooperation across different societies, rather than a tight linkage with market mechanisms. Nussbaum also pays attention to the role of institutions in enabling capability to be expressed in such a way that decentralized forms of governance are promoted. Further, she resists any idea of a 'world state' in that there would be no means to correct tendencies towards tyranny, hence a certain 'thin' account of structures at the global level are rather more desirable than 'thicker' accounts that might weaken diversity.[17]

This seems to me to be correct, for if natural law fostered notions of a global state, then echoes of fascism loom large. Natural law, therefore, could more properly be understood in terms of its first principle, that is, a general injunction to seek the common good, expressed through the virtues, rather than proscriptive rules for living. Her ten principles for a just global structure are therefore suitably modest in scope, encouraging responsibility towards other nations by those with greater wealth. She is, perhaps, like Sen, rather too acquiescent to market mechanisms, and in the light of the most recent global financial crash, consideration of a more radical restructuring would be appropriate.

Aquinas also believed in a form of universal law, so that 'that which natural reason constitutes between all men and is observed by all people is called the *jus gentium*' (Aquinas, 1974: 2a 2ae Qu. 57.3). The latter is necessarily a human construct, for 'only men share in it among themselves'.[18] I suggest that his vision of *jus gentium* corresponds with international law between nations and can be filled out by the kind of global principles that Nussbaum suggests. This implies the possibility of agreed global goals without a requirement for identical notions of the good.

[16] M. Northcott, A Moral Climate (London: Darton Longman and Todd, 2007), pp. 171–3.
[17] Nussbaum, Frontiers of Justice, pp. 306–15.
[18] Thomas Aquinas, (1974) Summa Theologiae, Volume 37, Justice, trans. Thomas Gilby (London: Blackfriars,1974), 2a2ae Qu. 57.3.

It is also worth noting that the most recent Encyclical of Pope Benedict XVI, *Caritas in Veritate* (2009), resonates with many of Nussbaum's ideas about enabling human capability and promoting human flourishing. He also proposes a form of world governance to oversee justice making between nation states, argues for the protection of all human life, including the most vulnerable and excluded members of society, and emphasizes the need for proper attention to all creaturely life. His approach is significantly different, in that he argues that global problems represent a moral and religious failure as much as a philosophical failure. Steering a middle course between capitalism and socialism, he presses for a much greater commitment by those in the richer, affluent nations towards those who are poor. He allows the market to have its place, but not at the expense of human lives. Above all, he presses for the idea of a humanization of those economic and political structures in society that seem to have a life of their own. In other words, he fills out some of the reasons why we might act on behalf of the most disadvantaged in society in a way that is missing in Nussbaum's approach, other than acknowledging the need for compassion. But compassion is not enough, for it betrays a lack of real respect for the intrinsic worth of all creatures; what is more important, therefore, is solidarity. I also believe that this solidarity needs to be extended to other creatures in a way not spelt out in this document. Pope Benedict XVI does, however, seem to welcome the idea of a form of global state in a way that is likely to be problematic. The difficulty, of course, is how to reach international agreements that are legally binding and effective in managing the global commons, without threatening the nationhood of individual states. This seemed to be one of the main sticking points at the UN Summit in Copenhagen – the objection to having emissions monitored for compliance by an international body seemed threatening to nations, such as China, built on different political structures compared with the Western world.

What Does Justice as Virtue Imply?

The transformation of human lives opened up in Pope Benedict XVI's Encyclical points to another way of envisaging justice, and that is according to virtue ethics. Certainly, for the classic tradition, justice is in the most general sense a habit of mind, that is, a virtue, whereby each is rendered his/her due. Justice in Thomism is also much more than simply following rules of the good. Nor is it simply a rendition of the values embedded in Biblical texts. For Aquinas, justice is not just a principle, but a virtue: 'justice is the habit whereby a person with a lasting and constant will renders to each his due'.[19]

The classical understanding of justice takes a number of different forms that are helpful to consider in the light of the more secular discussion on sustainable development, which often tends towards a narrowing of justice as principle in purely distributive terms. These forms include constitutive justice between

---

[19] Aquinas, Justice, 2a2ae, Qu. 58.1.

individuals, general justice between the individual and the state, and distributive justice between the state and individual. If we widen the notion of justice making to include those most commonly excluded, then justice making encompasses all human societies, regardless of ability, race, nation, gender, class or colour. Further, the term 'individuals' applies not just to other animals, but also to other creatures, as well. The measure of what might be due to different animals and creatures will be different, but justice making understood as 'what is due' is a reminder to consider what might promote flourishing of other creatures as well as human beings.

Adjudicating the respecting claims for the flourishing of these different kinds requires acting so as to promote the common good, understood as inclusive rather than exclusive of all creaturely kinds. Its premise is a theological understanding of all of creation as good, reflecting the intention of a good Creator. Human beings, through a deliberate act of solidarity, represent the interests of those of persons of other nations and cultures and other creatures.

The principled forms of justice have their counterparts as *virtues* of those persons executing the principles of justice. The virtue is, in other words, that quality of mind that permits justice as principle to be expressed in different ways and reaches even beyond this to challenge ways of living that do not come under the jurisdiction of positive law. This is why those who promote climate change legislation should press for a morally binding agreement, as well as a legally and politically binding agreement, since what justice requires in the moral sense goes further than legally binding measures could ever achieve, given the variety of perspectives on humans and other animals in the global sphere. A challenge to consumer habits, including day to day habitual choices about our food, clothing and travel, for example, is therefore still one of justice making as virtue, even if it is legal. It may be legal to consume large quantities of factory-farmed meat or Mange Tout grown in African countries already on the brink of drought, but are these acts of justice? Understanding justice as virtue also enables a deeper appreciation of the significance of what justice requires, for it opens up the possibility of an inner transformation of persons so that inner attitudes match outward practice. The CAFOD campaign entitled *Live Simply* tried to express this insight, for living simply, sustainably and in solidarity with those who are poor requires actions that express environmental justice making. Justice is about governance of behaviour towards others, yet knowing what a just deed might be is 'prescribed' not so much by justice itself, but by practical wisdom.[20]

Practical wisdom in the classic sense includes the qualities of foresight, envisaging what the future might hold, insight, reason and *memoria*, that is, taking account of the past. It is about decision making that works for the common good, understood as the good for the whole community. Prudence entails deliberation, judgement and action. A concrete example of the way in which practical wisdom might be expressed in a way that builds social justice finds its expression in the story of the Kenyan Nobel Peace Prize winner Wangari Maathai. Over 30 years

[20] Ibid., 57.1.

ago, she founded the green belt movement (GBM), which pushed for a community-led reforestation programme that takes account of threatened ecosystems, as well as the livelihoods of local populations. This movement supports local communities in tree-planting programmes and has been responsible for literally millions of tree plantings in over 4,000 community groups in Kenya. Wangari Maathai is also keenly aware of the importance of supporting women in the community, since women disproportionately experience the brunt of climate change impacts. The GBM has mobilized local women to act in such a way so as to bring communities together. It also serves to

> build a common purpose, more sustainable livelihoods, and over time, build resilience. Successful tree planting also requires capacity, commitment, proper financing, political will and good governance. It demands ownership by communities involved, respect for rights and, most importantly, that local people remain united behind a common vision. Preventing deforestation and increasing tree cover is challenging but the rewards to communities and country are manifold and provide benefits beyond simply absorbing carbon.[21]

This example shows how the vision of one woman has helped transform communities in Africa, and it offers a beacon of hope for how that transformation might come to be expressed in other contexts as well.

Towards Transformation

I have argued in this chapter that 'sustainable development' makes little sense if it is based on an exclusive model of justice making defined by a Western theory of justice according to social contracts between equal parties. Such a model assumes the universal validity of market mechanisms as the means through which to measure and judge 'progress' in development. It ignores the radical inequality between rich and poor nations, and the exclusion of those nations from reasoned decision making on global problems such as climate change. If there is to be a future for sustainable development, then sustainability needs to be grounded in the awareness of interconnected relationships between different peoples, other creatures and shared basic resources necessary for flourishing, such as clean air, food and water. This will, therefore, mean transforming the way justice is conceived in the Western world, so that it takes account of the stories of those suffering the most. In recent years, stories of climate change challenge and remind us of how interconnected different life forms have become in this overcrowded planet. Justice understood as capability puts more emphasis on what different peoples and other animals need in order to flourish. But the reason for putting this in place is based on a shared sense of solidarity with each other in a way that includes other creatures, rather than excludes them. Transforming cultures bent on consumerism

[21] W. Matthai, Foreword to GBM, *Responding to Climate Change*, p. 2.

away from self-interested needs towards a sense of shared solidarity based on global justice is a huge challenge. It is, however, more likely to be resisted as long as contract models of justice hold sway. The example of Wangari Maathai shows that mobilization of communities to take active steps towards environmental responsibility across a nation state is possible and beneficial to the health and well-being of those taking part. Fostering a strong sense of the common good and solidarity among people and between people and creatures is one contribution that the Church may make to this debate.

The global Church community may draw on different sources in order to support such a shift. Examples include the social teaching in the Roman Catholic tradition alongside more specifically biblical principles given more emphasis by Protestant denominations that stress the need for justice and right relationships between peoples. The call for an ecumenical approach to justice making, while it could go further than Christian communities and include other religious traditions, needs to start, at least, with the call for climate justice. This is one reason why the demonstration on 5 December 2009 known as *The Wave* held in London prior to the UN Summit on Climate Change attracted so many from different Christian denominations – including Methodist, Anglican, Roman Catholic and Eastern Orthodox – for the appeal to justice is one that is shared by different traditions. Ultimately, this rests on a basic Christian affirmation that all creation as good, whose goodness is affirmed not simply through the doctrine of creation, but also through the incarnation of Christ as the Word made flesh.[22] Further, humanity understood as made in the image of God points to the religious basis for the global demand for justice making beyond national boundaries.

Given the broad international basis for climate change and climate justice, the call for transformation is one that needs to be felt across those of different religious persuasions or none. This is one reason why, in Western societies, it is important to find strong philosophical and theoretical reasons for making such changes, as well as religious reasons that will inspire those of religious backgrounds. For morally binding agreements have their basis in particular philosophical presuppositions that have been aired in the present chapter. Those engaging in transformative action will find inspiration for motivation from a particular religious group or tradition, but the outcome of acting together in order to achieve such changes will of necessity be much broader and 'thinner' than this, in order to begin to encompass what is expedient at a global level. The danger of promoting such global change is hegemony of one particular tradition, but it seems to me that, as long as each tradition appropriates for itself its particular reasons for joint action, then solidarity across peoples and between people and other species is both a possible and realistic goal. Further, important lessons can be learnt from others on a similar journey from other religious traditions or none.

[22] Deane-Drummond, 2011, in press.

Although Wangari Maathai suggested to an audience in the Bella Centre at Copenhagen[23] that her Christian inheritance encouraged her to use natural resources for human ends and purposes, another strand in that tradition speaks of the goodness of all creation and its double affirmation in the story of Genesis and the drama of the incarnation. It therefore is consistent with the African celebration of all of life that inspired her to take up the challenge of a national reforestation programme discussed above. In a Western world, made complacent by its own financial difficulties, the stories of suffering and hope out of Africa call for a radical transformation of lifestyles, not only at an individual level, but also at the level of civic society and political action.

I. Response to Celia Deane-Drummond

Susy Brouard

In answer to the question 'does sustainable development have a future?', I feel the answer will only be affirmative if those of us in the global North can, in all humility, listen to those voices in the South who perhaps have a much greater understanding of development than we have. Celia has given the very concrete example of Wangari Maathai as someone whose vision transformed communities, and there are other voices, too, that we need to listen to. So what are these voices saying? What are their questions? Over 20 years ago now, the Bishops of the Philippines asked some very pertinent questions on this issue in their pastoral letter: 'We often use the word progress to describe what has taken place over the past few decades . . . but can we say there is real progress? Who has benefitted most and who has borne the real costs? The poor are as disadvantaged as ever and the natural world has been grievously wounded.'[24] Their questions display a profound critique of what development has offered to the people of the Philippines; a development which has not risen from the grass roots up, but one which has been imposed and driven by economic growth. Belatedly, we need to listen to and work with those whose experience and wisdom may well have been overlooked in the past, but who are now more than ready to speak out. It is they who have answers if we are prepared to listen; it is they who will show us the future of sustainable development.

On a recent visit to CAFOD, one of our partners from Brazil, Davi Yanomami, shared with us how beneficial it was when indigenous people were called to take part in meetings with international leaders to discuss the changing climate. He

---

[23] W. Matthai, 'Livelihoods, Forest and Climate with Nobel Laureate Ms Wangari Maathai, GBM and Partners', Framework Convention on Climate Change, UN Climate Change Conference, COP 15, Daily Programme, Part Two, Friday, 11 December.

[24] The Catholic Bishops' Conference of the Philippines, What is Happening to our Beautiful Land, A Pastoral Letter on Ecology (1988).

said the response to climate change of those in 'developed' countries had been slow and that: 'They didn't believe us because they are not in the forests. They don't see it. They sit in their homes, working, playing, drinking, unaware of what's happening'.[25] For this reason, Davi urged us to talk with the Yanomami authorities and with the younger generations, to learn from them. He reminded us what holistic and sustainable development might look like:

> You white people say that we, the Yanomami people, don't want development. You say this because we don't want mining on our land, but you do not understand what we are saying. We aren't against development, we are only against the type of development that you white people wish to impose on us. The development you talk about offering us isn't the same as that which we are familiar with. You talk about destroying our forest in order to give us money, saying we are disadvantaged, yet this isn't the development we know. For us, development is keeping our land healthy and allowing our children to live healthily in a place bursting with life.[26]

For the past seven years I have been privileged enough to work for an organization which *does* listen to the voices of the South and works in partnership with local communities, both in England and Wales and overseas, to bring about what we hope is sustainable development. So what do we mean by this exactly, and why would it be of importance to a Catholic development agency? To answer this question, we need to go back a bit and look at some of the Church's teaching. Even in 1979, in the documents from the Latin American Episcopal Conference in Puebla, Mexico, there was already a prediction that the depletion of natural resources and the pollution of the environment would become a critical problem: 'the consumptionist tendencies of the more developed nations must undergo a thorough revision', taking into account 'the elementary needs of the poor people who constitute the majority of the world's population'.[27] The theme of development had already been raised in 1967 in an encyclical by Pope Paul VI who, in contrast with the secular ideas of development at that time, saw development as much more than economic growth; rather, genuine development would mean that people would be 'artisans of their destiny'.[28] The Church, having acknowledged that 'the joys and the hopes, the griefs and the anxieties of the men (*sic*) of this age, especially those who are poor or in any way afflicted, these are the joys and hopes, the griefs and anxieties of the followers of Christ',[29] felt it had a unique contribution and indeed

---

[25] D. K. Yanomami, President of Hutukara Associação Yanomami (HAY), Open letter from the Yanomami people concerning development (Boa Vista, 25 February 2008).
[26] Ibid.
[27] Cited in A. T. Hennelly, (ed.), Liberation Theology: A Documentary History (New York: Orbis Books, 1990), p. 237.
[28] Pope Paul VI, Populorum Progressio, 65 (26 March 1967).
[29] Pope Paul VI (promulgated by), Gaudium et Spes, Pastoral Constitution on the Church in the Modern World (7 December 1965).

a duty to speak out on issues of human development, and also that which might stop or prevent authentic human flourishing.

Pope John Paul II was later to expand this teaching on development to include nature:

> In order to be genuine, development must be achieved within the framework of solidarity and freedom, without ever sacrificing either of them under whatever pretext. . . . A true concept of development cannot ignore the use of the elements of nature, the renewability of resources and the consequences of haphazard industrialization – three considerations which alert our consciences to the moral dimension of development.[30]

The present Pope has also spoken and written extensively on the theme of authentic development and the need to include the environment.[31]

So, sustainable development means, I think, taking into account the flourishing of both peoples and creation. I have already argued that in order for this to happen, the voices that need to be heard are those from the global South, but that is not to say that those of us who live in the North can remain passive; indeed, to remain passive would not be to adopt a neutral position, but to stay on the side of the oppressive hegemony. In a recent directions paper for its work in the next ten years, CAFOD acknowledges that, 'As global citizens, we need to understand the forces in our societies that block or undermine human flourishing with devastating consequences for the lives and dignity of the world's poorest people. This understanding must lead us to take responsibility and the necessary action.' So what kind of action might this response take, for those in the global North? What can we do to change unjust structures that keep the majority of the world in poverty? What can we do to stop or slow down the damage which is being done to creation?

Paulo Freire, the Brazilian educator, would be pessimistic about our ability to change the situation since we are the oppressors. I quote:

> Although the situation of oppression is a dehumanized and dehumanizing totality affecting both the oppressors and those whom they oppress, it is the latter who must from their stifled humanity, wage for both the struggle for a fuller humanity; the oppressor, who is himself dehumanized because he dehumanizes others, is unable to lead this struggle.[32]

I would be less pessimistic than Freire, as I feel that many today are prepared to play their part in the transformation of the world. They are looking at what prevents and stops humanity and creation from flourishing by supporting their brothers and sisters in solidarity, though there is no doubt, as Celia points out,

---

[30] Pope John Paul II, Sollicitudo Rei Socialis, 33 and 34 (30 December 1987).
[31] Pope Benedict XVI, Caritas in Veritate (29 June 2009), especially chapter four.
[32] P. Freire, Pedagogy of the Oppressed 30th Anniversary Edition (New York: Continuum, 2001), p 47.

that 'transforming cultures bent on consumerism away from self-interested needs towards a sense of shared solidarity based on global justice is a huge challenge' (p. 74–5). Over the years, I have worked with communities in England and Wales who have examined their lifestyles and made radical changes so that those in the global South have a chance of flourishing. In short, I have met and been inspired by people who are prepared to live a life of solidarity with those who live in poverty. I was involved with a grassroots initiative called *live*simply, which encouraged ordinary Christians to live more simply, sustainably and in solidarity with those who are poor. Individuals were asked to make promises on an online promise bank and communities were also asked to take on challenges, as working as a group of people often has a much stronger impact. The Make Poverty History march in 2005 and the recent peaceful demonstration in London ('The Wave') before the UN Summit on Climate Change show that people are willing to campaign for a fairer deal for those who will suffer the most and stand in solidarity with them.

The theme of solidarity has long been present in the social teaching of the Catholic Church and is perhaps best summed up in the words of John Paul II when he advocated that solidarity is not a feeling of vague compassion or shallow distress, but 'on the contrary, it is a firm and persevering determination to commit oneself to the common good; that is to say to the good of all and of each individual, because we are all really responsible for all'.[33] In his message on 1 January this year, Benedict XVI appealed for a greater sense of solidarity, enlarging the concept by advocating a solidarity which is intergenerational, embracing both time and space. He continues: 'We are all responsible for the protection and care of the environment. This responsibility knows no boundaries. In accordance with the principle of subsidiarity it is important for everyone to be committed at his or her proper level, working to overcome the prevalence of particular interests.'[34] Clearly then, in terms of sustainable development we can all play our part.

In the past, Catholic Social Teaching has advocated that those in power speak out for those who have no voice.[35] However, teaching and practice have moved on, and in 2005, at the annual CAFOD lecture, the liberation theologian Fr Gustavo Gutierrez said that, although he had respect for those who wanted to be the 'voice of the voiceless', he nevertheless had difficulty with the expression since 'our goal must be to help them obtain a voice; my intention is not to be the voice of the voiceless, as the poor themselves have a voice. We must direct our efforts and commitment towards this end'.[36]

I have tried, in this short paper, to argue that development will only be sustainable and have a future if those in the global North listen and work in partnership

---

[33] Pope John Paul II, Sollicitudo Rei Socialis, 38 (30 December 1987).

[34] Pope Benedict XVI, If You Want to Cultivate Peace, Protect Creation, Message of His Holiness for the Celebration for the World Day of Peace, 11 (1 January 2010).

[35] Cited in A. T. Hennelly, Liberation Theology: A Documentary History (New York: Orbis Books, 1990), p 135.

[36] G. Gutierrez OP, A Theology for Today: the option for the poor in 2005 (CAFOD's Pope Paul VI Memorial Lecture, 2005).

with those in the global South. For our part, we are called to live lives of radical solidarity, a call which has been central to the teaching of the Catholic Church. It is no longer appropriate to speak out on behalf of others but it is preferred that one ensures, all voices are heard. And so the last words belong to Davi Yanomami. He says: 'The forest is worth more than money. Today, there is a good struggle, to confront those who want to end the richness of nature, the water we drink. We all need to make a lot of noise so the government hears us. I hope we will win and that the men of the city will respect the land, our people, our earth.'[37]

II. Concluding Comments

Celia Deane-Drummond

Susy has developed, in her response to my paper, the importance of solidarity, and not just listening to the needs of those in the developing world, but also allowing those who are living in impoverished regions to articulate their concerns. She has also drawn on Roman Catholic social teaching and highlighted the way, from the beginning, it has sought to identify with the needs of the poorest communities and stressed the idea of a global community working for the common good. In addition, she cites liberation theology as that which tries to articulate, in theological terms, what might be the basis for human flourishing for those most disadvantaged in global society.

Drawing on her considerable experience of working with CAFOD, it would be impertinent of me to raise any objections. What I intend to do instead is to probe a little more deeply regarding what the implications are of following through with these different approaches in light of the agenda of sustainable development.

One key element needed for human flourishing, and therefore laying down the foundations for justice making, is respect for another in their own contexts. Liberation theology at its inception fought for deliverance from oppressive totalitarian regimes that epitomized what might be called 'structural sin'. The process of liberation has been a success in many cases, particularly in Latin America, and the situation of nations such as Brazil is a case in point. In such a context, we might ask, where does liberation theology now turn? Its original Marxist orientation now no longer seems necessary. This is why, perhaps, liberation theologians such a Leonardo Boff have turned to ecology: for now the earth itself stands in need of liberation.[38]

But we are immediately faced with a difficulty. The liberation theologies of what might be termed the 'first wave' were all grounded in grassroots social

---

[37] On a visit to CAFOD, 2009.

[38] L. Boff, Ecology and Liberation, trans. John Cumming (New York: Orbis, 1995); L. Boff, Cry of the Earth, Cry of the Poor, trans. Philip Berryman (New York: Orbis, 1997). See discussion in C. Deane-Drummond, Ecotheology (London: DLT, 2008), pp. 46–54; 204–5.

movements, struggling to articulate their concerns in the midst of a clearly identifiable enemy – the state. Some liberation theologians have transformed their
writing to keep pace with the changing political agenda and are now adding ecology, rather than engaging specifically with grassroots social movements. Boff, for
example, draws on the work of Thomas Berry and James Lovelock, both of whom
are white Western male writers. In as much as Boff shifts towards seeing the earth
as the basis for theological reflection, it veers close to the kind of pantheism that
Pope Benedict XVI is particularly critical of in *Caritas in Veritate*. This sets up yet
another tension between liberation theology and official church teaching, even
though some of the concerns of liberation theology have found a way into such
teaching, though now deliberately stripped of any Marxist influence.

The problems are not over yet, however, for the liberation theology that is struggling to speak on behalf of those without a voice is finding it difficult to reconnect
with the kind of grassroots movements that were once the bread and butter of its
original inspiration. Elina Vuola, writing from her experience of ethnographic
research on popular local cults of the Virgin Mary in Central America, believes
that the writing of liberation ecotheologians has become too theoretical. It may
mention the wisdom of indigenous traditions, but fails to base it on ethnographic
research or connect with contemporary political struggles of indigenous peoples.[39]
Such research shows that African-based religions, many indigenous religions and
forms of popular Catholicism form a rich diversity of local cults all over Latin
America, but their specific religious insights are ignored by liberation theologians.
Popular religiosity is therefore marginalized within the writings of liberation
theologians. There are a few exceptions, such as the work of Peruvian writer Diego
Irarrarzával, who has begun to map out a dialogue between indigenous beliefs and
Roman Catholic theology.[40]

There are other uncomfortable issues to address, such as following the process
of democratization in Latin America; the new social movements that are most
pressing are those to do with reproductive, sexual and gender rights. Such movements consider the Catholic Church – even in the guise of liberation theologians,
as working against their interests. The difficulty that needs to be addressed, therefore, is that while Roman Catholic social teaching presents the notion of the common good, it is a vision of the good that is filtered through a particular view of
what is acceptable or not according to traditional social teaching.

The question then arises, does this limitation in freedom of expression, that
seems to dominate even the work of theologians who are trying to give a voice
to the marginalized, have implications for what might be termed sustainable
development? I believe that it does, for if we took listening to the marginalized to

---

[39] E. Vuola, 'Latin American Liberation Theologians' Turn to Eco(theo)logy: Critical
Remarks', in C.Deane-Drummond and H. Bedford Strohm (eds), Religion and Ecology in
the Public Sphere (London: T & T Clark, 2011), in press.
[40] D. Irarrarzával, Inculturation: New Dawn of the Church in Latin America (trans. Philip
Berryman; Eugene: Wipf and Stock, 2008).

its limits, that would mean a richer intercultural exchange than has so far been possible. This need not, of course, necessarily mean a shift towards pantheism or paganism or any other latent fears. Rather, it means facing honestly and squarely religious and cultural differences within a common humanity, so that if theology makes any claim to give a voice to the oppressed, it recognizes the difficulty of doing so where that voice distances itself from traditional views. Further, a deeper understanding of other religious traditions and protecting that diversity is one more aspect of what the future of sustainable development means if it is going to have any future that really protects the interests of different peoples.

5 The Problem with Human Equality: Towards a Non-Exclusive Account of the Moral Value of Creatures in the Company of Martha Nussbaum

David Clough

The basis of our rhetoric against exclusion of particular groups of human beings is a proclaimed belief in human equality. In fact, however, we do not believe that human beings in general are equal: not in height, weight, age, strength, speed, health, beauty, moral virtue, intelligence, wealth, power or in any other respect. In proclaiming the equality of human beings, neither do we believe that human beings should be treated equally: instead we think that those who are thirsty should be given water, rather than those who have just drunk, that those who are sick should receive medical care, rather those who are healthy, that those who are unable to feed themselves should be fed by others, rather than those who are capable of feeding themselves independently, and so on. What we mean by the claim that all human beings are equal, then, is not that they are all equal or that they should all be treated equally, but that we should not base unequal treatment on irrelevant characteristics of persons. Thus, for example, the electorate in a democracy should be defined according to those capable of voting, rather than those of a particular gender, judges should reach decisions based on the merits of a case, rather than on the relative privilege of the contesting parties, and academic examiners should decide grades according to the quality of work assessed, rather than on the basis of their personal relationship with students.

While this non-discriminatory equal regard seems non-contentious in a liberal society, if we ask about the basis for such a policy, it is surprisingly hard to give a satisfactory response. For the Stoics and a long tradition originating in their philosophy, the possession of rationality was the characteristic of human beings that was the primary reason for respecting them. This idea was influentially taken up by Kant in the formulation of the categorical imperative that rational beings – and only rational beings – should never be treated merely as a means, but always

as an end in themselves. There are at least three difficulties with this justification of equal regard, however. First, there is the plausibility of the justification.
It is not clear why the possession of rationality is particularly worthy of equal
moral regard: if we encountered two extraterrestrial alien species, one of which
was rational, but solitary and selfish, and the other of which was irrational, but
relational and altruistic, it is not clear that we would be right to give moral regard
only to the first. The second problem is that of boundary matching. The category
of rational beings cannot ground equal regard for human beings and only human
beings, because its boundaries do not match those of the category of human beings:
whatever substantive definition of rationality we use will exclude some beings we
usually think of as human – such as newborn infants or those with severe learning difficulties – and many definitions of rationality will include some non-human
species – such as chimpanzees. The third difficulty with using rationality as a basis
for equal regard of human beings is the problem of degree. Persons can be more
or less rational, and so rationality is a matter of degree, rather than an absolute
property. If rationality is the basis of our respect, it is not at all clear why we should
respect the most and least rational of human beings equally, rather than valuing
the superrational most highly.[1]

A second tradition, represented by Locke and given recent impetus by John
Rawls, grounds equal regard in a supposed social contract, rather than rationality.
Persons in society are considered to have consented to a fair set of social arrangements, and they are respected as those who have contracted rights and responsibilities under such a regime. While presumed consent to a social contract avoids
the third objection to the justification based on rationality, however, in that it is
not a matter of degree, it is vulnerable to the two first objections to the previous
scheme. In relation to the first consideration of the plausibility of justification, it
is not clear why we should have moral regard only for those capable of consenting
to a social contract and undertaking responsibilities under it. In relation to the
second difficulty of boundary matching, clearly newborn infants and those with
severe learning difficulties will not be included in the category of those deserving
equal regard.

Those campaigning against the exclusion of persons considered to be marginal
have been understandably critical of these justifications for equal regard, primarily because of the boundary-matching problem. If rationality or social contract
are used as the basis for equal regard, the status of those who do not fit into these
categories is problematic. Kantians and Rawlsians will commonly seek to find
ways to extend moral protection to human beings who do not fit the standard
categories, but the fact that such a secondary strategy is necessary implies that
non-rational or non-contracting human beings are marginal to the equal regard
framework.

---

[1] Richard J. Arneson terms the problem of degree the 'Singer Problem', in recognition of
Peter Singer's role in first noting it: R. J. Arneson, 'What, if Anything, Renders All Humans
Morally Equal?', in *Singer and His Critics*, (Oxford: Blackwell, 1999), p. 105.

One notable attempt to circumvent the boundary-matching problem is to suggest that the justification for equal regard of human beings is their possession of human DNA. On this account, every human being is entitled to equal regard merely on the grounds of species membership. While attractive in its inclusivity, however, this strategy is not a justification for equal moral regard of human beings, but a refusal to provide such a justification. It therefore fares particularly poorly in relation to the plausibility objection, as it is difficult to see why a particular DNA structure should be the exclusive basis of equal regard. If a community of near-human ancestors were discovered living in some remote location, it is hard to judge that they should not be given moral regard simply because the DNA in their cells did not match ours exactly. Encountering a humanoid extraterrestrial race would provoke the same issue.

Others have proposed alternative justifications for the unique moral status of human beings, such as their capacity for relationships. In some accounts, the capacity of human beings to engage in reciprocal relationships receives emphasis, although this remains open to the boundary-matching issue in relation to human beings that are incapable of significant interaction. It is also open to the objection concerning degree: should those most capable of relationships be valued more highly? Alternatively, the emphasis may be placed less on the capacities of the individual, and more on their place within a complex of intersecting relationships. This has the advantage of being able to give an account of the value even of unresponsive patients in a persistent vegetative state, but has the unwelcome additional implication that the moral value of those living in isolation is threatened. Other proposed justifications include intelligence or self-consciousness, though arguments very similar to those noted above can be rehearsed against them.

Some utilitarians abandon the attempt to preserve the boundary between the human and non-human with the claim that the only necessary moral guideline is to maximize utility of beings capable of suffering or satisfaction of their aims. This has the attraction of simplicity, but gives up on major features of traditional moral thought, such as the relevance of intention, virtue, character and absolute moral norms – the idea that some things, such as torturing children, would be wrong to do whatever the situation. Utilitarian schemes can also be criticized for not, in fact, leading to viable calculations of utility. Furthermore, the apparent simplicity is often complicated with additional norms, such as privileging the satisfaction of higher order desires over lower ones.

Theologians have often been tempted to short-circuit the difficulties of justifying equal moral regard through the invocation of some divine rationale. Foremost in these attempts has been the use of Genesis 1.26 to undergird the affirmation that all and only human beings are made in the image of God. As Gordon Wenham has noted, however, whenever an attempt is made to define the content of this image there is the suspicion that the commentator is merely reading their own values as to what is most valuable about human beings into the text.[2] For a large part of the Christian tradition,

---

[2] G. J. Wenham, *Genesis*, Word Bible Commentary (Waco: Word, 1994), p. 30.

the consensus view has been that rationality is the image of God in human beings, threatening to return us to the set of problems identified above. It is almost certainly a mistake to identify any human characteristic with the divine image: the reference to the divine image both in Genesis 1 and Genesis 9 seems to relate more closely to a human task that mirrors God's task, than to an attribute of human beings.[3] This makes the image of God a moral responsibility, rather than an indicator of moral status. The fact that Jesus Christ became incarnate as a human being to bring redemption is an alternative theological grounding for equal moral regard, suggesting that we should respect equally those for whom Christ died. As I have argued elsewhere, however, it is unnecessary and inappropriate to restrict the significance of God's work in Christ to the human realm.[4] Some theologians suggest that human relationships with God are a ground for respecting them, though this would apply to all creatures of God, unless some additional strategy is employed to show why the human relationship is unique. In any case, the same plausibility challenges apply to these proposed theological solutions as were raised in relation to philosophical strategies. In particular, if we discovered alien life with similar attributes to human beings, it seems to me that it would not be defensible to judge that we should give no moral regard to these other creatures of God because Genesis did not record them as made in the divine image.

If I am correct to suggest that it is inappropriate to reach for a quick theological fix to demarcate a field of equal moral regard coterminous with the human species, it seems that we are hard pressed to justify the non-discriminatory equal regard for human beings that seems to be the modern liberal consensus. There are several possible ways forward. First, we could continue to attempt to find an adequate justification for this consensus. The strength of the consensus provides strong motivation for this quest, though given the efforts that have been employed to date, this seems unlikely to succeed. Second, we could consistently accept a particular criterion of moral regard despite the arguments against them advanced above. For example, we could specify that rationality was the proper ground of moral regard, despite its implausibility, the consequence of excluding non-rational human beings and the consequence that the most rational should be respected more than those less rational. Third, we could decide to become utilitarians, despite the strong reasons specified above against doing so. Fourth, we could decide that we would give equal regard to human beings and no other species without justification, despite the morally tenuous and inconsistent position we are left in as a result. This last seems to be the default option we are in fact operating.

An alternative to all these strategies is to question whether the identification of a field of equal moral regard coterminous with the human species is the most appropriate moral framework. One motivation for such a reconsideration, beyond the difficulties noted above, is that the mirror image of radical inclusion of all

---

[3] On Genesis 9, see S. Mason, 'Another Flood? Genesis 9 and Isaiah's Broken Eternal Covenant', *Journal for the Study of the Old Testament* 32:2 (2007), pp. 177–98 (193).
[4] D. Clough, *On Animals: I. Systematic Theology* (London: T&T Clark/Continuum, forthcoming), chs 4–5.

human beings within a magic circle of equal moral regard is the radical exclusion of every member of every non-human species from this circle. This exclusion is becoming harder to justify as we learn more of the cognitive, social and moral aspects of the lives of non-human animals. We now have reason to believe that sheep are capable of recognizing hundreds of faces;[5] crows are able to fashion tools in order to solve problems;[6] chimpanzees exhibit empathy, morality and politics;[7] dolphins are capable of processing grammar;[8] parrots can differentiate between objects in relation to abstract concepts, such as colour and shape;[9] and that sperm whales and orcas have developed culturally specific modes of life and communication.[10] Particular non-human species are like human beings in particular ways. Particular species are also very unlike other non-human species, just as we are, so to think we have arrived at a useful basic categorization of species in the terms 'human' and 'animal' (where the latter is used as exclusive of the human) is bizarre. Jacques Derrida has expressed the absurdity of this position most clearly:

> Confined within this catch-all concept, within this vast encampment of the animal, in this general singular, within the strict enclosure of this definite article ('the Animal' and not 'animals'), as in a virgin forest, a zoo, a hunting or fishing ground, a paddock or an abattoir, a space of domestication, are all the living things that man does not recognize as his fellows, his neighbors, or his brothers. And that is so in spite of the infinite space that separates the lizard from the dog, the protozoon from the dolphin, the shark from the lamb, the parrot from the chimpanzee, the camel from the eagle, the squirrel from the tiger or the elephant from the cat, the ant from the silkworm or the hedgehog from the echidna. I interrupt my nomenclature and call Noah to help insure that no one gets left on the ark.[11]

In short, it is increasingly obvious that to judge that protozoa, sharks, squirrels and chimpanzees belong in the category of creatures without moral value, and human

[5] K. M. Kendrick, 'Sheep Don't Forget a Face', *Nature* 414:4860 (2001), 165–6.
[6] A. A. S. Weir, Jackie Chappell and Alex Kacelnik, 'Shaping of Hooks in New Caledonian Crows', *Science* 297:5583 (2002), p. 981.
[7] F. de Waal, *Good Natured: The Origins of Right and Wrong in Humans and Other Animals* (Cambridge, MA: Harvard University Press, 1996); F. de Waal, *Chimpanzee Politics: Power and Sex Among Apes* (Baltimore: Johns Hopkins University Press, 2000).
[8] L. M. Herman, Stan A. Kuczaj and M. D. Holder, 'Responses to Anomalous Gestural Sequences By a Language-Trained Dolphin: Evidence for Processing of Semantic Relations and Syntactic Information', *Journal of Experimental Psychology: General* 122:2 (1993), pp. 184–94.
[9] I. M. Pepperberg, *The Alex Studies: Cognitive and Communicative Abilities of Grey Parrots* (Cambridge, MA: Harvard University, 2000).
[10] H. Whitehead, *Sperm Whales: Social Evolution in the Ocean* (Chicago, IL: University of Chicago, 2003); D. H. Chadwick, 'Investigating a Killer', *National Geographic* 207:4 (2005), p. 99, cited in C. Southgate, *The Groaning of Creation: God, Evolution, and the Problem of Evil* (Louisville; London: Westminster John Knox, 2008), ix.
[11] J. Derrida, and D. Wills, 'The Animal That Therefore I Am (More to Follow)', *Critical Inquiry* 28:2 (2002), pp. 369–418 (402).

beings alone belong in a different one, where moral value is uniquely and equally bestowed, is radically implausible. Together with the incoherence of the justifications offered for such positions, the clear injustice of this exclusion of all non-human creaturely life from moral consideration indicates the need for an alternative account.

In a theological context, the reason for caring for and attending to the well-being of another creature is that we recognize its place in God's good purposes and are thereby enabled to appreciate its value. Since, as I have argued elsewhere, it is a significant theological mistake to understand God's purposes in creation and redemption as limited to the human species, we are not free in a theocentric context to make the anthropocentric error of considering the purpose of non-human creation as exhausted in its utility to human beings. We cannot assume our species to be the centre of God's interest in a huge and astonishingly diverse creative project. Instead, we must recognize that God intends each creature for its own sake, for its contribution to the glorification of God and for its participation in the Trinitarian divine life.[12] Such an understanding of God's purposes for creation means refusing to accept the Neoplatonic hierarchies of value that have been influential on Christian theology, picturing a 'Great Chain of Being' from God downwards.[13] This leads us to a radical theological extension of the Kantian principle: to treat not only all human persons, but all creatures, as ends in themselves. This is, in one sense, a call for the equality of all creatures, but only in the sense already mentioned in relation to equality of persons. Extended to non-human creation, the principle becomes: we should not base unequal treatment on irrelevant characteristics of creatures. For example, it is not a disadvantage to a mouse not to have the same access to education as human beings do: the capacity to benefit from education is a relevant characteristic by which to make decisions about how to distribute the good of education. But to decide that it is legitimate to conduct experiments on mice that cause them suffering and premature death on the grounds that they are not human is to base unequal treatment on an irrelevant characteristic: species membership.

One important recent proposal for an account of ethics that refuses to bestow moral value on the basis of the binary categories of human/non-human is the capabilities approach of Martha Nussbaum, grounded in Aristotelian moral philosophy. Nussbaum's approach begins with the discussion of the capabilities of human beings in order to provide a foundation for considering how they should be treated. She identifies ten central capacities that are required for human life with dignity: life; bodily health; bodily integrity; sense, imagination and thought; emotions; practical reason; affiliation; other species; play; and control over one's environment.[14] These are understood by Nussbaum as a minimum account of

---

[12] Clough, *On Animals: I. Systematic Theology*, ch. 1.
[13] See, for example, A. O. Lovejoy, *The Great Chain of Being: A Study of the History of an Idea* (Cambridge, MA: Harvard University Press, 1942).
[14] These are set out in M. Nussbaum, *Frontiers of Justice: Disability, Nationality, Species Membership* (Cambridge, MA; London: Belknap Press, 2006), pp. 76–7, and were

social justice: 'a society that does not guarantee these to all its citizens, at some appropriate threshold level, falls short of being a just society'.[15] While Nussbaum's approach is not unique as an alternative to Kantian and Rawlsian theories, and has some overlap with the lists of basic human goods in some recent accounts of natural law theory,[16] what is particularly notable about her thinking in the present context is her openness to the question of whether justice should be considered beyond the sphere of the human. She cites with approval a ruling of the Kerala High Court in India in 2000 concerning cruelty to circus animals, recognizing the rights of animals to protection, and argues that 'the fact that humans act in ways that deny animals a dignified existence appears to be an issue of justice, and an urgent one'.[17] Human responsibilities to other animals are not indirect, as Kantian and contractarian accounts suggest, and do not merely arise from compassion, but arise from the recognition that animals are entitled to not be treated in ways that are not consistent with their dignity. Utilitarian approaches, Nussbaum argues, are similarly insufficient because they suggest that the suffering of one group can be traded off against the pleasure of another, in the case of the circus, for example.[18] Nussbaum bases her account of the good of animals on the capabilities of an individual animal, rather than a species as a whole, which means she does not consider extinction of a species as more than the injustice done to members of that species.[19] She does, however, consider that species-specific norms will be relevant to judgements about what constitutes the good of a particular creature. While she recognizes that the capabilities approach can recognize the good for an animal independent of its sentience, she sees some wisdom in utilitarian concerns about sentience, and makes the pragmatic judgement that 'we have enough on our plate if we focus for the time being on sentient creatures'.[20]

With regard to the question of whether the dignity of non-human animals should be understood as fully equal to that of human beings, Nussbaum makes a range of comments. First, she notes James Rachels's comment that less complex creatures are not subject to the same range of harms and benefits, so that 'nothing is blighted when a rabbit is deprived of the right to vote, or a worm of the free exercise of religion'.[21] Second, she recognizes that in a capabilities approach, the

---

developed in earlier works such as M. Nussbaum and J. Glover (eds), *Women, Culture, and Development: A Study of Human Capabilities* (Oxford: Oxford University Press, 1995) and M. Nussbaum, *Women and Human Development: The Capabilities Approach* (Cambridge: Cambridge University Press, 2000).

[15] Nussbaum, *Frontiers of Justice*, p. 75.

[16] See, for example, J. Finnis, *Natural Law and Natural Rights* (Oxford: Clarendon Press, 1980); G. Grisez, *The Way of the Lord Jesus*, vol. I (Chicago: Franciscan Herald Press, 1983).

[17] Nussbaum, *Frontiers of Justice*, p. 326.

[18] Ibid., p. 343.

[19] Ibid., p. 357.

[20] Ibid., pp. 361–2.

[21] Ibid., p. 361.

question of equality is not quite so pressing as it is for utilitarians, for example, who have to sum up the interests of all creatures.[22] Beyond these two points, Nussbaum seems personally convinced of the force of the argument – 'It seems there is no respectable way to deny the equal dignity of creatures across species' – but sceptical that the overlapping moral consensus on which she seeks to establish her theory could support such a radical claim.[23] For this reason, she argues for an overlapping consensus around 'the looser idea that all creatures are entitled to adequate opportunities for a flourishing life'.[24] Notably, one of the chief reasons she considers it problematic to gain a sufficient moral consensus for equality across species is the way that Judaism, Christianity and Islam, among other comprehensive doctrines, 'rank the human species metaphysically above the other species and give the human secure rights to the use of animals for many purposes'.[25] It is not clear what giving all creatures adequate opportunities for a flourishing life will mean for Nussbaum: she notes that the capabilities approach disagrees with the Benthamite utilitarian view that a painless death is no harm for a creature with no interest in the future: even if a creature had no sense of the future, a painless death could well be cutting short its capability to pursue its good.[26] She seems to favour norms against the killing of 'at least the more complexly sentient animals for food', but considers that progress towards the development of a consensus on this will have to be gradual, and begin with banning cruelty towards animals.[27] Nussbaum is also cautious in relation to the consequences of moving, globally, to vegetarian sources of protein, and of the health of the world's children under these circumstances,[28] although it is very clear that not using 40% of the world's grain as feed for animals raised for meat would have a very substantial effect on releasing food resources for human use.[29]

Nussbaum's approach has the benefits of recognizing both the injustice of excluding non-human creatures from moral consideration, of providing a framework for considering the way in which their flourishing might be respected and protected, and of being realistic about what kind of consensus might be achievable in improving human treatment of other animals. Her reliance on the achievement of moral consensus as a basis for her ethic, however, has the weakness that she is not able to advocate clearly what it would mean to respond adequately to the dignity of the lives of non-human creatures, because unless she can claim a moral consensus for her position, it has no moral authority. Obviously, the task of changing attitudes towards the treatment of animals will always depend on gaining

---

[22] Ibid., p. 383.
[23] Ibid.
[24] Ibid., p. 384.
[25] Ibid., p. 390.
[26] Ibid., p. 386.
[27] Ibid., p. 393.
[28] Ibid., p. 402.
[29] D. Pimental and M. Pimental (eds), *Food, Energy and Society* (Boulder, CO: University Press of Colorado, 1996), p. 74.

this kind of moral consensus, but from the perspective of theological ethics, it is disorientating to find that discovering what is right would have to await the development of a moral consensus. Instead, it seems preferable to argue for a clear account of the place of non-human animals in theological ethics and then seek to gain consensus for movement towards that position. With this goal in view, it is necessary to consider what a theological account of human responsibilities towards animals might learn from Nussbaum's account.

The first and most obvious area of common ground between a theological ethic such as the one I have proposed and Nussbaum's capabilities approach is the reason it is attractive in the first place: its openness to the moral value of non-human creatures. While Nussbaum is right that Christianity, together with the other Abrahamic faiths, has often been interpreted in ways that subordinate non-human creation to human ends, this is by no means a necessary result of a theological account. Indeed, once the mistake of confusing Christianity with anthropocentrism has been recognized, theological accounts have a key advantage over modern atheistic philosophies in recognizing continuity in moral value between human beings and other animals. If we imagine a universe without a creator, we are likely to be over-impressed by the differences between different species and especially by those characteristics of our own species that seem to make us distinctive amid the vast mass of life that surrounds us. Once we confess God as creator of the universe, we acknowledge a single fundamental binary opposition, that between creator and creature, that relativizes all creaturely differences to points of detail. It is much easier to avoid anthropocentrism in the context of an account that recognizes a basic duty of giving honour and worship to a being beyond the human. A teleological understanding that sees a purposive unity in the flourishing of living creatures also helps avoid exaggerating the significance of the human species. This common ground between Nussbaum's Aristotelianism and Christianity may account for their similarity on this basic question of the relationship between the human and non-human parts of creation – Platonic accounts may share this feature, too.[30] A second and related point of commonality between the theological approach for which I am arguing and Nussbaum's account of capabilities is the common cause they make in relation to alternative approaches to ethics, such as Kantian, Rawlsian and utilitarian ones. While neither Nussbaum nor I wish to dismiss the insights of these other approaches, their merits and demerits look similar from a theological and Aristotelian perspective. A third point that a theological ethic of human relationships with other animals can learn from in Nussbaum's account is her express intention to take seriously the particularity of the lives of other creatures. This is an important and necessary response to the Derridian critique of the totalitarian use of 'Animal' in the passage cited above. Instead of believing that we have completed the moral task in assigning a particular creature to the status of '(non-human) animal', we need to

---

[30] See, for example, C. Osborne, *Dumb Beasts and Dead Philosophers: Humanity and the Humane in Ancient Philosophy and Literature* (Oxford: Clarendon, 2007).

recognize, as Nussbaum does, a responsibility to understand what constitutes a good life for this creature and how human beings may impact on the exercise of its capabilities, positively or negatively. Finally, theological ethics would do well to attend to some of the hard questions Nussbaum raises. For example, she asks whether humans 'should police the animal world, protecting vulnerable animals from predators', recognizing that this seems absurd, but confronting the implication of her capabilities approach that what matters is whether a creature's capabilities are curtailed, not whether this is done by a human or non-human agent.[31] The contrast with a standard ecological norm of non-interference with wild nature is striking, and it is unrealistic to think that human beings would benefit prey animals through large-scale interventions, let alone their predators. There is something, however, in Nussbaum's question that resonates with a biblical vision that sees predatory relationships between creatures as failing to express the fullness of the creator's will.[32]

In assessing the merits of the new approaches to thinking about moral value beyond the human that Nussbaum and I are commending, it is tempting to rush to situations of conflict between humans and other animals. Examples such as the following might be used to show the necessity of the absolute moral boundary our approaches reject. If one sees a puppy and a human baby drowning, and could only save one, on what grounds can we justify preferring the human? If rabbits or other herbivores are consuming crops and thereby imperilling human life, is it permissible to kill them? If the diseases carried by mosquitoes are resulting in the deaths of many human beings, can the extermination of mosquitoes be defended? It is possible to give answers to these questions in a variety of ways. In relation to the preference for saving a human baby over a puppy, I would be inclined to say that in extreme and artificially forced choices of this kind we might appeal to species loyalty or intra-species responsibility as a legitimate but limited moral principle. Parents are responsible for providing for their own children in a way that they are not responsible for other children, but this does not mean they have no moral responsibility for the welfare of other children or that the interests of other children are subordinate to those of their own. It may be that we are responsible for fellow members of our own species in a similar way. In response to the question of defending food resources for human beings from other animals, it must make sense to appeal to the legitimacy of a creature seeking to obtain the resources necessary for its survival – though there would also be a responsibility to do this without endangering other animal lives where possible, which in the case of the rabbits would prefer fences to shotguns. In the third case, the legitimacy of seeking what is necessary for survival would generate a right to defend this against aggressors, even when they are morally innocent, such as is presumably the case in relation to mosquitoes. In a theological context, a recognition of the inevitable conflict between creatures in the world as we know it can be seen in the context

[31] Nussbaum, *Frontiers of Justice*, p. 379.
[32] See, for example, Gen. 1.29–30, 6.13; Isa. 11.6–9, 65.25–6.

of lamenting the fall of creation from the harmony intended by its creator and a longing for the new creation in which this conflict will be no more.[33]

It is natural to rush to such examples of conflict and important to be able to give answers to such challenges, but I suggest that there is a good reason to resist the temptation to pause too long over such cases. If it is the case that the flourishing of creatures other than human ones should be a part of human moral concern, we must recognize that the vast majority of killing, injury and cruelty practiced by humans towards other animals does not take place in situations where the lives of human beings are in irreconcilable conflict with the lives of other creatures. Human beings do not need to consume meat to survive, but around 56 billion animals are raised and slaughtered for human consumption annually,[34] many of which are raised in intensive conditions that cannot begin to be defended as enabling their flourishing. Therefore, the moral issue where action seems most urgent coincides with where the moral question is simplest: where not human life, but human convenience is in conflict with the lives and well-being of other creatures. We would do well, therefore, to devote our attention to the obvious and clear moral cases in this area before we take the luxury of reflecting on those at the borderline.

The proposal of moving beyond a situation where only humans are recognized as possessing moral status may provoke the concern that if the barrier between moral regard for human and non-human animals were broken down, human interests, and especially the interests of the most vulnerable human beings, would suffer. It is the case that if a position such as the one I am proposing were to be adopted, human life would have to change in some ways and would be more costly in some respects. A good comparison is the cost of ending slavery in the United States of America: labour became more costly once the moral principle that slavery was illegitimate had been conceded. We can agree, I take it, that this economic cost of redressing a moral wrong was well worth paying. We can go further, and recognize that the economic cost of righting the wrong was a measure of the unfair economic advantage white slave owners took over their black slaves. In a similar way, if we come to see it is no longer appropriate to use non-human creatures for our ends as if they were merely intended for our use, we will have to find other ways to feed ourselves, conduct research, entertain ourselves and so on. In recognizing these costs, however, we should avoid exaggerating them. Beyond the inconvenience of changing our dietary habits, for example, switching to a vegetarian diet would bring human benefits, making more food and more healthy food available for human beings. There are harder questions to face, such as whether growth in human population and the

---

[33] See Clough, *On Animals: I. Systematic Theology*, chs 6–7.

[34] Food and Agriculture Organization of the United Nations, *Livestock's Long Shadow: Environmental Issues and Options* (Geneva: Food and Agriculture Organization, 2006), p. 36, cited in M. C. Halteman, (Washington, DC: The Humane Society of the United States, 2008), p. 25.

consequent destruction of habitats of other kinds of creatures is legitimate, but there are many significant changes that can be made before we reach this kind of competitive decision. Where there are costs, however, it does not seem to me that they will fall disproportionately on those sometimes considered marginal within human communities, as is sometimes feared. To gain the sense that all creatures should be respected as ends in themselves strengthens, rather than weakens, the recognition that all humans should be respected that way.

There are serious problems with our belief in human equality. The current array of accounts that seek to defend the case that human beings, and only human beings, should be respected equally fail to provide a plausible account that both supports equal regard and restricts it to human beings. If we add the consideration that the exclusion of non-human creatures from moral consideration is in itself morally problematic, it becomes very clear that we are in need of accounts of ethics that are able to see beyond the human/non-human boundary. Utilitarianism has been prophetic in raising awareness that the suffering of non-human animals is of moral consequence, but for many reasons it cannot give a satisfactory account of ethics, not least its inability to explain why the welfare of some creatures may not be sacrificed in order to benefit others. Nussbaum's capability approach, grounded in an Aristotelian philosophical tradition, looks very much more promising as a dialogue partner for theological ethics in this area, with interesting common ground at key points. The development of a theological ethic that makes a radical extension to Kant in affirming that every creature is intended by God as an end in itself, informed by Nussbaum's attention to the capability of particular creatures, promises to be a coherent and consistent new framework for theological ethics, with significant consequences for the ordering of human practices in relation to animals.

I. Response to David Clough

Wayne Morris

Introduction

David offers an important and persuasive critique of the ways that many theological and philosophical perspectives on what it means to be human serve to perpetuate a hierarchy of human animals over non-human animals. Further, David shows how such perspectives have also served to dehumanize certain groups of people who in some way do not 'fit' established criteria of what it means to 'be human'. Subsequently, David works towards a constructive theological and philosophical ethic, drawing on the work of Martha Nussbaum, to propose an alternative way of thinking, and as a result acting, towards non-human animals. David offers an important contribution to thinking about the challenge of how all human animals must negotiate how best to live alongside and in relationship with non-human animals.

The 'Voice' of the Non-Human?

David's critique of Christian attitudes towards non-human animals echoes the critiques of many whose voices and perspectives have historically been marginalized in theology. John Hull became blind as an adult and, on becoming blind, he returned to the Bible, only to realize that the Bible was written by sighted people and, as a result, led to Hull feeling alienated from it.[35] The language, imagery and content of much theological and biblical literature throughout the ages reflects the experience of ancient near-Eastern or European, able-bodied, educated men. Likewise, and with good reason, David notes the anthropocentrism of Christian theology, which does not simply ignore animals, but has often actively justified the hierarchy of human over non-human. In deconstructing the anthropocentrism of Christian theology, David seeks to reconstruct a theology that takes non-humans seriously, seeking to transform both human attitudes and practices towards non-human animals.

I recognize at once the anthropocentric criticism David makes of Christian theology, but as a contextual theologian, my starting point for all constructive theology is that it emerges out of a particular person's or group's experience. Any theology that claims to be feminist must emerge from the experience of women. Any theology that calls itself black theology must emerge from the experience of black people. Any theology that seeks to speak about the experience of an historically marginalized group, but that is not constructed by a member of that group, must take great care and time to show how they have engaged with that group's experience. Theologies of disability, some of which seek to speak theologically about persons who do not have the opportunity or capacity to construct and articulate a theology for themselves, must show how the theologian has engaged with disabled experiences. But what of a theology of non-human animals? How might their experience be used to form and shape a theology of non-human animals? How might such experience be understood and engaged with? How might we judge whether a theology of non-human animals is truly liberating, or else a form of unwelcome paternalism? Can a theology of non-human animals written by human animals ultimately be another form of oppression? My question of David, in his deconstruction of anthropocentric theologies and reconstruction of new theologies is, where is the 'voice' of non-human animals, and how might we engage with them? If we don't discover such 'voices', is any theology of non-human animals potentially a form of paternalism (humans know best) or even 'oppression'? Nussbaum provides an example of the dangers of ignoring experience, when thinking about a particular group, that helps to illustrate this point.

Nussbaum's quest to discover and articulate a set of criteria that gives a 'minimum account of social justice' that leads to a 'life with dignity' is a noble and important quest. Any attempt to transform for the better the way societies, cultures, institutions and governments think about human, and indeed, non-human life, deserves consideration while also being open to people asking, can this truly

---

[35] J. Hull, *In the Beginning there was Darkness* (London: SCM Press, 2001), p. 3.

make lives better? But like many of the accounts that aim to define what it means to be human that David criticizes, Nussbaum's ten capabilities, while liberating for some people, may be oppressive to others. Nussbaum's ten capabilities do offer a constructive way of thinking about a 'life with dignity', but they must also, I think, be treated with suspicion.

Nussbaum presents her ten capabilities as having universal significance. While she recognizes that the 'minimum thresholds' of her capabilities need to be established in context, even individually, it is essential to be suspicious of anything that claims to be universally applicable. When she addresses herself to people with disabilities, and in particular people with severe intellectual disabilities, the problem of her universalizing comes to the fore. Drawing on an example of someone with a severe intellectual disability, someone who will never have the opportunity to experience some of Nussbaum's capabilities, such as 'senses, imagination and thought', 'practical reason' or 'control over one's environment',[36] she concludes that the life of such a person must be considered to be 'extremely unfortunate'.[37] In such a view, Nussbaum exposes her ten capabilities as not being a basic account of social justice with universal significance, but a Western, liberal, able-bodied account of social justice. Anything that does not conform to Nussbaum's ideal for herself must be considered to be, at the very least, 'unfortunate'.

Many hearing people find it difficult, if not impossible, to understand why many Deaf people view their Deafness so positively. This is because too often a hearing person imagines what it would like to lose their hearing, and this is something they consider to be traumatic.[38] But Deaf people often do not understand their Deafness in terms of loss (a hearing perspective), but rather in terms of what is good about their lives, their culture, language and community. It seems to me that Nussbaum begins her reflections on what constitutes a life with dignity by thinking about what it would be like to live a life without certain opportunities given to her (opportunities she values in her Western, liberal tradition). She concludes that a life without such capabilities is 'unfortunate'. For many people, that will be true, but it will not be true for everyone. Of significance in Nussbaum's arguments is that she does not attempt to understand the world from the perspective of the person with a severe intellectual disability. She can only imagine what life would be like for her if she were 'like them' and conclude that their lives are 'unfortunate'. Such perspectives, when engaged with the lives of people with severe intellectual disabilities, might lead societies to conclude that their lives are so unfortunate they are not lives worth living or supporting because they are lives that are essentially not fully human. When Nussbaum's theory is imposed on others, such a view may marginalize, even exclude, those whose lives will never conform to Nussbaum's

---

[36] M. Nussbaum, *Frontiers of Justice: Disability, Nationality, Species Membership* (Cambridge MA/London: Belknap Press/Harvard University Press, 2006), p. 76-7.

[37] Ibid., p. 192.

[38] W. Morris, *Theology without Words: Theology in the Deaf Community* (Aldershot: Ashgate, 2008), p. 61.

norms. Above, I asked of David, where is the voice of non-human animals in his theological ethic? Here, then, I am warning that if we view the life of a human or non-human animal through the lenses of what makes a good life 'for me', we are in danger of imposing our own view of what constitutes a good life on to others, however we categorize human and non-human animals. Non-humans animals may have a quite different 'perspective' on their own lives, if only we could understand what that was.

Imago Dei

Finally, I recognized in David's critique of the philosophical and theological traditions that justify an 'inequality' between human and non-human animals many of the questions that have been raised by theologians of disability. That humans should be respected above other creatures for their capacity to reason, connected with ideas about what it means to be made in God's image, for example, have served, as David rightly points out, to dehumanize people who do not have the capacity for reason; people with intellectual disabilities, people with mental illnesses, people with dementia and infants. Perhaps David, agreeing with Wenham, is, however, a little cynical about how Genesis 1.26 has or could be used. While the concerns raised about the use of *imago Dei* are important, *imago Dei* has, nevertheless, been for many a liberating concept.[39] With Nussbaum, I would not want to so readily reject something that has 'illuminated so much about core issues of social justice'[40] and offered a transformative way forward. Neither do I think that theologians read into *imago Dei* their own values and biases any more than any theologian does this in any theology they develop.

There can be no doubt that the notion of *imago Dei*, both in terms of how it is presented in Genesis 1.26 and how it has subsequently been used, is anthropocentric. Nevertheless, within the Christian tradition, there are images for God that draw on non-human metaphors. For example, in the biblical tradition, Jesus is portrayed directly or indirectly as a 'lamb' (John 1.36), or the 'lion of Judah' (Revelation 5.5) or a 'hen' (Matthew 23.37), while the Holy Spirit is portrayed as a 'dove' (Matthew 3.16), to name just a few examples. So, while there can be no getting away from the anthropocentrism of Genesis 1.26, it is worth acknowledging that the Judaeo-Christian tradition does make use of animal imagery to speak of their deity. If humans in their perspectives on God find it appropriate to use animal metaphors to speak of God, it may be that our images of God need not be so anthropocentric. Indeed, such metaphors challenge the Christian community to think about the place of animals in God's life and whether God's future eschatological embrace is one that is inclusive of non-human animals.

---

[39] *Imago Dei* is used to think positively about disability, for example, in Thomas Reynolds, *Vulnerable Communion: A Theology of Disability and Hospitality* (Grand Rapids, MI: Brazos Press, 2008), pp. 177–88.

[40] M. Nussbaum, *Frontiers of Justice*, p. 69.

To speak of *imago Dei* begs the question, 'what is God like?' Such a question brings me to the doctrine of the Trinity. If non-human animals might in some way be included in God's eschatological embrace alongside humans, as I have suggested, the doctrine of the Trinity provides a model for understanding the kind of existence that humans and non-humans might have together in God's presence and so provide a model for human existence on earth. John Zizioulas's understanding of the Trinity as a place of 'communion and otherness'[41] is useful here, for the Trinity provides a way of speaking about how we can coexist in a context of respect and difference. This may not only be between human persons, but also between human and non-human animals. Such a concept takes us beyond seeking equality (the use of such a term David and I would treat with suspicion), to working to discover what it means to live in communion with one another and the whole of creation, in a context in which difference is respected and affirmed. This potentially removes the possibility of imposing human perspectives on what constitutes a good life onto non-human animals, and instead acknowledges that different species may have different ways of being themselves, while recognizing that different creatures need to find ways of appropriately living together.

II. Concluding Comments

David Clough

I am grateful for this response, which raises four key issues with the argument I develop in the chapter: a problem with what attending to the voice of other animals could mean, a problem with Nussbaum's attempt to specify universal capacities (and therefore my use of her work), a concern about whether I am unduly cynical about the *imago Dei* and the significance of non-human divine imagery and the doctrine of the Trinity. I will treat them in turn.

First, I am asked about the dangers of theologizing about other animals without being able to attend to their own voices. I think there are two important notes to strike in this context. On one hand, we should recognize that the inability of other animals to speak to us does not mean we are unable to understand some aspects of their experience. For the past two years we have shared our home with a cat. Most of the time in her relationship with me she is an independent and stand-offish kind of creature, who will resist attempts to entice her onto a lap and retreat from expressions of affection. Sometimes, however, she solicits attention and will delight in being stroked for as long as I have the patience to continue doing so, purring loudly all the while. I cannot ask her how she feels about the prospect of receiving affection at a given moment, but she can certainly tell me. Similarly, on the days we need to take her to the vet, her own view of the desirability of the project is very clear indeed. It is possible, therefore, to have some

---

[41] J. Zizioulas, *Communion & Otherness* (London: T&T Clark, 2006).

sense of the voice and experience of other creatures in a way that cannot plausibly be reduced to mere projection of human experience onto them or of inappropriate anthropomorphism. I would argue, therefore, that some theological accounts of non-human animals could be falsified by the voice of non-human creatures. Accounts of religious sacrifices of non-human animals that hold that the victims consent to their slaughter, for example, I take to be false on the basis of the observed responses of non-sedated animals to the prospect of their killing. On the other hand, however, I think there is more that needs to be said by theology about the place of other animals before God than can be shown to be consistent with their own voice. I do not expect to come across other animals who are able to anticipate the peaceable relations between creatures prophesied by Isaiah, but I do not feel bound by this expectation to stop talking about their place in such a peaceable new creation. I wonder if this indicates a limit to the applicability of contextual theology: that in this case (as perhaps in others?) it is crucial to be able to speak of others in a way that cannot originate or be governed by their own voice or experience.

Second, there is the question of whether Nussbaum's identification of capacities is oppressive, and in particular whether she is right to judge it unfortunate that some human beings are unable to exercise senses, imagination, thought, practical reason or control over their environment. While I would welcome further discussion of this point, my sympathies are currently with Nussbaum here. I see the danger of identifying a norm of human functioning, and judging humans that fail to meet its basic criteria as inadequate, but this is not how I understand Nussbaum's project: she is not attempting any kind of scale of value, but trying to set out what human capacities need nurturing and supporting. I appreciate the importance of taking seriously the voice of those who cannot hear saying they do not experience their condition as disabling, but I am not yet convinced that this voice should be interpreted as a universal truth about human disabilities. To take an extreme case: the appropriate response to an anencephalic infant – usually born blind, deaf, unconscious and unable to feel pain – is not the construction of a theology of liberation that denies that such a creature is unfortunate, but rather pity, mourning and care. The fact that some persons with disabilities would be offended by being seen as unfortunate does not make it inappropriate to see any person with disabilities in this way.

The third issue concerns the interpretation of the image of God. I am convinced that this has served as a liberating and egalitarian concept for many human beings, and am glad it has. My query is twofold: one theoretical – it does not seem a good reading of the text to think it names particular attributes that distinguish human beings from other creatures – and one practical – the routine invocation of the term to be inclusive of all human beings has had the unintended side effect of providing grounds for disregarding other creatures. I do not consider that this is a zero-sum game: we could find a way to affirm appropriate moral regard for all human beings without at the same time disregarding non-human creatures.

Finally, what of the non-human images used of God, and the meaning of God's Trinitarian existence, as incorporating communion and otherness? I greatly appreciate the reminder of the wealth of imagery used of God that is based on non-human animals. In connection with the previous point, it is hard to avoid the claim that, in the examples given, the lion is an image of God as Father, the lamb an image of God as Son and the dove is an image of God as Holy Spirit. God is therefore imaged in the human, but also in the lion, the lamb, the dove, and perhaps, we might say with Aquinas, in every part of creation in some way (*Summa Theologica* I.93.2 *ad*.1). As regards the idea that the redemption of every creature in all their particularity and otherness will be their communion in the Trinitarian life of God: Amen!

6 Does Size Really Matter? A Feminist Theological Response to Secular Dieting and Weight Loss

Hannah Bacon

A quick look at a few popular magazines may be all we need to answer the question of whether size really matters. The front cover of one edition of *Now* magazine, for example, was dominated by the headline, 'Celebs' Weights Exposed' and was followed quickly on the contents page by images of Gwyneth Paltrow working out. Many of the pages that followed apparently 'exposed' the 'real' weights of celebrities such as Cheryl Cole, J-Lo, Victoria Beckham, Alesha Dixon, Jordan and Catherine Tate.[1] While such stories and images will no doubt be unsurprising to us, they do nevertheless reveal the strongly pervasive power of Western cultural expectations surrounding thinness and its inseparable association with femininity. As Kandi Stinson notes, 'to be female is to diet'[2].

While it is true that dieting is not an exclusively female enterprise, it is still the case that women continue to be the main focus and key players within the dieting industry. Part of this chapter, therefore, aims to consider the ways in which cultural discourses surrounding body size interlink with cultural discourses having to do with gender and the construction of femininity, serving to categorize the 'fat' female body as 'deviant' and 'other'. As a feminist who is also a theologian, however, I am also keen to ask about the role of Christian theology in perpetuating such patriarchal and anti-fat discourses. Specifically, I want to interrogate the relationship between Christian theology's seeming suspicion of desire and appetite and some of the central principles which seem to underpin secular forms of dieting.

In seeking to address these concerns, this chapter is separated into two halves. The first takes a close look at the Christian tradition, using Augustine as

---

[1] *Now*, 29 September 2008.
[2] K. Stinson, *Women and Dieting Culture: Inside a Commercial Weight Loss Group* (New Brunswick, New Jersey and London: Rutgers University Press, 2001), p. 3.

a significant example of Western theology and its stigmatization of female desire. This section considers the multiple ways in which Christian ideas about the dominance of the will over the body and the need to control desire map onto the principles and practices of secular dieting, using my own fieldwork inside a UK secular diet group as a focus. The intention here is not to argue that Augustine is directly responsible for the principles which appear in this particular diet group, but that Augustine, like other Christian thinkers in the West, has contributed to a profound theological suspicion of the body and female desire which has become so culturally powerful and pervasive that it continues to inform a number of secular institutions and practices,[3] including current secular forms of dieting.

The second section of this chapter turns toward thinking about a way forward. If there is a powerful congruency between the principles which underpin this secular diet program and those which seem to underpin aspects of Christian thought surrounding the body and desire in the West, how might we go about constructing a theological response to secular dieting which does not simply reinforce an understanding of female desire as dangerous? How might we *transform* this discourse? In addressing this, this chapter argues strongly for a theology of abundance – a theology which, I argue, is modelled in the lovers' exchange in the Song of Songs, is grounded on the Trinitarian and incarnational identity of God and is performed by believers through participation in the Eucharistic meal.

Inside a UK Diet Group

Before beginning this analysis, it is appropriate to say something about the fieldwork I am currently conducting, especially given that reference will be made to this at various stages throughout the chapter. Since the end of June 2009, I have been attending an organized commercial diet group on a weekly basis.[4] The group is part of a well-known UK-based diet organization and makes up one of the 6,000 groups which meet across the UK every week. The organization was founded in 1969 and so is just into its 41st year of existence.

So far, my research has involved participant observation and informal conversations with members, but it will involve semi-structured interviews with up to 15 group members in the coming months. The group I attend varies in size from week to week, ranging from around 10 to 30 members. Members also vary in age, but the group is predominantly female with only two male members, neither of whom attends regularly. The group is mostly white and middle class, and the female leader reflects this demographic. The meeting takes place in a church hall

---

[3] S. Bordo, *Unbearable Weight: Feminism, Western Culture, and the Body* (Berkeley, Los Angeles, London: University of California Press, 1993), pp. 13–14.
[4] The reader should note that this Chapter was written following the Symposium in 2009 at which time I was still participating in the diet group. Fieldwork inside this diet group did, however, end in September 2010.

inside a church centre and usually lasts for around one and a half hours. There are new members most weeks, but many of these do not return. Meetings tend to consist of the same components: before the meeting, members will sign in, pay, get weighed, and then socialize with other members. If there is a particular theme which is being followed, food 'tasters' may be provided by members and so some of the time before the meeting may be spent eating, much to my surprise! During the meeting, the leader will welcome new members, present awards to those who have reached significant targets (as identified by the diet program), address each individual in the group about their weight gain, loss or maintenance that week and invite members to respond. The meeting usually ends by the leader taking a raffle and commissioning the group to 'go forth and shrink!' After the meeting, members tend to leave quite rapidly, but some will stay and help the leader pack up. It is not uncommon for members to go directly from the meeting to the take-away.

Exclusion and the 'Fat' Female Body: Fat is a Feminist Issue

What is clear from this research so far is that weight loss and slimness are considered essential for making the female body 'fit'. In one sense, this is evidenced literally by a desire expressed by many female members to fit into smaller clothes. Rachel, for example, told me that she wasn't particularly bothered about what the scales showed, as long as she could fit into her size 12 jeans. At another level, however, this is expressed as a desire to make the body 'fit' with what society holds to be culturally normative and socially acceptable. Of course, it is true that according to dominant Western culture, 'fat' bodies do not fit and must be pulled back into shape. This is especially true of the fat *female* body, given that femininity is culturally tied up with slimness. Female bodies which adhere to the white, Western cultural expectation of slenderness – a vision of the ideal feminine woman which Elizabeth Schüssler Fiorenza refers to as the hegemonic 'White Lady'[5] – are normalized, and those who fail to fit this mould are marginalized and outcast. Michelle Lelwica also notes that 'the tightly contoured female body delineates an elite white-Western vision of womanhood, produced and circulated by the popular media and employed for commercial purposes.'[6] This white-Western image of womanhood, she maintains, is so universal, that it operates as the lens through which all other female bodies are judged and evaluated. The 'fat' female body is defined as 'deviant', thereby establishing thinness as central to today's white, Western feminine ideal.[7]

To be 'fat' and female, then, means to occupy a position of otherness in relation to the normative Western slender female body. Because 'fat' is often perceived as

[5] E. S. Fiorenza, *Sharing Her Word: Feminist Biblical Interpretation in Context* (Edinburgh: T&T Clark, 1998), p. 144.
[6] M. Lelwica, 'Spreading the Religion of Thinness from California to Calcutta', *Journal of Feminist Studies in Religion* 25:1 (2009), pp.19–42 (25).
[7] Ibid., p. 26.

'unfeminine, unattractive, and a sign of a body "out of control" '[8], dieting often emerges as a way back into femininity, as well as a way back into selfhood. Not only do women gain affirmation as being truly feminine, they are also empowered to find the real them *underneath* their body fat; a self which we must assume can only emerge through weight loss.

Dieting, however, also importantly provides a method for controlling and curtailing female *desire*. Indeed, at the heart of the secular diet industry is an attitude of suspicion towards female desire, and this is shown most obviously by the requirement placed on members to monitor and police what they eat. Dieters, for example, in the group I am currently observing, monitor their own body weight on a week-by-week basis and are required to calculate the 'syn'[9] value of all foods. There is also a strong tradition of surveillance within the group itself, which is generated both by group members and by the leader. The leader will habitually ask members to give an account of their weight gain or weight loss and has in the past handed out a fake eyeball to members to keep inside their lunch boxes as a reminder that she is watching them. Added to this, there is also a ritualized enquiry process which follows each weigh-in, in which members will ask how others 'got on' that week. When members have 'gained', an explanation is always offered as to why this was so. Joanne, for example, explained that it had been her dad's birthday and that this had involved cake. Work colleagues had also recently returned from summer holidays, bringing with them a host of foods, and there was only so much she could resist. There is, therefore, in addition to the leader's policing of members, a process which involves members policing other members, and this seems to necessitate the need to explain and rationalize weight gain.

At the heart of the diet group I am observing, as well as the diet industry more generally, there rests an underlying assumption that it is morally valuable, as well as practically necessary, for women to 'watch' their weight and to police their (and other women's) desire for food. That this is the case particularly for women arises as a result of women internalizing what has come to be known as the 'male gaze'. Under patriarchy, it is men who gaze or look and women who are gazed upon. As such, women come to be evaluated and learn to evaluate themselves in terms of their appearance.[10] Culture therefore develops specifically in order to please the eye and appetite of the male, and women consequently learn to police their size and shape in keeping with this imaginary gaze. It does not take much, however,

---

[8] J. Germov and L. Williams, 'Dieting Women: Self-Surveillance and the Body Ponopticon', in J. Sobal and D. Maurer (eds), *Weighty Issues: Fatness and Thinness as Social Problems* (New York: Aldine de Gruyter, 1999), pp. 117–32 (119).

[9] 'Syn' here is short for 'synergy' and is a reworking of the original trademark spelling 'sin' formerly used by the organization. 'Syn' depicts the organization's view that restricting the amount of food treats dieters enjoy (typically things like cakes, crisps, chocolate, alcohol etc.) works alongside other elements of the diet to optimise weight-loss.

[10] N. M. McKinley, 'Ideal Weight/Ideal Women: Society Constructs the Female', in Jeffery Sobal and Donna Maurer, *Weighty Issues: Fatness and Thinness as Social Problems* (New York: Aldine de Gruyter, 1999), pp. 97–116 (98–9).

to realize that such scrutiny serves conveniently to ensure that women do not take up too much space. It provides what Susan Bordo refers to as a 'concrete expression' of the central rule which underpins the construction of femininity within the patriarchal world: that female hunger and desire – whether for power, independence, or sexual pleasure – must be contained and kept under control.[11]

God and Desire

Considering the role of Christian theology in developing and perpetuating this discourse about female desire is deeply important. Indeed, Christian theology has played and continues to play a profound role in the development of Western anxiety towards female desire and has, I want to suggest, served to fuel secular discourses about self-control and the need for weight loss.

In the opening to her book, *Veiled Desire*, Kim Power notes that female desire has proved particularly problematic within Christianity because woman, as well as God, constitutes the object of man's desire. 'The Christian discourse of desire', she argues, 'sets up a choice between woman and God, wherein the sexually desirable woman is represented as being in direct conflict with God for the hearts of men'.[12] According to this discourse, it is only possible to achieve an uncompromised and unreserved focus on God through the eradication of sexual desire for women. For Augustine, for example, to live according to the order of God demanded that man should not be controlled by the sexuality of his wife. Even sex within marriage constituted a 'lowering of the male to his inferior self'.[13] Woman thus symbolized the law of sin, luring man away from God, and so needed to be controlled by him in order to prevent his own moral and spiritual downfall.

The ordering of male intellect *over* female desire was, however, according to Augustine, intrinsic to the ordering of the world as God intended it. What happened at the fall was that Eve, rather than willingly accepting this, turned such a 'holy' order upside down; she acted on her *own* authority, so that female desire now came to control the male rational mind and so destroyed the natural hierarchy of reason ruling *over* desire.[14]

Of course, the influence of Hellenistic Greco-Roman culture on classical theology made clear that in order to control male desire it was necessary to control female sexuality and so women more generally. Eve often came to symbolize the dangers of female appetite and desire, and women's capacity to tempt men away from God into sin. Tertullian, for example, famously cast all women in the role of

[11] Bordo, *Unbearable Weight*, p. 171.
[12] K. Power, *Veiled Desire: Augustine's Writings on Women* (London: DLT, 1995), p. 3.
[13] R. R. Ruether, 'Augustine: Sexuality, Gender and Women', in Judith Chelius Stark (ed.), *Feminist Interpretations of Augustine* (The Pennsylvania State University: Pennsylvania, 2007), pp. 47–68 (61).
[14] Ibid., pp. 56–7.

Eve, asserting that women were 'the devil's gateway' and ultimately responsible for destroying the image of God and man, as well as causing the death of Christ.[15] Augustine also asserted that Eve represented women's capacity to pull men away from their prime object of desire, God. While Adam reflected what Augustine saw as the masculine dimension of the mind, Eve reflected the feminine dimension.[16] Whereas the feminine aspect was concerned with the senses and human appetite/desire and was to be identified with 'the reason of knowledge' and, as such, with the corporeal and temporal, the masculine was concerned with what Augustine called the 'reason of wisdom' and with the contemplation of eternal things.[17] The reason of knowledge, or *scientia*, was responsible for discerning good and evil in the corporeal world and, as such, made recommendations to the masculine reason of wisdom, or *sapientia*. Although these recommendations could be good, they could also be found wanting because of the feminine's proximity to the senses, guilty of seeking after personal pleasure and the fulfilment of carnal appetite. If the masculine dimension acted on such wanting advice, this was akin to the serpent once more addressing the woman and the woman once more luring the man, as well as herself, into sin.[18] The upshot of this was that the feminine was seen as dragging the masculine away from the 'heady' knowledge of God into the corruptible realm of the senses and the corporeal. It followed then, for Augustine, that the masculine must always ensure that the feminine was 'kept in check'.[19]

Dieting, Desire and God: A Healthy Recipe?

The parallels between this kind of theological position and the position of secular diet plans such as the one in which I am currently conducting research are striking. Both suggest that it is good and right to subject the body and its appetites to the superior rule of reason, intellect and the will. If Christianity traditionally teaches that 'appetite is a lure that ensnares the soul and prevents its pious impulses',[20] then the secular diet I am investigating in my research would seem to reflect a similar opinion.

Of course, there are dangers with focusing too heavily on Augustine, since he provides but one example of how Christian theologians have traditionally reflected upon desire. We also need to be careful that we do not imply that Augustine is

---

[15] Tertullian, *On the Apparel of Women*, trans. Revd. S. Thelwall (Whitefish: Kessinger Publishing, 2004), p. 4.

[16] Augustine, *On the Trinity*, ed. Gareth B. Matthews; trans. Stephen McKenna (Cambridge: Cambridge University Press, 2002), 12.12, p. 95 and 12.3, p. 84.

[17] Ibid., 12.12, p. 95.

[18] Ibid., 12.12, pp. 95–6.

[19] Ibid., 12.7, p. 90.

[20] R. Klein, 'Fat Beauty', in Jana Evans Braziel and Kathleen LeBesco (eds), *Bodies out of Bounds: Fatness and Transgression* (Berkeley, Los Angeles, London: University of California Press, 2001), p. 28.

directly responsible for current emphases on will power and its dominance over desire and appetite, which seem to characterize this secular diet, as well as many others. What is clear, however, is that Augustine, although only constituting one example, evidences a theological suspicion of desire which perfectly echoes that evident within secular forms of dieting. For Augustine, for example, although both masculine and feminine are rational, the feminine is that aspect of the mind which must not act on itself, which only discerns the corporeal, rather than acting on what is discerned; it is, therefore, that aspect of reason which is susceptible to temptation and which is more readily associated with desire; it is that aspect which must be rightly subdued by the heady and superior reason of wisdom. Similarly in this diet programme, the body and its desires are made accountable to the heady intellect of members. Members must avoid temptation and are frequently asked by the leader how they will go about doing so. When members recount instances when desire has taken over and they have given into temptation, the leader responds by asking them to provide a plan of action for the following week. Emphasis here then, just as with Augustine, is placed on reasserting the power of *action*, regaining *control*, and perhaps most importantly, restoring the proper and original *order* of things. Desire is placed back in its rightful place as subject to the dieter's will and superior intellectual decision to lose weight.

Just as with Augustine, this secular diet maintains that to avoid sin (or 'syn') it is necessary to curtail desire by making the body subject to the will. Just as with Augustine, this secular diet stresses that uncontrolled desire and appetite drag the 'person into sin/'syn' and demand a response of self-discipline and a careful and deliberate policing of the body. Of course, that there is a specific focus on *female* appetite in this, like all other diet groups, simply reinforces Augustine's mandate that it is necessary to curtail female desire in particular.

It is interesting that part of this diet group's shared discourse includes reference to so-called safe foods, those foods which are 'free' to eat and which can be eaten without limitation. Of course, this implies that some foods can be dangerous, and this is reflected in the group. When speaking about the syn value of a sausage roll, for example, the leader once remarked that it was 'scary' how many syns were in this particular food. She also warned the group that it was the syns dieters didn't see which were to be feared and watched. The bits at the end of a packet of cereal, the syns in salad dressing or the syns in manufactured soups. All, according to the leader, mattered and could get well-intentional dieters into trouble. Such an identification of food with danger, of course, resonates with the narrative of the fall in which food paves the way into sin. Although Eve thinks that the tree of knowledge is 'good for food', 'a delight to the eyes' and 'to be desired to make one wise' (Gen. 3.6) – insights which, according to Phyllis Trible and others show Eve to be discerning, autonomous and independent[21] – classical interpretations of the Genesis account render Adam and Eve's eating as the cause of 'the fall'. Just as with

---

[21] Also see D. F. Sawyer, 'Hidden Subjects: Rereading Eve and Mary', *Theology & Sexuality* 14, 3 (2008), pp. 305–20.

this secular diet, food here is linked with danger, and we are told that what might appear harmless or even good to eat may, in fact, turn out to be otherwise.

Of course, it is Eve in particular who has been blamed for sin and who has been charged with bringing evil into the world. Certainly, as the doctrine of original sin developed in the fourth and fifth centuries through the theologies of Ambrose and Augustine, so the culpability of Eve intensified.[22] Augustine, for example, maintained that the serpent approached the woman first because she was less rational and more susceptible to deception. Adam, on the other hand, was not deceived by the serpent, but went along with Eve out of companionship.[23] Although the fall couldn't have taken place without Adam (given that it was his role to act on Eve's recommendations), it was Eve who was nevertheless responsible for luring Adam away from obedience to God. The desire and lust associated with concupiscence, which for Augustine made the sexual act sinful, was primarily established by Eve and by her eating of the forbidden fruit in Eden. So pervasive is this classic association of sin with women and eating in our contemporary Western mindset that *Walls* ice cream could successfully launch its '7 Deadly Sins' range of *Magnum* ice creams in 2002 through advertisements which personified each sin as female.

How, then, might such associations be resisted and even transformed? How might we challenge the central premise at the heart of Augustine's theology and secular diets like the one mentioned here, that the body and its appetites can't be trusted and threaten to drag us away from what is right and holy?

Theology, Dieting and Transformation: Towards a Theology of Abundance

Female Desire in the Song of Songs
It seems to me that there are a number of valuable resources within the Christian tradition which might help with this. The Song of Songs in the Hebrew Bible seems an obvious place to start, given its obvious celebration of sexuality and desire, especially female desire. Although frequently in the past interpreted as a text which speaks analogously about God's relationship with God's people, Israel, current scholarship questions the authenticity and accuracy of this view.[24] What we have in this text is a poetic story of two human lovers and a passionate and intimate telling of their erotic desire for one another.

Within this text, sexual desire is explored without any indication of marriage and without any reference to procreation.[25] Interestingly also, it is the *woman's* desire which in many respects forms the centrepiece of the story. She speaks for

---

[22] Ibid., p. 315.

[23] Ruether, 'Augustine', p. 54.

[24] See, for example, D. Carr, 'Gender and the Shaping of Desire in the Song of Songs and its Interpretation', *Journal of Biblical Literature* 119:2 (2000), pp. 233–48 (233–34).

[25] K. A. Stone, *Practicing Safer Texts: Food, Sex and Bible in Queer Perspective* (London & New York: T&T Clark, 2005), p. 98.

herself and controls the way we view her lover by conjuring up scenarios and the words he speaks (e.g. 5.2–8).[26] Indeed, Cheryl Exum notes that the attention the woman receives in the Song is unique to the Bible, as is her characterization. Here we see a woman initiating sexual encounters, passionately searching for her lover in the streets, speaking openly and explicitly about her erotic desire for him, all of which were not commonplace within Ancient Israel.[27] 'He is altogether desirable' (5.16) and her 'inmost being' yearns for him (5.4). She also begins and ends the Song and directs her lover to act in certain ways: to draw her after him (1.4), to sustain her with raisins and to refresh her with apples (2.5), to 'be like a gazelle or a young stag' (2.17), to 'go out early to the vineyards' (7.12), to come to the garden.[28] Although her body is an object of the man's gaze, he is undeniably also an object of her gaze.[29]

Importantly, we also see the lovers' desire and sexual love expressed through various images of nature, food and drink. He is like an apple tree among the trees of the wood (2.3) and his fruit is sweet to taste (2.3). Her cheeks are 'like halves of a pomegranate' (4.3) and her love better than wine (4.10). Although it was common in ancient Israel, as well as elsewhere in the ancient Near East, to describe sexual activity through agricultural imagery, such imagery tended to be deeply patriarchal.[30] Here, however, we see that the woman is not simply objectified, for as Lisa Isherwood notes, 'she eats and is eaten, she indulges in a riot of taste and smell'.[31] What we have in this text, then, is a hearty celebration of desire and of female desire in particular. The woman rejoices in her own beauty (1.5), she openly and explicitly calls upon her lover to taste the fruit from her garden (4.16), and rather than leading to sin, as with Eve, this sets the scene for a tantalizing play of desire between the two lovers. Rather than receiving punishment and death for eating, eating serves as an expression of life and livingness. The use of fruit imagery draws this home, as this was an important supplement to the ancient Palestinian grain-based diet, adding juiciness, sweetness and an explosion of tastes, smells and textures.[32] Such imagery then importantly communicates the excitement and adventure of sexuality, as well as the life-enhancing nature of sexual desire. Overall, the Song rejoices in the anticipation and thrill of desire, encouraging all to 'eat' and 'be drunk with love' (5.1).

Of course, we need to be careful that we do not over romanticize this book, for it does not escape the clutches of patriarchy altogether. According to the Song, the woman is abused (5.7), she remains nameless and is mindful of the cursory gaze of

---

[26] J. C. Exum, *Song of Songs: A Commentary* (Louisville: Westminster John Knox Press, 2005), p. 15.

[27] Ibid., p. 25.

[28] Also see Carr, 'Gender and the Shaping of Desire', p. 241.

[29] Stone, *Practicing Safer Texts*, p. 103.

[30] Exum, *Song of Songs*, p. 21, and L. Isherwood, *The Fat Jesus: Feminist Explorations in Boundaries and Transgressions* (London: DLT, 2007), p. 43.

[31] Isherwood, *The Fat Jesus*, p. 43.

[32] Stone, *Practicing Safer Texts*, p. 100.

others (1.6). However, many feminist theologians have understandably seen in this text a subversive message which flies in the face of classical Christian accounts of desire, such as those expressed by Augustine previously. Rather than encouraging the curtailment of desire, desire is presented here as something to be celebrated and embraced.

As such, this passage provides an important example of how Christianity might resource a voice of challenge and transformation from within its ranks. Of course, there are other examples, but it is not my intention to discuss these here. Instead, what I want to suggest now is that running through the very veins of Christianity is a subversive strand which, rather than constituting one example among many, exposes Christian theology as fundamentally a theology of abundance.

The Theological Foundations of a Theology of Abundance

Theology, in my view, has to be first and foremost a theology of abundance. It has to speak about God's 'extravagant affections', to use the title of Susan Ross's book, and it has to speak about crossing and challenging boundaries. It has to talk like this because it speaks of a God who is by nature expansive and limitless; because it speaks of a God who is Trinity and because it speaks of a God who is incarnate. As Trinity, God cannot simply be reduced to oneness because God is always more than this; God is both three and one at the same time, both transcendent and immanent, both temporal and eternal. As Trinity, God explodes these kinds of boundaries. Indeed, according to this doctrine, Father, Son and Holy Spirit give to one another in an unending and limitless exchange of love. This community is characterized by reciprocal living and the overflowing of boundaries. While there is distinction between the triune persons, there is also *perichoresis* and so the mutual indwelling of each person in the others, ensuring that relations within the Trinity always remain fluid and dynamic.[33]

As such, there is a deep ambiguity at the heart of the being of God, for God is never either this or that, but always both together. The doctrine of the Trinity also tells us that God's generous love knows no limits and cannot simply be contained within the inner Trinitarian life. Because it is God's nature to give and to give generously, this love spills out in abundance to invite the rest of creation into communion with the eternal God. John Zizioulas expresses this well through the term *ekstasis*, identifying that God creates an 'immanent relationship of love "outside Himself"'.[34] In other words, this God is not only incapable of being inwardly bounded, but also outwardly so. There are no limits to the inclusive embrace of this God.

---

[33] H. Bacon, *What's Right with the Trinity? Conversations in Feminist Theology* (Farnham: Ashgate, 2009), pp. 188–89.
[34] J. D. Zizioulas, *Being as Communion* (New York: St Vladimir's Seminary Press, 1993), p. 91.

In many respects, though, it is the doctrine of incarnation which speaks most profoundly about God's generosity and abundance.[35] Here we have the notion of God becoming human, which not only signifies the place of humankind within the eternal identity of God, but also the role of the body in revealing God: the body, we are forced to admit, *is* sacramental.[36] What is significant about the body of Christ, however, is that this body, according to the Gospel accounts, cannot be reduced or limited to a specific form, time, space or place. It is, as Graham Ward describes, a 'displaced' body, whose identity is always unstable and deferred.[37]

According to Ward, Jesus's body takes various forms: as male flesh and bone, but as a man who is unlike other men, as a man who performs miracles, who walks on water and who heals the sick; as a transfigured body who the disciples see glorified in the company of the prophets Moses and Elijah; as bread at the Eucharistic supper where his physical presence is extended to incorporate the 'body' of the bread; as a crucified and broken body who is abused and killed by the misuse of power by other men; as a resurrected body who passes through walls and disappears but who, at the same time, is tangible and able to eat; and finally, as an ascended body who is now present in those who identify themselves with Christ and in those who 'live the story in their own lives, even in their own bodies'.[38] Essentially, Ward's point is that the body of Christ is an ambiguous body which transgresses boundaries and cannot be contained.

Of course, Ward has a good point. What he shows with finesse is that an orthodox Christology can be a subversive one; one which presents the logic of incarnation as a radical voice of challenge to static and one-dimensional accounts of the Christian God. Framing this within the context of the Trinity, however, means that incarnation further reflects the ambiguity which lies at the heart of the Christian God. What, then, does this help us to say about the role of desire, and of female desire more particularly, within Christian thinking? What of the role of food and eating within Christian theology?

At the most basic level, a theology of abundance, which is grounded on an orthodox account of the Trinitarian being of God and the incarnate Christ, identifies that God is not a containable or bounded God. If fear of the excessive and uncontrollable nature of desire is what fuels attitudes of suspicion towards female desire and appetite, both within much Christian thought as well as within contemporary secular diet programs such as the one mentioned here, then a theology of abundance provides a strong voice of challenge asserting that the Trinitarian and incarnate God is a God of unbounded excess!

---

[35] Ibid., p. 6.
[36] See Bacon, *What's Right with the Trinity?*
[37] G. Ward, 'Bodies: The Displaced Body of Jesus Christ', in J. Milbank, C. Pickstock and G. Ward (eds), *Radical Orthodoxy: A New Theology* (London & New York: Routledge, 1999), pp. 163–81 and also *Cities of God* (New York: Routledge, 2000).
[38] Ward, 'Bodies', p. 225.

The obvious subordination of the material and corporeal in Augustine's thought (like much classical thought) is also challenged, since both doctrines assert that God has a body and a material presence which cannot be contained. In this sense, the assumed dichotomy Augustine (much like this secular diet) constructs between the body/desire and God/that which is 'good' or holy, is overturned. God, the most holy, has a body which cannot be bounded. The need expressed by this diet group then, like many others, to control the size and shape of the body, especially the female body, is now radically exposed as operating in contradistinction to a theology of abundance which takes the incarnational and Trinitarian identity of God seriously. According to a theology of abundance, the 'fat' body can no longer be identified as freakish, sinful or abnormal, but must instead be theologically affirmed through identification with an expansive God.

You Are What You Eat! Eating as Transformative Praxis

This kind of theology, then, challenges the anti-fat, desire-denying and body-denying discourses within the contemporary West which serve to exclude fat bodies from gaining acceptance. Such a theology, however, is practically demonstrated within Christian communities by the sharing of bread and wine in the Eucharist. It is here that we see, perhaps most profoundly, that God is an expansive God, and that food, rather than dragging us away from God as our prime object of desire, actually provides a gateway into life and into participation in the Trinitarian community.

It is, after all, by eating and consuming the body and blood of Christ which Jesus provides as *food* for us (i.e. the bread and wine) that we come to participate in the body of Christ (the Church) and so to share in the eternal life of God. The Eucharist confirms, at a basic level, the unbounded and extendable nature of the body of Christ, as well as the expansive and open nature of the Trinitarian God. By digesting the gifts of bread and wine we not only affirm our identity as sharers in Christ, but also as sharers in the Trinitarian life of God – as people in 'holy communion' with God.[39] Indeed, through the giving and receiving of these gifts, we echo the reciprocal giving and receiving of love within the Trinity[40] – a love which, we should remember, does not seek to possess or appropriate the other, but which seeks to welcome the other into a mutual and unbounded relationship of love and exchange.

Besides this, however, eating provides a means by which we might be made whole. Rather than eating our way into death (as traditionally depicted through the figure of Eve), eating now becomes the way into life and fulfilment, as echoed by the lovers in the Song of Songs. Eating becomes a *transformative* praxis, because

---

[39] A. F. Méndez Montoya, *The Theology of Food: Eating and the Eucharist* (Wiley-Blackwell: Chichester, Oxford, Malden, 2009), p. 146.
[40] Ibid.

we literally become what we eat – we *become* the body of Christ, the restored and redeemed community of God, through the act of eating. Desire for food, thus, rather than dragging one away from God, as was maintained by the likes of Augustine, propels one closer to God. Food, rather than being a 'danger' which threatens to drag one 'off track' and away from one's ultimate goal, as proposed by the dieting group mentioned here, becomes a means by which we might join with others as the body of Christ to share in the life of God. Understood this way, food is not only 'safe', but to be celebrated and enjoyed!

Of course, we must remember that there have been those who have seen the Eucharistic meal as the only food necessary for sustenance. Catherine of Siena, for example, was one of a number of women in the Middle Ages who sought to discipline the body through fasting, and for her the consecrated Eucharistic host was, in the end, the only meal she was prepared to consume. She starved to death at the age of 33.[41] What I am not suggesting, then, is that the Eucharistic meal constitutes the only food which leads to life. Instead, what I think the Eucharist communicates is that food in itself is a source of life, and life in abundance, because it *expands* our relationships with one another and *expands* our relationship with God. It leads to 'fullness'. We do not become *more* by eating *less* and by taking up a *smaller* space, as is maintained by the dieting organization mentioned here. As members of the Christian community, we are called to assert with confidence that eating transforms us for the better, and this beckons a hearty appreciation of desire, rather than a suspicion of it. 'Food and eating' are, as Lisa Isherwood rightly notes, 'performative acts displaying the Christian life'.[42]

Conclusion: Food for Thought . . .

If the doctrines of Trinity and incarnation point towards a theology of abundance, revealing the Christian God as a God who cannot be contained or bounded, but as a God who is welcoming, expansive and representative of difference and multiplicity, it is disturbing that Christian theology has developed throughout its history a suspicion of the body which serves to sanction a fear of desire and an understanding of the fat female body in particular as deviant, dangerous and wayward. Although it is undeniable that Christian theology continues to endorse a suspicion of desire and appetite, what I have hopefully shown is that there are a number of valuable resources within the Christian tradition which tell a different story. If we are to take the Song of Songs seriously – and this is a big question, given that it is not common practice to hear sermons on this, in my experience – then what begins to emerge is a story about the utter excitement and uncontainable joy of desire. If we are to take the doctrines of incarnation and Trinity seriously, then

[41] N. M. Lahutsky, 'Food and Feminism and Historical Interpretation: The Case of Medieval Holy Women', in R. N. Brock, C. Camp & S. Jones, *Setting the Table: Women in Theological Conversation* (St Louis, Missouri: Chalice Press, 1995), pp. 233–48 (234).

[42] Isherwood, *The Fat Jesus*, p. 136.

what emerges is a fundamental principle which runs through the very veins of Christianity, that God is a God of excess, vastness and unboundedness. If we are to take the Eucharist seriously, then what becomes apparent is that food enables us to consume the identity of Christ, to become what we eat – the body of Christ and the redeemed community of God – and to partake in the eternal life of the Trinity. Food and desire for food lead to life and fullness, as opposed to death and destruction, and this marks the beginnings of a truly subversive theology which stands to challenge the anti-fat, anti-desire motifs evident both within aspects of the Christian tradition and also within the secular diet industry.

I. Response to Hannah Bacon

Lisa Isherwood

I am delighted to respond to Hannah Bacon's chapter 'Does Size Really Matter: A Feminist Theological Response to Secular Dieting and Weight Loss', because just like Hannah, I think it does, and that as, in my view, Christianity has been part of the problem for women, it should attempt to be part of the solution. I am broadly in agreement with Hannah's argument, that is to say, that women's bodies have been the objects of unbearable scrutiny via the male gaze for millennia, and some of this can be traced to the creation of women as the 'other' within Christian dualist thinking. The issue of women and desire, so cruelly shaped by a suspicious theological rhetoric which sees women at the heart of the fall of man [sic!] has played its part in making both women and men cautious over the matter of women and their ability to trust themselves or to be trusted by others. We find ourselves at a time when the body is spoken about more freely; it takes up a great deal of secular and increasingly theological debating time, yet we are strangely ill at ease with it and at times even uncertain about its significance in our value and meaning. We often speak as though our bodies were something other than ourselves. Further, we live in a time when the fitness culture appears to be at its height, yet more women are dying from the harsh ways in which they sit in their skins and the society that enables them to view themselves with such suspicion, guilt and, at times, hatred.

As Hannah says, the skinny woman is the norm, yet surgical enhancement of breasts, and now even buttocks, is on the increase. The female body is under pressure to, at one and the same time, be less and be more – with the added irony, of course, that dieting decreases the secondary sexual characteristics first, precisely the attributes women are under pressure to get enhanced. The male gaze and the capitalist culture that is never far behind benefit, and diet industries and surgical industries make billions of pounds annually and women fight with their bodies. However, skinny girls have not always been welcome at the cultural party, and in religious circles they were at one time almost unknown, a sign of ill omens and scarcity. There was a time, we are told by experts, when there was an ecologically friendly, non-competitive and peaceful relational society during which the divine was imaged as a large, fleshy mound of divinity; as our Divine Mother. Crucially, they remind us that obesity is not an ahistorical concept; it is, like all others, rooted in time and place; it is historical, created by the power dynamics of gender, class and race. Hannah does not deal with this, and I feel this is an important part of the argument, because once we ask about the ideological underpinning of notions of size we begin to move the debate from one of moral weakness, abnormality and pathology on behalf of the fat woman, to one of control and power and exclusion on behalf of cultural forces and those who create them. Indeed, the female body has never in human history been viewed as desirable when as 'close to the bone' as it is today. The full-busted, full-bodied, tall, mature woman has been replaced by the anorexic ideal and the worryingly 'little girlish waif' look that goes with it. This is achieved through diets that place Western women on less calories per day then even the poorest women in India, which is approximately 1,400 calories and, most alarmingly, less than was calculated to keep humans functioning in Nazi concentration camps. The UN Health Organization calculates that 1,000 calories a day is semi-starvation, and this will be associated with irritability, lack of focus, tension and preoccupation with food, but this and less is what women are encouraged to achieve if they are to reach and maintain the perfect size and shape.[43]

Another aspect I think is missing and could well be included in Hannah's piece is the now well-established argument that the female body acts as a signifier of the state of the nation, the culture or the clan, and thus has to be controlled.[44] The interesting question for feminists today, then, is why it is the slender, almost anorexic body that signals the edges of a decent society? Susie Orbach,[45] whose research in the area of women and size has been transformative, believes a fat female body simply challenges too much in a patriarchal society. She demonstrates that fat subverts the male gaze, and as such claims a subjectivity for women that has far-reaching effects, as it challenges the ever-sacrificial nurturer role, replacing it with a body that begins to understand and value its own needs as worthy of inclusion in male discourse. Women begin to tentatively engage with their own desire, and this appears to be a far more relational and empowering embodiment than patriarchal structures allow, be they secular or theological. Further, it places women outside the competitive and power-driven world of rivalry with other women and frantic consumption of goods and products to achieve that envied perfect state. In short, then, she and others are arguing that fat female bodies carry a different set of culture messages than those perpetuated by patriarchy – they are certainly not corporate enough – and this is important when we engage with these bodies as a Christological starting point.

---

[43] L. Isherwood, *The Fat Jesus: Feminist Explorations in Boundaries and Transgressions* (London: DLT, 2007), p. 13.

[44] A. Howson, *Embodying Gender* (London: Sage, 2005), p. 22.

[45] S. Orbach, *Fat is a Feminist Issue* (London: Hamlyn Press, 1979), pp. 45–8.

Hannah points out that Christianity, with its inability to deal with women and desire, has helped create the problem that we are faced with, and I would go further and argue that this inability is deeply rooted in dualistic metaphysics that beat at the heart of much traditional Christian doctrine. It is for this reason that I would part company with Hannah in attempting to find a way ahead that is based in Trinitarian theology, which appears a little abstract and metaphysical for such an enfleshed issue. I prefer to start from feminist Christology, a place that declares that the divine became incarnate, a place that need not fall foul of the worst excesses of dualistic metaphysics.[46] Women need, as Nelle Morton proclaimed, to journey home, and in this case that is back to our bodies, to a place of once again inhabiting this flesh that holds within it the divine. We are asked to touch and revel in our passions, and I do agree with Hannah that this may be an invitation laid out on the Eucharistic table; one that has become rather sterile with its metaphysical overlay, but was once a radical space of sensuous engagement and commitment. It was here that the exchange model of a patriarchal society was challenged by sharing bread and wine and declaring that the fullness of divine/human incarnation was enfleshed through radical praxis – eating together!

Shannon Jung reminds us that eating and food have always been an expression of humans' relationship with God, and he also argues that they are an expression of our deepest values. He claims 'eating is a spiritual practice that reminds us who we are',[47] not only in our own bodies, but also in relation to the world economy. For Jung, there are very embodied consequences that stem from the impoverishment of diet cultures. Two world views actually emerge; one is holistic and revolves around relationships and sharing, while the other is business orientated and involves slicing life up into bits.[48] The latter, of course, also denies passion and desire, since both aspects of the human person become moral weaknesses to be overcome for the good of the regulated systems, whether theological or economic.

Feminist Christology stems from 'dunamis', the raw and passionate energy that calls us into relationality, that is spoken of as our birthright and as central to divine incarnation both in Jesus and in us.[49] A feminist Christ delights in human desire as the force that will redeem the world and connect us with others, and so placing women at war with themselves in a battle to control desire is akin to blasphemy, since it splits us off from what is our divine potential. As followers of Jesus, we are 'sensuous revolutionaries', living our deepest passions and connections in order that our free and full embodiment may sing of abundant incarnation as a counter to the worst excesses of our genocidal and disconnected world. A feminist Christological starting point allows for a challenge to patriarchy in its global

---

[46] L. Isherwood, *Liberating Christ* (Cleveland: Pilgrim Press,1999).
[47] S. Jung, *Food For Life, The Spirituality and Ethics of Eating* (Minneapolis: Fortress Press, 2004), p. 6.
[48] Ibid., p. 8.
[49] C. Heyward, *The Redemption of God* (Washington: University of America Press, 1982).

forms, as well as agency for women in their personal embodiment – it allows the bodies of women to be valued beyond the male gaze and for fat female bodies to be the starting point of a liberation theology. The personal becomes political and theological, and in so doing beckons us to see further than individual moral censure and distaste. The large bodies of women are speaking a profound truth about the patriarchal environment in which they live, and slimming clubs, even if it is slimming for Jesus,[50] are not the answer. We need the courage to hear what they are saying and to begin Christological reflection from this divine/human encounter.

The fat body, rather like the grotesque body before it, represents multiplicity, a bulging, open body in the process of becoming which is completely out of keeping with a bounded theology and a bounded society. What emerges, then, is an obscene Christ, one who challenges all the boundaries and opens up the whole divine process. Marcella Althaus-Reid has spoken of an obscene Christ, by which she means that obscenity uncovers what needs to be made visible. For example, the black and feminist Christs are obscene as they uncover both racism and sexism inherent in Christology. Althaus-Reid says, 'any uncovering of Christ needs to follow that pattern of obscenity at the same time because Christ and his symbolic construction continue in our history, according to our own moment of historical consciousness.'[51] Our consciousness needs to shift in order to create an obscene Christ in matters of shape and size. Why? Well, because we have seen the worlds that are created by fat phobia, fear of the maternal, and the phallic world this gives birth to and the glorying in anorexic that is killing millions of women; all these worlds are in themselves a crime against the incarnational glory of individuals, but they also play into larger systems of oppression. A corpulent Christ is obscene and asks us profound questions which we need to answer in our skin. As followers of an incarnational religion, it is within that skin, that policed body, that our revolution lies since it is here that the God we claim to believe in situated the power to transform the world.

II. Concluding Comments

Hannah Bacon

I am grateful to Lisa for her thought-provoking response. We are in agreement that Christian theology has played and continues to play an important role in the establishment and sanctioning of weight-loss ideology and that given its culpability, must be part of any solution. What this 'solution' looks like, however, is slightly

---

[50] M. R Griffith, *Born Again Bodies, Flesh and Spirit in American Christianity* (Berkeley: University of California press, 2004).

[51] M. Althaus-Reid, *Indecent Theology. Theological Perversions in Sex, Gender and Politics* (London: Routledge, 2001), p. 111.

different for Lisa and me. For Lisa, we must develop an obscene Christology through the notion of the 'corpulent Christ'; for me, such a focus on Christology can be extended further to include reflection on the Trinity and so towards an image of a corpulent God.

Lisa's charge is that an appeal to the Trinity seems too abstract and metaphysical to be useful when dealing with such an embodied issue as dieting. Christology, she argues, is a more effective starting point, because it locates theological reflection in the body and within fleshy history. Of course, Lisa is right, and I would want to second the importance of this. However, I do not think it is enough to limit theological reflection to Christology alone, partly because I am not altogether comfortable with equating the incarnation of God in Jesus with the incarnation of God in the rest of human flesh. For me, it is important to preserve something of the uniqueness of Christ and I have written on this elsewhere.[52] Also, as someone who wants to maintain the orthodox confession of God as Trinity, I think there is something additional to be gained from this. If we locate Christology within the broader and larger context of the Trinity, then the fleshiness and bodiliness of Christ exposes bodiliness as part of God per se. Bodiliness becomes integral to God's eternal self-identity to the point that it becomes nonsensical to talk about a disembodied God. All of a sudden, the Trinitarian God starts to look far fleshier. Faced with the fleshiness of God, but also with a community of relationship, typified by dynamism, fluidity, flux, the unbounded sharing of mutual love and the overflowing of boundaries between persons, we might conceive of the Trinitarian God as a 'corpulent God'.

The corpulent God exceeds all limitations, all boundaries and all measures. Rather than being an image grounded on metaphysical abstraction, it takes its root from the fleshy incarnation of God in Jesus and from the position of fleshy humankind within the Godhead. Such a God provides a model of relationship and mutual love which knows no end. As such, the Trinitarian space is a massive, fleshy space; a space of desire and hunger for the other, for communion and for connectivity. It is a vast, warm and welcoming space which is big enough for all; not in spite of one's body size, but in celebration of it. In a time when, as Lisa notes, we are strangely ill at ease with our bodies, encouraged to reduce the body through dieting in pursuit of the 'anorexic ideal', such an understanding of the Trinity can, I believe, provide an important countercultural voice of resistance, in addition to that offered by a focus on the corpulent Christ.

Lisa also rightly identifies the importance of locating ideologies of size within a cultural setting and as resulting from the power dynamics of gender, race and class. This is an important point, and one that is worth expanding upon. One of the most striking things which has become apparent throughout my research is that 'fat' is assumed to be universally 'wrong' by most, if not all, members within the dieting group. There is little recognition that regulations about body shape

---

[52] H. Bacon, 'A Very Particular Body: Assessing the Doctrine of Incarnation for Affirming the Sacramentality of Female Embodiment', in J. Jobling and G. Howie (eds), *Women and the Divine: Touching Transcendence* (New York: Palgrave Macmillan, 2009), pp. 227–52.

and size are culturally determined, simply an assumed consensus that fat must be fought. It is not surprising, then, that this weight-loss organization recently launched a 12-week fight against obesity in an attempt to encourage members of the local community to shed their excess weight. Promotional balloons were produced for this campaign, on which were written the words, 'Let's Beat it Together!', 'it' presumably meaning 'fat', confirming quite clearly that 'fat' is not something relative to time or place or indeed to cultural constructions of gender, race and class.

Obesity, though, we must remember, is a socially determined phenomenon. Not only is the apparent obesity epidemic in the UK disputed – a report by the Social Issues Research Centre (SIRC) in 2005, for example, concluded that the British government's reference to an 'obesity epidemic' was unsubstantiated[53] – the toned and trim female body is a relatively recent invention, emerging in the late nineteenth century. It was only towards the end of the Victorian era that those who could eat well deliberately chose not to,[54] with body management and the regulation of food becoming a preoccupation of the middle class and a visible sign of wealth.

It is certainly true that today, the ideal thin female body is a body not only constructed through gender inequalities, but also through economic and racial inequalities. In essence, thinness characterizes white-Western, middle-class privilege[55] – and so, as Lisa notes, becomes a marker of a 'civilised' nation – presenting a particular 'type' of femininity (i.e. white-Western, affluent) as a universal norm.[56] What this all means, though, in reality, is that the diversity of female embodiment is ignored with women across the globe (independent of racial or economic location) feeling the need to squeeze their bodies into a homogenized space.

The image of the corpulent God becomes helpful here, then, because that which is most holy, most perfect, is that which is vast and space-taking, encouraging women to occupy their *own* space – both physically and politically – within the world. And yet because God as Trinity does not occupy the space of the other, the homogenizing agenda of the white-Western, thin female ideal is challenged. Aligned with a corpulent God, 'fat' no longer becomes indicative of a person's moral failing, neither is it seen as an objective wrong befitting of theological judgment. Instead, we are led to ask questions about why the variety of women's shape has been degraded and why 'fat' has come to be viewed as both threat and unattractive,[57] the answers to which must be rooted in power dynamics (as we have already seen) and challenged by theology.

[53] Social Issues Research Centre, *Obesity and the Facts: An analysis of data from the Health Survey for England 2003* (February 2005), p. 3

[54] S. Bordo, *Unbearable Weight: Feminism, Western Culture, and the Body* (Berkeley, Los Angeles, London: University of California Press, 1993), p. 185.

[55] M. Lelwica, 'Spreading the Religion of Thinness from California to Calcutta', *Journal of Feminist Studies in Religion* 25:1 (2009), p. 26.

[56] M. Nasser and H. Malson, 'Beyond Western Dis/orders: thinness and self-starvation of other-ed women', in H. Malson and M. Burns (eds), *Critical Feminist Approaches to Eating Disorders* (London & New York: Routledge, 2009), pp. 74–86 (75).

[57] See S. Orbach, *Fat is a Feminist Issue* (London: Arrow Books, 2006), p. 203.

Admitting with Lisa that the fat female body carries a different set of cultural messages – refusing to pander to the expectations of a patriarchal, colonialist and capitalist system – it seems to me that the image of the corpulent God is important precisely because it celebrates, rather than demonizes, the fat body, encouraging larger women to take pride in their bodies. As followers of Jesus and as lovers of the triune God, we can be the 'sensuous revolutionaries' Lisa talks about, revolutionaries not only committed to the celebration of appetite and desire, but also revolutionaries who seek to subvert fat phobia on the grounds that God, as Trinity, is a corpulent, flesh-loving and abundant God!

7 Transforming Tyrannies: Disability and Christian Theologies of Salvation

Wayne Morris

Introduction

Commenting on the work of Grace Jantzen, Elaine Graham describes Jantzen's writings as being structured according to a process of 'diagnosis' and 'transformation'.[1] Drawing on her own earlier work in feminist theology, Graham argues that such an approach to theology 'exposes what is assumed to be taken for granted and objective knowledge as androcentric, before moving on to develop a more representative or authentic tradition, often founded on the inclusion of formerly excluded voices and experiences'.[2] This chapter follows that same model of 'diagnosis' and 'transformation', whereby it aims to identify the ways in which many Christian theological approaches to understanding salvation are based on able-bodied experience and serve to exclude and dehumanize many people with disabilities. I then aim to reconstruct a theology of salvation that takes seriously the experiences of people with disabilities. In arguing that all disabled people are central to God's salvation plans, this theology of salvation in turn challenges constructions of 'normality' and 'able-bodiedness'. It is hoped that such a change in thinking about salvation might also contribute towards a change in attitudes and practices towards disabled people in churches and in society more widely, so that disabled people's humanity might be affirmed and their lives valued more fully by everyone.

The Problem with Labels: Not All Disabled People are the Same!

'Disability' is a term that is used to refer to a wide range of people with varying experiences. How one chooses to define 'disability' will determine who is classified

---

[1] E. Graham, 'Redeeming the Present', in E. L. Graham, *Grace Jantzen: Redeeming the Present* (Farnham: Ashgate, 2009), pp. 1–19 (3).
[2] *Ibid.*, p. 3.

as 'disabled'. For the last 20 to 30 years, disability studies, and indeed disability theology, has been informed by ways of thinking about disability which set up a dichotomy between the 'social model' and 'medical model' of disability.[3] The social model argues that disabled people can be better included in society, by society more widely becoming more accessible. The medical model treats disability as an illness that needs to be cured. The social model intends to replace the medical model as a way of thinking about disability that emerges out of disabled people's reflections on their own lives. The notion of setting medical and social models of disability in opposition to each other, while instrumental in influencing a transformation in recent thinking about disability in society, is increasingly proving to be a false dichotomy. The creation of an inclusive society is not achieved by trying to 'cure' people with disabilities, but sometimes medical intervention is important in the lives of some people with disabilities. Much in society can be changed to make society more inclusive, but not every issue of inclusion is solved in this way. Alternatively, Amos Yong makes a distinction between 'disability' and 'illness', a new dichotomy to distinguish people who may need contrasting responses in order to be included and so participate fully in society. He distinguishes the two, suggesting that 'disability delimits specific areas of functioning while illnesses result in whole-body debilitation'.[4] However, to make such a distinction between illness and disability fails to take into account the reality of many people's lives. My own mother, for example, had a brain tumour, which made her blind, and later she became a wheelchair user. Was she ill, disabled or both, and if we can decide, does that make the task of inclusion easier? While it is important to have a language with which to speak about the experience of people who are labelled as disabled, as well as people who are ill, the distinctions between illness and disability are no more easily definable than the distinctions between disabled and non-disabled. Such umbrella terms do not do justice to the diversity of human experiences, the social and cultural contexts that can help to determine how disability, illness and able-bodiedness is understood, and such definitions fail to recognize the many lives in which the boundaries between such categories overlap and blur. So how should disability be understood?

Mary Grey argues that 'one does not have to be a cultural analyst to notice how Western society conceals and shuns death; by association, people with disability share in this marginalization because their very presence is a reminder of death'.[5] This provides another way of thinking about disability, as an experience that society labels in a particular way because that experience reminds others of death. Grey's suggestion that the marginalization of people with disabilities in society is

---

[3] J. Swain, S. French and C. Cameron, *Controversial Issues in a Disabling Society* (Buckingham: Open University Press, 2003), p. 22–5.
[4] A. Yong, *Theology and Down Syndrome: Reimagining Disability in Late Modernity* (Waco: Baylor University Press, 2007), p. 245.
[5] M. Grey, '*Natality and Flourishing* in Contexts of Disability and Impairment', in E. L. Graham, *Grace Jantzen: Redeeming the Present* (Farnham: Ashgate, 2009), pp. 197–211 (202).

because they remind others at least of their own vulnerability is not unique. From the perspective of some in the disability movement, the notion that non-disabled people are only 'temporarily non-disabled' reflects the idea that no human person is immune from the possibility of disability – anyone could be disabled. So, if disability is a reminder of death and vulnerability, and disability is a state into which anyone might enter at any moment of their lives, then to avoid the reminder of the potential for disability and human mortality, disabled people, it is argued, are marginalized. Grey, however, like many others who have written on disability over the past 20 years or so, is guilty of homogenizing the experience of disability.

It may well be true that the presence of a person living with a degenerative and disabling disease does, indeed, remind others of their own mortality and vulnerability. It is also true that no person is immune to the possibility of becoming disabled. Nevertheless, this is not true in every case. While many non-disabled people would fear the possibility of blindness, for example, and so a blind person may remind others of the vulnerability of their own vision, it is difficult to understand how a blind person could remind others of death. Many blind people live very full and fulfilled lives. It is also true that unless a person is born with a condition such as Down's syndrome, they will never develop that condition at a later stage in their lives. Not all disabled people are the same; it is a term used to speak about a range of different people with different experiences. So far I have argued, therefore, that the medical or social models of disability, a distinction between illness and disability, and an understanding of disability as a condition that reminds others of death do not adequately express how disability should be understood. Below, I will argue that disability, while a positive and subversive term for many who live with disabilities, is used more widely in society to label people who do not conform to societal norms and whose contribution to society is considered as a result to be less valuable than that of others. It is in understanding what society considers to be 'normal' and valuable that we begin to understand how an able-bodied notion of disability is constructed.

Disability and the 'Tyranny of the Normal'

The idea or concept of 'disability' is, I argue, essentially a social construction devised as a way of categorizing certain people who have conditions that society deems to be of less value than the so-called able-bodied or non-disabled. The *Disability Discrimination Act (1995)* defines someone as being disabled if they have 'a physical or mental impairment which has a substantial and long-term effect on his [*sic*] ability to carry out normal day-to-day activities'.[6] The language of this legislation reflects what has historically been an acceptable way to talk about disability. A society constructs concepts and images about human persons that it

[6] United Kingdom, *Disability Discrimination Act 1995* (United Kingdom: Office of Public Sector Information, 1995), paragraph 1(1).

determines to be normative, often based on what that society considers to be the most valuable and productive. Disabled people are invariably perceived in some way to deviate from normality, whether in their bodies, minds or senses and, as a result, they are usually marginalized and excluded, even dehumanized. Reynolds refers to such constructions of 'normality' and 'abnormality' and the subsequent marginalization that occurs as 'the tyranny of the normal'.[7]

The social construction of 'Disability' provides a wider social framework for labelling and categorizing some of those people considered by society to be 'less than normal', and in this sense 'disability' is a negative term. However, it should also be noted that the term 'disability' has more recently been used by people with disabilities to refer to something much broader than a label or category that results from living with a particular condition or impairment. It refers to an identity, culture and shared experience in which individuals have found solidarity with others in a shared experience of oppression and subsequent struggle for trans-formation. While for people with disabilities, the term 'disability' speaks of shared experience, identity and culture, and for this reason is a term that I continue to use here. However, that is not the origin of the term disability, nor is it the way most non-disabled people in society think about disability. 'Disability' is used to refer to people who are Deaf, deafened, blind, visually impaired (though not generally to people whose vision is corrected by wearing glasses), wheelchair users and people with learning and intellectual disabilities, including mild forms of dyslexia and Down's syndrome, among many other conditions. In the definition used in the *Disability Discrimination Act*, people who have disabling conditions as a result of cancer, HIV/AIDS and various other conditions are also protected by disability legislation.[8] These conditions are invariably thought to make people 'not normal' and therefore less productive and valuable in society, and for these reasons disa-bled people experience social marginalization and exclusion.

Such a broad, umbrella term for a diverse range of experiences only leads to the homogenization of experience, which in turn can suggest that the way to be inclusive of people with disabilities is also universal and singular (see the medical and social models above). People with disabilities, however, are not all the same. A person who is Deaf has a very different life experience to someone with HIV or someone with Down's syndrome. But when we look at different cultures and contexts, what is considered to be a 'disability' itself also varies. Avalos et al.'s collection of essays on biblical texts[9] demonstrates this; in particular, one chapter which shows how some women and some people we might today say are 'disa-bled' are all categorized together as being in some way less 'normal' because their

[7] T. Reynolds, *Vulnerable Communion: A Theology of Disability and Hospitality* (Grand Rapids, MI: Brazos Press, 2008), p. 69.
[8] Equality and Human Rights Commission, *Disability Discrimination Act: Guidance on matters to be taken into account in determining questions relating to the definition of disability* (London: The Stationary Office, 2005), p. 6.
[9] H. Avalos, S. J. Melcher and J. Schipper, J. (eds), *This Abled Body: Rethinking Disabilities in Biblical Studies* (Atlanta: Society of Biblical Literature, 2007).

contribution to society was considered to be of less value than that of *able-bodied* men, in particular in times of war.[10] To say that disability is a social construction is not to say that conditions like spinabifida, Down's syndrome, blindness, Deafness and so on do not exist except as constructions of society. It is rather to say that the homogenization of people with such conditions into one category is the result of a social construction of normality and abnormality. It is such constructions of normality that underpin many Christian theologies of salvation which have subsequently been used to marginalize and oppress many disabled people in churches and in society more widely.

Disability and the 'Tyranny of Salvation'

Because disability is a relatively new term referring to a group of people who may not have been categorized together at different periods of history, it is important that care is taken when looking at what theological traditions have to say about disability, for it was not a 'label' familiar to people of past generations. There are many ways in which traditions and theologies within Christianity have served to marginalize, exclude and dehumanize many different people in society and the church, including those who fall under contemporary Western constructions of disability. One such way is through some theologies of salvation which perpetuate ideas that God only saves those who are 'normal' and so rejects those who cannot hear the Gospel, understand the Gospel, articulate or express a faith in Christ, or whose bodies, it is supposed, are 'disabled' because of sin; to be saved, the sin, and therefore the disability, must be removed. To illustrate the point that many theologies of salvation are shaped by the 'tyranny of the normal', a discussion follows which exposes as exclusive of people with disabilities both the view that faith is necessary for salvation and that in order to participate in the present and future kingdom of God a person must be able-bodied.

Salvation and Faith

Geivett and Phillips express a way of understanding salvation that is prevalent in many parts of the Christian tradition. They say, 'except perhaps in very special circumstances, people are not saved apart from explicit faith in Jesus Christ, which presupposes that they have heard about his salvific work on their behalf'.[11]

[10] C. R. Fontaine, '"Be Men, O Philistines" (1 Samuel 4.9): Iconographic Representations and Reflections on Female Gender as Disability in the Ancient World', in H. Avalos, S. J. Melcher and J. Schipper (eds), *This Abled Body: Rethinking Disabilities in Biblical Studies* (Atlanta: Society of Biblical Literature, 2007), pp. 61–72.

[11] R. D. Geivett and W. G. Phillips, 'A Particularist View: An Evidentialist Approach', in S. N. Gundry, D. L. Okholm and T. R. Phillips (eds.), *Four Views on Salvation in a Pluralistic World* (Grand Rapids, MI: Zondervan, 1995), pp. 213–45 (214).

To talk about an 'explicit' faith is invariably to suggest that faith must be received and understood, even if only in part, intellectually, and heard and expressed through language. Such an understanding of salvation could only lead us to conclude that people with certain learning and intellectual disabilities could not be saved because they would not have the capacity to know, intellectually, anything of Christ's salvific work or have a faith that could be explicitly expressed to others through language. That is, unless of course, it is to this group of people that Geivett and Phillips are referring to as having 'special circumstances'. The 'tyranny of the normal', it can be argued, is present in such understandings of salvation and of faith, because faith and subsequently salvation can only be attained through being 'normal'. Let us explore the relationship between faith and salvation further.

Yong suggests that if faith is necessary for salvation, it would be right to ask, 'what is faith?' One response he offers is to distinguish between *pistis* (faith) and *gnosis* (knowledge); all people relate to God through *pistis*, even if they do not 'articulate that in terms of gnosis'.[12] Yong, however, perceives a problem with such a distinction, because 'faith seems stripped of almost all human content and that there is an implicit universalism that undercuts libertarian human freedom'.[13] On first glance, such a distinction between faith and knowledge, where faith ceases to be something that is experienced intellectually, does appear to overcome the problem that people with learning disabilities cannot be saved. In the minds of many who argue that faith is necessary for salvation, however, knowledge of God at the level of the intellect is essential. There is no reason why an intellectual understanding of God should not form a part of faith for those with the capacity to have such an understanding, and so Yong is right to be concerned if faith is universally stripped of content. However, when Yong objects to a distinction between faith and knowledge, his objection implies that the intellect is in some way necessary for salvation, for presumably, unless a person's freedom is removed, a person must choose whether they wish to be saved or not. As a result, in seeking to separate faith from the intellect, Yong does the exact opposite, for to have freedom, he implies a person has the capacity to choose in the first place. It may well be the experience of many that faith is something understood and responded to intellectually, but should this be the normative way of speaking about faith and salvation? Or is making such a way of talking about faith and making it necessary for salvation a way of the 'normal' in society excluding those it considers to be 'less than normal'? If the 'normal' can defend the idea that God excludes people with learning disabilities from his kingdom, why should humans behave any differently in society and the churches?

While Geivett and Phillips suggest that explicit faith in Christ is necessary for salvation, excluding people with profound learning and intellectual disabilities, they also allude to the importance of hearing for faith. The necessity of hearing for faith, and therefore salvation, is articulated in the work of some of the most

---

[12] A. Yong, *Theology and Down Syndrome*, p. 235.
[13] *Ibid.*

influential of theologians in Western Christian history. St Paul explains that 'faith comes from what is heard' (Romans 10.17), which St Augustine at one point takes literally. Responding to the Pelagian, Julian of Eclanum, Augustine wrote, 'since you deny that an infant is subject to original sin, you must answer why such great innocence is sometimes born blind; sometimes, deaf. Deafness is a hindrance to faith itself, as the Apostle says: "Faith is from hearing"'.[14] While some will no doubt wish to argue that if we look at other parts of St Augustine's work, we might find a different attitude, a survey of literature by people who engage with historic attitudes towards Deaf people shows that it is this approach and attitude to Deaf people that stands out in Augustine.[15] The impact of such attitudes towards Deaf and blind people is further found in the much later work of St Thomas Aquinas, who expresses similar sentiments to Augustine: 'Now man [sic] attains to belief both by seeing miracles and by hearing the teachings of faith . . . it is said that faith is through hearing. Therefore man [sic] attains to faith by acquiring it'.[16] While neither Augustine nor Aquinas speaks directly of salvation in the references above, they do suggest that certain people with disabilities cannot have a faith, because they cannot hear or see. If faith is necessary for salvation, then we must conclude that Deaf and blind people, along with people with intellectual and learning disabilities, will almost certainly not be saved.

Salvation as Healing

In Luke's Gospel, Jesus declares that 'The Spirit of the Lord is upon me, because he has anointed me to bring good news to the poor. He has sent me to proclaim release to the captives and recovery of sight to the blind.' He goes on to say 'Today this scripture has been fulfilled in your hearing' (Luke 4.18–21). Such texts are often used as 'proofs' that one of the signs of the future kingdom of God is the healing, indeed curing, of people with disabilities. Many of the healing narratives are then interpreted as signs of who Jesus was and the future kingdom he represented. As a result, such Gospel texts have been used to suggest that disabled people will not experience salvation, or if they do, then it cannot be in their disabled condition. Such a view is further supported by the way the Greek word *swzw* can be translated as either 'to save' or 'to heal'. Healing, invariably interpreted as cure, is understood as a prerequisite for entry into the kingdom of God. Implied in all of this, therefore, is that disabled people cannot experience salvation

---

[14] Augustine of Hippo, *The Fathers of the Church*, trans. M. A. Schumacher (New York: CUA, 1957), p. 115.

[15] See, for example, A. F. Dimmock, *Cruel Legacy. An Introduction to the Record of Deaf People in History* (Edinburgh: Scottish Workshop Publications, 1993), p. 2, and H. Lewis, *Deaf Liberation Theology* (Aldershot: Ashgate, 2007), p. 78.

[16] Thomas Aquinas, 'Question VI: On the Cause of Faith', A. C. Pegis, (ed.), *The Basic Writings of Saint Thomas Aquinas* (vol. 2; Indianapolis: Hackett Publishing, 1997), pp. 1115–18 (1115).

as disabled people, but only as non-disabled people. Yong notes that 'the complaints about Pentecostal-charismatic healing practices are legion in the disability literature',[17] traditions that interpret healing to mean, for disabled people, the removal of their disability and subsequent normalization. Such an understanding of the kingdom of God, in which disabled people are normalized, is not, however, unique to Pentecostal-charismatic traditions, but is present across most Christian traditions, to varying degrees.

Like the association of faith with salvation, the association of cure with salvation reflects a salvation shaped by the tyranny of the normal. Disabled people must be seen as part of God's salvation plan, in their disabled condition, and such a view must challenge the 'tyranny of the normal', whereby it is assumed that salvation is achieved by a certain process so that those who cannot participate in that process are excluded. Such theologies of salvation, informed by the tyranny of the normal, then perpetuate the tyranny of exclusion. They determine normative mechanisms by which salvation is achieved which reflect the experience and vision of the ideal body of the most powerful. It is essential that the tyranny of the normal that informs the tyranny of salvation is named and deconstructed as above. For such exclusion, whether of some or all disabled people, does not seem consistent with the idea of a God who comes alongside the marginalized and stands in solidarity with the excluded, who 'brought down the powerful from their thrones and lifted up the lowly' (Luke 1.52). And, if disability is indeed a social construct, it does not seem at all reasonable that God excludes from God's salvation plan those whom a particular culture at a particular time deems to be 'disabled'.

Alternative Salvations: Transforming Tyranny?

Thus far, it has been argued that many theologies of salvation have been developed in light of the 'tyranny of the normal'. In particular, examples of the association of faith and healing with salvation have been used to illustrate how ideas of normality are used to speak theologically about who will or will not be saved. At this point, having attempted to 'diagnose' the problem of the tyranny of salvation, I now turn towards 'transformation', by attempting to construct a more inclusive theology of salvation, drawing on motifs within the liberation theology of salvation of Jon Sobrino. First, however, I will begin with a response to those who propose that faith and healing are necessary for salvation.

Faith and Being Able-bodied are *not* Prerequisites for Salvation

Valuing attributes such as hearing, seeing and the intellect, and thereby marginalizing those who do not have such capacities, is a reflection of the 'tyranny of the

---

[17] A. Yong, *Theology and Down Syndrome*, p. 242.

normal'. When such capacities become prerequisites for salvation, then salvation is dependent on social constructs of normality and abnormality. Whatever faith may constitute, whether it involves *gnosis* (knowledge) or not, the necessity of faith for salvation must be rejected. The consequence of such a proposal would be that salvation is universal, inclusive of everyone. While this may mean that being saved is no longer a matter of human choice or freedom, it must be remembered that not all humans, such as infants, many people with learning disabilities and the unevangelized, can choose anyway. Such a theology of salvation is not negative, as Yong suggests, because it takes away human freedom. Rather it is a positive theology, because it does not discriminate, and it is a theology that is inclusive and open to all humanity, irrespective of human capacities to choose. If everyone is saved, irrespective of intellect or choice, it may be argued that such a proposition makes faith redundant. That is not, however, a necessary consequence of removing a link between faith and salvation. There is no time to explain in detail why that should be the case here. However, suffice to say, faith could be said to represent a state of being that emerges in response to an encounter with God. A person may grow in relationship with God as a result of faith, and a life may be transformed. Faith is not devalued in any way by being separated from salvation. Indeed, faith becomes something that is not entered into out of fear of what might happen otherwise, but rather entered into positively in anticipation of what it might bring for the good.

While the notion that faith is necessary for salvation must be resisted, it is also important to resist any suggestion that to be healed, or more specifically to be 'cured', is necessary for salvation. Reflecting on the notion of 'cure' in relation to people with Down's syndrome, Frances Young notes, 'every cell in the body is affected by this (Down's syndrome). The whole person is as she is because the basic make-up of this person is as it is. What sense does it make to speak of healing? It would be a different person who would appear'.[18] Similarly, it makes no sense to speak of healing for people who understand their disability positively, as being so central to their identity that it shapes a person's life to such a degree that the impact of disability on identity can be compared to race, gender or sexuality. This is not so for all disabled people, as disabilities can be so very different. For those who live with considerable pain on a daily basis, a 'cure' would no doubt be a desirable aspect of salvation. But for those who do think about their disability as something positive, the healing narratives in the Gospels become particularly problematic. They are problematic in the first instance because, as John Hull notes, every time Jesus encounters a disabled person, he rids them of their disability.[19] If disability is perceived to be positive, good and a part of a person's identity, then this would not be the desired outcome of an encounter with Jesus. Further, in

[18] F. Young, *Face to Face: A Narrative Essay in the Theology of Suffering* (Edinburgh: T&T Clark, 1990), p. 63.
[19] J. M. Hull, 'From a Blind Disciple to a Sighted Saviour', in T. Woodcock, and I. Merchant (eds.), *Fleshing out Faith: A Reflection on Bodies and Spirituality* (Birmingham: Student Christian Movement, 2000), pp. 6–7.

some instances, Jesus says to some of those he cures, 'your faith has made you well' (or saved you) (e.g. Mark 5.34, Luke 17.19) and 'your sins are forgiven' (e.g. Luke 2.5). Such texts imply and have been interpreted to mean that disability is a punishment for sin, faith is necessary for salvation and that disabled people cannot be saved unless they are 'normalized' so as to be 'able-bodied'.[20] Such interpretations must be rejected and resisted by arguing that such normalization is not necessary for salvation. That is not to say that to be 'cured' cannot be a part of salvation for some, but it is rather to say simply that 'cure' is not *necessary* for salvation.

Towards a Transformative Theology of Salvation

Drawing on the work of liberation theologian Jon Sobrino, I would like to argue that it is important not only to ask who is saved or how we are saved, but also, what does it mean to be saved; what difference does salvation make to human existence? Sobrino responds to such questions by defining salvation as follows:

> salvation is *life* (satisfaction of basic needs), over against poverty, infirmity and death; salvation is *dignity*, (respect for persons and their rights), over against disregard and disdain; salvation is *freedom*, over against oppression; salvation is *fraternity*, among human beings who are brought together as *family* . . . salvation is *pure air*, which the spirit can breathe in order to move toward that which humanizes (honesty, compassion, solidarity, some form of openness to transcendence), over against that which dehumanizes (selfishness, cruelty, individualism, arrogance, crude positivism).[21]

These five liberationist characteristics of salvation that Sobrino identifies above will now be briefly reflected upon in turn, in light of the experience of people with disabilities. In so doing, I aim, finally, to articulate what a liberationist theology of salvation might look like and how that might provide an alternative theology of salvation that speaks more positively to the lives of people with disabilities subjected to the 'tyranny of the normal', both within and without church contexts.

Salvation as Life

When Sobrino speaks of 'salvation as life', to 'have life' means more than simply to be alive; it is rather to have life in all its abundance (John 10.10). With disabled people, however, questions abound about whether disabled people should be alive at all. Pre-implantation genetic diagnosis and tests during pregnancy for so-called 'genetic defects' are just two examples of ways society tries to avoid the birth of people

---

[20] These ideas are discussed further in R. McCloughry and W. Morris, *Making a World of Difference: Christian Reflections on Disability* (London: SPCK, 2002), pp. 94–110.
[21] J. Sobrino, *No Salvation Outside the Poor: Prophetic-Utopian Essays* (New York: Orbis Books, 2008), p. 57.

with disabilities. In contrast, public outrage rises when Deaf parents argue that they should be allowed to have Deaf children, to have a foetus that is likely to be Deaf implanted, and are accused of not considering the best interests of the child. Presumably, a child's best interests are rooted in fulfilling the social construct of normality. In addition, the widely publicized case of Daniel James, a 22-year-old man who became paralysed from the neck down as a result of a rugby accident,[22] provides an example of a person concluding that their disabled life was not worth living. He died in 2008 in Switzerland, choosing suicide as the only option left to him. While the seriousness of James's condition cannot be underestimated, society must surely take some of the responsibility, through the way disability is socially constructed, for a young man feeling he does not have a life worth living in his disabled condition. The examples just given are not being used to say that the choices people have to make about their own lives and caring for the potential life of a disabled baby are ethically wrong. What is being argued is that 'salvation as life' challenges society to reflect on how disability is understood, and how that shapes subsequent actions and practices in society more widely, not least social perceptions that some disabled lives are not worth living.

Salvation as Dignity

'Salvation as dignity' develops the idea of 'salvation as life', as having a dignified life is to have a life that flourishes. Mary Grey, reflecting on Grace Jantzen's concept of flourishing, defines flourishing using a horticultural metaphor of flowering or blossoming, reflecting the etymological roots of the term 'flourishing'. To have life in all its abundance means to have a life that is able to flourish, to grow to its full potential, to blossom so as to fully display the beauty and uniqueness of the creation. Grey notes, however, that 'for many poor communities . . . where no flourishing is experienced on earth, hope in heaven is all that sustains'.[23] The importance of a future hope for many who are oppressed or who suffer must remain as a part of Christian understandings of salvation. For those who suffer, it is a hope of release from pain that is all that sustains. For those who are oppressed, it is a hope of release from exclusion and marginalization, but if they are hopes only for the future, there is no reason to act to transform the present. What must be avoided is the tendency to use such a future hope to cause people with disabilities to accept their current situation, to suffer in pain or oppression. 'Salvation as dignity' speaks of a God who stands in solidarity with disabled people in their struggle to have a life that flourishes, and in particular to resist those persons and powers who try to suppress such flourishing through oppressive attitudes, practices and theologies.

[22] British Broadcasting Corporation, 'Mother defends rugby suicide son', (URL: http://news.bbc.co.uk/1/hi/england/hereford/worcs/7677706.stm, 18 October 2008, accessed 11 January 2010).
[23] M. Grey, '*Natality and Flourishing* in Contexts of Disability and Impairment', p. 199.

Salvation as Freedom

Salvation as freedom is an important liberation motif. In the case of people with disabilities, however, it is important to ask, 'freedom *from* what?' and 'freedom *for* what?' The answer to the question 'freedom *from* what?' can be answered by 'freedom from the tyranny of the normal' and its expression in the societal and ecclesial marginalization and exclusion of people with disabilities. The answer to the second question, 'freedom *for* what?' requires further exploration. Hans Reinders is critical of Nancy Eiesland's liberatory theology of disability[24] which, he argues, emerges out of a 'disability-rights' approach to thinking about the place of disabled people in society. The disability-rights approach, he argues, that Eiesland uses, is too dependent on an 'anthropology of liberal citizenship' that is based on 'the notion of purposive agency aiming at self-representation'.[25] While Reinders overemphasizes Eiesland's singular dependence on disability-rights thinking, he is right to warn of the dangers of a theology of liberation that equates human freedom with personal autonomy over one's own life and the right to represent one's self fully in society. While this must no doubt be one characteristic of freedom for many people with disabilities, such a singular understanding of freedom is not open to people who do not have the intellectual capacities to make decisions about their own lives.

Freedom, therefore, must mean something more than independence, autonomy and the possibility of self-representation. Perhaps Sobrino deliberately made freedom the central characteristic of salvation in his list of five, as it brings together the other four. Freedom means, first, the right to a life, and secondly, the right to a life that flourishes. As we have seen, a flourishing life may not be one in which a person achieves agency and self-representation, but it may be for some disabled people. To specify what it means to flourish in practice is an impossible task. Freedom as flourishing means to be free to be yourself. But the discovery of what that means, be that an intellectual, sensory, spiritual or some other kind of discovery, however, must be worked out contextually, in particular, in contexts of community, the fourth characteristic of salvation to which we now turn.

Salvation as Fraternity

'Salvation as fraternity' may more usefully be described as salvation as community. The importance of community as the context in which disabled people's lives might flourish best is not new.[26] Much of what has been suggested and which is affirmed here is that many people with disabilities do not flourish only by their rights being

---

[24] N. Eiesland, *The Disabled God: Toward a Liberatory Theology of Disability* (Nashville: Abingdon, 1994).

[25] H. Reinders, *Receiving the Gift of Friendship: Profound Disability, Theological Anthropology and Ethics* (Grand Rapids/Cambridge: Eerdmans, 2008), p. 165.

[26] A. Yong, *Theology and Down Syndrome*, pp. 250–3.

protected in law, but rather, like all people, disabled people flourish most as the result of positive and life-affirming relationships with others. Twelve years ago, I was involved in the care of people who were Deaf and blind with severe intellectual disabilities. I wore a band around my wrist with beads on it that was unique to me. Those with whom I worked began to recognize me through this wristband. In recognizing my presence with them, a relationship of trust developed as a result and so we began to be comfortable and relaxed in each other's company. Relationships occur in many ways – intellectual, emotional, spiritual – but perhaps the most important characteristic of a positive relationship is the development of trust between persons. As persons grow in trust of one another, so they become more fully themselves, able to flourish as those among whom they live provide a context for that to be realized. Rather than living in communities and contexts that oppress and marginalize, where mistrust is rife, disabled people need to be able to form relationships of trust with others, so that they can be themselves and live a life that flourishes.

Salvation as Pure Air

Sobrino's 'salvation as pure air', finally, speaks of something that the spirit can breathe in order to work towards those things that humanize. That 'pure air' is the Spirit of God, who collaborates with the struggle of disabled people for lives transformed for the better. Yong describes salvation as 'the transformative work of the Spirit of God that converts human hearts from lives of sin, estrangement, and inauthenticity to lives of peace, wholeness and reconciliation between human beings and God'.[27] 'Salvation as pure air' is not simply about the transformation of human lives for the better, drawing on anthropological insights alone. Rather, salvation is initiated by God and is something in which God actively participates alongside and in solidarity with human persons. When Yong talks about 'sin, estrangement and inauthenticity', he speaks mainly about a conversion of the individual, a reorientation towards God. Sobrino's 'salvation as pure air', however, suggests that such transformation must take place not only with individuals, but in communities as well. It involves the conversion from societal and institutional sin, the social marginalization that leads to estrangement and the constructions of normality that set human persons up in opposition to one another. The Spirit of God as 'pure air' participates with disabled people in such struggles for conversion.

Conclusion: Think Differently to Act Differently

The approach to salvation proposed here intends to place disabled people not at the margins of God's salvation plan, but right at the heart of it. It challenges the 'tyranny of the normal' and the tyranny of theologies that perpetuate exclusion by challenging all members of Christian communities to seek to 'construct the

---

[27] *Ibid.*, p. 229.

kingdom'[28] that is inclusive of everyone here on earth. A saved existence is one in which human persons have 'life, and have it abundantly' (John 10.10), where they are treated with dignity, where they experience freedom and inclusion, where they can engage with the Spirit in whatever way is appropriate to them and, in so doing, have their humanity affirmed. A criticism that may be launched at such a proposal is, that by focusing on salvation as an earthly goal, the future 'heavenly possibilities' that salvation might offer are ignored. Zizioulas speaks of salvation as a reality that is rooted in the future with branches that reach out into the present,[29] and so future and present are always in communion with each other. Those branches reach into the present to call the whole of creation forward to a better future. Further, however, when salvation is understood as an earthly, as well as a heavenly, possibility, the kingdom begins to be constructed on earth; so by looking at the present, perhaps we will begin to glimpse something of the future that awaits all humanity.

I. Response to Wayne Morris

Elaine Graham

The tragic case of Fiona Pilkington, who killed herself and her daughter following years of torment at the hands of her neighbours, has brought to light the prevalence of bullying and harassment of people with learning disabilities. Writing in *The Times*, Neil Dando, who himself has a learning disability, and sponsored by MENCAP, argued that, 'It is time that the police started to treat crime against someone with a learning disability as seriously as racist hate crime'.[30] Other commentators argued for programmes of public awareness, in order to counter misunderstanding and prejudice. This raises the question of whether society is prepared to move beyond mere tolerance of those with intellectual and physical disabilities, and to proactively uphold their basic human right to be treated with dignity. But is religious belief and practice contributing positively or negatively to that process? In this response to Wayne Morris's chapter, I will develop two of his themes: his search for alternative models of salvation, and his plea to end the 'tyranny of exclusion' against people with disabilities.

Wayne's chapter notes that those with disabilities, intellectual and physical, have long laboured under assumptions about what is normative – or indeed, 'normal' – in human experience, and that this has often diminished their ability to be regarded as fully human (p. 124). He argues that certain theological understandings amount to a 'tyranny' by privileging certain models of humanity in relation to God that are exclusive both in their assumptions of what it means to be made in

[28] J. Sobrino, *No Salvation Outside the Poor*, p. 91.
[29] J. D. Zizioulas, *Being as Communion* 2nd edn (London: DLT, 2004), p. 59.
[30] N. Dando, 'The Victim', *Times* (30 September 2009), p. 26.

the image and likeness of God and of what it means to be 'saved'. 'Faith and being able-bodied are not prerequisites for salvation', he argues (p. 135), and in particular, the connection between salvation and propositional faith must be broken, because it excludes those unable to muster intellectual assent.

This suggests that both our models of humanity and our narratives of salvation may need reframing. A number of writers have attempted the former from the perspective of disability. David Palin and Frances Young have both struggled with questions of how far someone with a severe cognitive disability can exercise agency or be considered an autonomous person.[31] They conclude that such lives need not be considered diminished, but ones in which relationships with others assume a heightened importance. More recently, Hans Reinders has developed this theme, arguing that the value of those with disabilities rests in their capacity to call forth compassion in others, in what Reinders terms the 'gift of friendship'.[32] This strongly echoes an influential thread in feminist ethics (such as Nell Noddings, for example), which insists that dependence on the care of others should not be regarded as weakness, but as a 'normal' part of human experience. Implicitly, of course, this delivers a judgement on the values of a society that elevates invulnerability, success and individualism; but what of the implications for theology? To see the 'image of God' in those with profound disabilities would, as Nancy Eiesland reminds us, really require us to contemplate the scandal of a God who is not powerful, but stigmatized and on the margins.

And what of 'salvation'? Here, I think of the work of the feminist philosopher of religion Grace Jantzen, who adapted much of Hannah Arendt's work to argue that an emphasis on salvation as the end of religion fuelled an 'other-worldly' spirituality that longed to be 'rescued' from finitude and mortality and cultivated a contempt for the affairs of the material, created world. Instead, she argued for an ethic of 'flourishing', which promoted the values of life, creativity, diversity and justice, rather than death or fear of death, and identified new horizons of becoming that allied humanity with *amor mundi*, love of the world and the realization of the ultimate preciousness of all natals.[33]

Wayne refers to liberation theology as an alternative route by which a new paradigm of salvation might be articulated. One powerful strand of that came from a generation of German political theologians, such as Dorothee Soelle, Jean-Baptist Metz and Jurgen Moltmann, who challenged Western Christianity's reduction of the Gospel into a form of spiritualized and privatized piety. They criticize Western liberal theology for colluding with an intellectualized preoccupation with conscience, propositional belief and intellectual coherence at the neglect of

[31] D. A. Palin, *A Gentle Touch: from theology of handicap to a theology of human being* (London: SPCK, 1992); F. Young, *Face to Face* (London: Epworth, 1985).
[32] H. Reinders, *Receiving the Gift of Friendship* (Grand Rapids: Wm. B. Eerdmanns, 2008).
[33] G. M. Jantzen, *Becoming Divine: Toward a Feminist Philosophy of Religion* (Manchester: Manchester University Press, 1998); 'Flourishing: Towards an ethic of natality', *Feminist Theory* 2:2 (2001), pp. 219–32.

involvement in communities of faith, action and transformation.³⁴ To echo Karl Marx, theology cannot simply understand the world, but must also seek to change it. The test of authentic theology within the crucible of *orthopraxy*, rather than *orthodoxy*, central to theologies of liberation, flows from this claim that to be saved is more than a question of 'right belief' and extends to a participation (which is as much collective and structural as individual) in God's 'drama' of salvation.³⁵

I wonder, however, whether Wayne's chapter acknowledges the full implications of a liberationist soteriology. All theologies of liberation – including the emergent voices in theologies of disability – claim the right to speak from experience as a fundamental starting point, and to theologize about that experience as worthy of offering legitimate insights into the nature of God. The 'tyranny of exclusion' is more than a matter of equality of access. At its most radical, it names those formerly excluded and rendered invisible within the theological canon as fully made in the image of God, and capable of bearing witness to God's saving work – not in spite of, but because of, their marginalization. But this requires us to move beyond equality – a theology of inclusion – towards the theological embrace of difference or even *alterity* (otherness).

Wayne notes Mary Grey's synthesis of a liberation theology of disability with Grace Jantzen's feminist philosophy of natality, in which the dynamics of exclusion are prompted in part by fear of differently-abled persons, who may embody forms of vulnerability, contingency or imperfection that remind us of our own finitude.³⁶ The philosopher Julia Kristeva has explored similar territory, arguing that prejudice against foreigners and other 'minorities' is an expression of a pathology in which difference – of any kind – must be objectified and expelled from an economy of the same. As Kristeva has argued, 'the foreigner is a "symptom": . . . psychologically he [sic] signifies the difficulty we have of living as an *other* and with others'.³⁷ Culturally, the alien's difference can be both exotic and unsettling, as it exposes the contingency of that which we formerly took for granted. Psychoanalytically, it awakens the strangeness and dividedness of our own identity, the parts of ourselves we wish to repress.

However, the logic of this begs the question as to whether inclusion and liberation for those with disabilities (in church and society) can come about simply by effacing differences. The danger is that such inclusion advocates a form of homogeneity; but theologies of liberation argue that God is revealed in unexpected,

³⁴ J. B. Metz, *Faith in History and Society: Toward a Practical Fundamental Theology* trans. D. Smith (London: Burns & Oates, 1980), esp. pp. 32–6. See also P. M. Scott and W. T. Cavanaugh (eds), *The Blackwell Companion to Political Theology* (Oxford: Blackwell, 2004), pp. 231–17, 227–40, 241–55.
³⁵ R. Haughton, *The Drama of Salvation* (New York: Seabury Press, 1975).
³⁶ M. Grey, '*Natality* and *Flourishing* in the Contexts of Disability and Impairment', in E. L. Graham (ed.) *Grace Jantzen: Redeeming the Present* (London: Ashgate, 2009), pp. 197–212.
³⁷ J. Kristeva, *Strangers to Ourselves* (trans. L. Roudiez; New York: Columbia University Press, 1991), p. 103.

often scandalous, circumstances. The central premise of God's 'preferential option for the poor' is testament to this insistence that exclusion and oppression, as continuing historical realities, are places in which the costly suffering of Christ – and thus the ongoing drama of salvation – continues to be enacted. Morris notes:

> Surely, the representation and exploration of human experience is incomplete as long as disability is either missing from or misrepresented in all the forms that cultural representation takes. It is fear and denial of the frailty, vulnerability, mortality and arbitrariness of human experience that deters us from confronting such realities. Fear and denial prompt the isolation of those who are disabled, ill or old as 'other,' as 'not like us.'[38]

As Tom Shakespeare has argued, disability can be likened to gender as an element of difference which is objectified as 'otherness'.

> I am . . . suggesting that disabled people could also be regarded as Other, by virtue of their connection to nature; their visibility as evidence of the constraining body; and their status as constant reminders of mortality. If original sin, through the transgression of Eve, is concretized in the flesh of woman, then the flesh of disabled people has historically, and within Judaeo-Christian theology especially, represented divine punishment for ancestral transgression. Furthermore, non-disabled people define themselves as 'normal' in opposition to disabled people who are not.[39]

Like Kristeva and Grey, Shakespeare identifies the fear of those with disabilities as the cause and symptom of their deviation from a norm, since 'disabled people remind non-disabled people of their own vulnerability'.[40]

For Shakespeare, this is the dynamic of objectification which marks the difference between 'having an impairment' and 'being disabled'. The former is an experience (possibly individually owned?) and the other the socially ascribed identity of a group that becomes a 'scapegoat', or 'dustbin', for the anxieties of the majority. Yet this renders the presence of disabled bodies in the body politic as all the more vital, since their visibility represents a refusal to collude in the fantasy of the human condition 'as perfectible, as all-knowing, as god-like: able, over and above all other beings, to conquer the limitations of their nature through the victories of their culture'.[41]

The affinities between Shakespeare's argument and the core premises of liberation theology should be apparent; and emergent voices in the theology of disability are beginning to adopt a stance in which assimilation, or equality to a hegemonic norm, are rejected in favour of alternative paradigms that reconstruct received

---

[38] J. Morris, *Pride against Prejudice* (London: The Women's Press, 1991), p. 85.

[39] T. Shakespeare, 'Cultural Representations of Disabled People: dustbins for disavowal?' in L. Barton and M. Oliver, (eds) *Disability Studies: Past, Present and Future*, (Leeds: The Disability Press, 1997), pp. 217–33, (p. 229).

[40] *Ibid.*, p. 230.

[41] *Ibid.*, p. 230.

notions of personhood, salvation – and even God. Yet a claim for 'equality' alone risks the loss of the specificity of experience of those with disabilities – not least, as Wayne himself remarks, there is a tendency to homogenize a range of experiences of impairment. So in keeping with the spirit of the 'preferential option', therefore, theologians such as Deborah Creamer are insisting on a movement beyond inclusion, towards a model of diversity which embraces difference and renders it theologically significant. Like other authors, such as Nancy Eiesland, Creamer is especially concerned to address the specificity of the disabled body as a vantage point from which to do a new kind of theology; as, for example, how it might serve as a hermeneutic through which to reinterpret classic Christian doctrine on the body of Christ.[42] This should be regarded as a gift to the rest of the Church, since to refuse 'to recognize and reflect on *difference* as an important aspect of the metaphor of the body of God leaves us theologically impoverished'.[43]

Wayne's essay is a helpful demonstration of the way in which the voices and perspectives of those who have been traditionally excluded from theological discourse challenge the ethical and pastoral behaviour of the 'mainstream'. They challenge us also to return to fundamental questions of how to speak of God and how to conceive of the ends of faith. Yet arguably, there is a more radical step beyond exclusion and the abolition of the tyranny of normality: a theology of *alterity*, in which the scandal of difference and otherness is embraced as a sign of God's work of salvation in the world.

II. Concluding Comments

Wayne Morris

Elaine's proposal, that we need to move beyond a theology of inclusion towards a theological embrace of difference and otherness (p. 163), suggests that I need to define more clearly what I mean by 'an inclusive theology of salvation'. In response, drawing on my work with the Deaf community in Birmingham, I would like to draw on their understanding of 'inclusion' as a concept that contrasts 'integration' as a way of defining what underpins my proposed inclusive theology. The original language in which these concepts are expressed is British Sign Language (BSL). Drawing on this Deaf understanding of inclusion, I suggest that an inclusive theology is indeed a theology that embraces difference and otherness.

In the Deaf community, 'integration' is a concept that often refers to institutional and governmental agendas to end specific provision and services for Deaf people, with the result that Deaf people are 'integrated' with hearing people and

---

[42] D. B. Creamer, *Disability and Christian Theology* (New York: Oxford University Press, 2009); Eiesland, N., *The Disabled God: Toward a Liberatory Theology of Disability* (Nashville: Abingdon, 1995).

[43] Creamer, *Disability and Christian Theology*, p. 69, my emphasis.

provided for in hearing contexts as much as possible. This has led to the closure of such things as schools for Deaf people and, in some instances, churches for Deaf people. Such 'integration' has often led to marginalization in those institutions which pursue integrative policies and often leads to the further exclusion of Deaf people in society more widely. A society in which Deaf people can flourish is not necessarily a society in which everyone is treated in the same ways in the same places, but rather where people are treated differently according to their particular contexts and needs. In BSL, 'integration' is signed as follows:

- The left and right hand are placed in front of the body, fingers extended away from the body with the palms facing the floor.
- The two hands are at equal height indicating equality.
- Fingers are often used as ways of articulating how a person (one finger) or group of people (many fingers) behave (such forms of expression are known as 'classifiers' in BSL).
- The fingers on the left hand may represent Deaf people and the fingers on the right hand may represent hearing people.
- 'Integration' is signed by the right hand moving over the left and the fingers of the right hand resting between the fingers of the left.
- At first glance, it appears as though hearing and Deaf people are mixed together equally.
- However, in the movement of one hand over the other, the notion of domination and oppression is evoked.

Policies and practices that intend to bring a minority group of people, such as the Deaf community, into the institutions and groups of a dominant majority, invariably are policies and practices that cater to the majority and seek ways to make the minority 'fit' what works for the majority. From the perspective of the minority group, in this instance the Deaf community, such 'integration' is often oppressive. That is so, because Deaf people become more fully a part of society not by having to conform to hearing norms and ways of living, but by being allowed to live as Deaf people in their Deaf condition. The opposite of 'integration' is not 'segregation', however, but inclusion.

The sign, roughly translated as 'inclusion', is almost identical to that for 'integration' described above. However, when the two hands move together, they rest alongside each other. This reflects a recognition that Deaf and hearing people need to be alongside each other, but not necessarily always in the same contexts. Inclusion means retaining the distinctive culture, identity and language of the Deaf community as something equal to that of hearing people. Subsequently, policies and practices informed by 'inclusion' rather than 'integration' are, as a result, not always orientated towards treating Deaf and hearing people the same. Rather 'inclusion' recognizes that sometimes Deaf and hearing people, because they are in some ways different to each other, need to be treated differently.

Elaine proposes that we move beyond an inclusive theology towards a theology of alterity. I have chosen the term 'inclusive', conscious of the problems this term raises, because the understanding of 'inclusion' that underpins my chapter is one that contrasts and subverts notions of 'integration' and is a particularly Deaf understanding of what inclusivity means; not being made like hearing people, but coming alongside hearing people in their Deafness. I would like to suggest that, when I refer to an inclusive society or an inclusive theology, I am indeed referring to a society and theology in which 'the scandal of difference and otherness is embraced' (p. 138). In my deconstruction and critique of the 'tyranny of the normal', here I am resisting any attempt to homogenize the lives and experiences of people with disabilities. When I use this deconstruction of the 'tyranny of the normal' to argue that faith may be important, but not *necessary* for salvation, I am arguing that we do not all need to be the same in order to 'be saved'. When I suggest that for some, salvation is release from their condition in this world, but for others it is not, I am proposing multiple ways of understanding both disability and salvation. Such an inclusive approach to salvation acknowledges that difference and otherness are important and, as a result, it is necessary to acknowledge that God engages differently with different people, rather than only engaging with people when they fit social constructs of 'normality'. I am therefore grateful to Elaine for prompting me to clarify what I mean by 'inclusion'.

However, I wish to go beyond such inclusive ways of thinking about disability and salvation to reflect on how such thinking might inform praxis. My liberationist construction of salvation, drawing on the theology of Jon Sobrino, can help us to think differently about disability and salvation, but also challenges those for whom a Christian theology of salvation matters to act differently as well. Here it is important to reiterate my earlier conclusion that the future vision of the kingdom of God, whether that is expressed as a place in which 'difference and otherness are embraced' or a place of 'inclusion', while rooted in the future, has branches that must reach into the present to transform the present. Thinking differently about salvation has the potential to transform praxis by providing a theology that might empower the churches and their disabled members to resist normalization or homogenization, and to embrace difference and otherness as a reality that is part of the intention of God both for this world, and the world to come.

8 Participation for All?

Dot Gosling

Since the meaning of participation has many variables, I propose to use my own working definition as follows: the positive, voluntary and active involvement of an individual or group in shaping something in order for transformation to take place for the good of all involved. Participation can create feelings of joy and affirmation, and is fundamentally based on an ethic of respect between persons. In the context of work with young people, participation uses anti-oppressive practice and empowers individuals or groups to shape decisions.[1]

This chapter will explore why the full participation of young people in the life of the Church is important for the Church, focusing on my own Church context within the Church of England, although recognizing that what I have to say may be important for other Churches, too. It seeks to make clear why creating a Church in which everyone can participate fully should be an important part of the strategy, especially for working with those on the outside and the margins of Church. It will use core youth work values, alongside theological reflection, to develop a notion of participation in Churches that enables young people to more fully become members of the Church. It will argue that creating an inclusive Church is a theological imperative and will consider how the relationship of the Trinity might have an impact on directing the Church towards more inclusive practice, both today and in the future. An exploration of community and learning and their influence on participation will be discussed in recognition of the fact that all people participate in lifelong learning and in community at every stage of their lives. It is suggested that because of this, individuals within the Church, as well as the Church more generally, must be engaged in working towards greater participation in the life of the Church for all.

---

[1] For example, see Participation Works Partnership, 'National Participation Strategic Vision Launched', retrieved from: www.participationworks.org.uk/news/national-participation-strategic-vision-launched, accessed 5 January 2010.

Dot Gosling

Why Participation?

At the heart of my notion of participation are the core values (which draw on youth work values) of equality of opportunity, lifelong learning, belief that everyone has something valuable to contribute, anti-oppressive practice, empowerment, active listening and affirmation.[2] From a Christian point of view, this understanding of the nature of participation is further reinforced by the mandate set out in Galatians 3.28 that 'There is no longer Jew or Greek, there is no longer slave or free, there is no longer male and female; for all of you are one in Christ Jesus'.

Creating opportunities for full participation in the Church can have an extremely positive and often very significant effect on young people.[3] I, for example, experienced positive active participation as a young person at Church, and this experience was formative for me and has shaped me up to the present day. As part of my profession as a Christian youth work lecturer within the context of higher education, I work closely with Christian youth work students with the specific aim of trying to encourage them to empower young people within the Church to become active participants (rather than passive receptors) in their own faith journeys. Encouraging young people to participate in this way is advantageous, because it enhances their growth as people and their development as disciples of Christ. It also promotes an ownership of their faith and of the Church to which they belong. Having an ethos of equality of opportunity is advantageous for the Church, because it can empower and provide a space for more people to take ownership of the issues of their particular locality and to get involved, rather than remaining passive and expecting those in positions of authority (such as clergy, readers and others on Church leadership teams) to do everything.

Lifelong learning and a belief that everyone has something valuable to contribute are linked with equality of opportunity. When individuals are treated with respect, there is more likelihood of them having things to say that are constructively positive, rather than negative. Empowering people is a skill that involves all the core values of youth work and is vital for transforming the Church into a positive place where those on the margins are welcomed and listened to, valued and loved as Christ commands us to love.[4]

This could be a means of transforming the culture of Churches so that active listening to those on the margins of the Church, those who do not feel part of the Church in different ways and for whatever reason, become part of the whole Church's thinking and behaviour.

Active listening refers to the type of listening in which all the attention of the listener is focused both on the spoken and the unspoken, and on the emotional

---

[2] Smith, M. K., 'Young People, informal education and association', retrieved from: www.infed.org/youthwork/b-yw.htm, accessed 23 July 2010.

[3] L. Ward and B. Hearn, *An Equal Place at the Table* (Published for Participation Works by NCB, 2010) p. 6.

[4] Matthew 22.37–8

and physical attitudes of the speaker.[5] In the context of work with young people, this means leaving aside the prejudices that older people sometimes have, for example, that young people do not have things of worth to offer to Churches. Although the merits of active listening are self-evident, this form of listening is not always experienced by individuals (especially young people) within a Church environment. In some Church contexts, young people do not experience a diversity of beliefs, which quite often leads to narrow theological views and perspectives. Implementing a strategy of active listening would allow these beliefs to be explored through discussion and debate. Young people could be encouraged to experience different Christian Church traditions as a start, and informal and non-formal education (which is core to youth work practice) could be used to further develop the young person's understanding of Christian belief and practice. One of the main difficulties here, however, is that Church communities often do not recognize the urgency that is needed to listen to those on the margins, in particular young people, and to purposefully include young people in its work. The aim of active listening is not just to stop the decline in Church attendance, but for a theology of inclusion to be part of the theology of the Church for everyone, because inclusion matters; it is a Gospel imperative. Having outlined some of the ways that core youth work values may contribute to creating Church communities in which all people, in particular young people, can participate, I now move on to consider how the structures of the Church of England (the Church on which I focus here) often limit the participation of young people in the Churches.

The parishes of the Church of England have many members who participate passively in Church, and I would suggest that one question that may need to be asked is whether the structures of the Church of England are helpful in promoting active participation for everyone. The following section will give a brief overview of the structures found within the Church of England, but it is also worth noting that each parish and context will be different in how they do things, as is the case for each deanery and diocese.

The Church of England has two provinces and 43 dioceses. Within each diocese are (in some, episcopal areas) archdeaconries, deaneries and parishes. Deaneries have different ways of working, and each parish, while linked to the wider Church in many ways, has freedom to exercise a certain amount of autonomy over the way it operates. In my former parish, for example, the leadership team included a vicar, an ordinand (me), three lay readers, and two Churchwardens. The Parochial Church Council (PCC) was elected by members of the congregation and met (usually) once a month to discuss various issues. From that particular PCC, three members were voted onto the Deanery Synod. From the Deanery Synod there are elections onto the Diocesan Synod and General Synod. In each of the synods, and also in the parish, there is a provision for being co-opted onto various committees.

---

[5] See, for example, Mind Tools, 'Active Listening: Hear What People are Really Saying', retrieved from: www.mindtools.com/CommSkll/ActiveListening.htm, accessed 23 July 2010.

However, many people (young and old) do not see the importance and value of committees in which much of the language and methodology do not allow for the more creative style of learner.[6] While there are some Churches that do include young people in their structures, who want to get their voices heard and who recognize the value of committee and working group membership, in all of these committees an individual has to be voted on or co-opted, and it is often quite difficult for young people to get on to these committees and make a contribution. Many young people do not want to be seen as pushing themselves forward, or they might have low self-esteem and so would not want to be put forward. Attitudes towards young people, that they have nothing useful to contribute to such committees, may often make it difficult for a young person to be elected. Also, since many of these committees are made up of a high majority of older people, this may leave many young people feeling out of their 'comfort zone'. The way that the structures of the Church of England operate, therefore, often preclude young people from being fully involved in Church life.

On the other hand, there are examples of strategies the Church of England has used to enable greater participation of young people in its structures. The Church of England has a Youth Council (CEYC)[7] that seeks to represent a youth voice to the wider Church. To do this, they meet as a Council twice a year, once in November for a residential, and once in April for a day meeting. Discussion and debate take place on topics relevant to the Church and to young people – anything from the environment to women bishops to the well-being of young adults today. This provides an important forum for the voices of young people to be heard, enabling individual members to gain confidence, self-worth, knowledge and understanding of a range of different areas of life, which they can then communicate to their respective dioceses and to their youth groups and Churches. Often young people involved in the CEYC become involved in leadership in the Church in different guises, and the Council often serves to encourage a sense of vocation in the lives of these young people. Three of my former students, all of whom were involved with either CEYC or their own denomination's youth council, are now youth officers, one for a Roman Catholic diocese, one for the Salvation Army, another in a Church in Canada, and two are ordinands within the C of E, with another one already discerning a call to ordained ministry.

Much of the work done with the CEYC is through informal education in their regional groups, where a diocesan youth officer empowers the young people to engage with topics through informal discussion or experiential workshops. It is often the case that as the young people gain confidence in speaking out in the safe space that is provided and learn to reflect, elements of theological reflection are included into the discussion. For example, at one event, a group of young

---

[6] Peter Honey Publications, 'The Learning Styles Questionnaire', retrieved from: www. peterhoney.com/content/LearningStylesQuestionnaire.html, accessed 20 July 10.
[7] Church of England, 'Church of England Youth Council', retrieved from: www.ceyc.org/, accessed 20 July 10.

people were involved in a discussion of women in leadership in the Church. This discussion took place within the context of a Diocesan Youth Synod where the lead worker was male, and the volunteer helpers were parents of the young people within the group. The group was 60% male and 40% female, and all but two of the young people came from Churches where the leadership was all male. In providing a safe space for conversation in which active listening took place and where young people were empowered to articulate their own points of view, young people participated fully and left feeling valued and challenged. So, there are examples of good practice in which young people are able to participate fully in Church contexts, and this good practice needs to become the norm, rather than the exception. Having considered the problems that many young people experience with regard to participation in Churches, I would now like to move on to engage with some thinking about models of the Church and how this can help to provide a theological foundation for the view that Churches should be places in which all people can participate fully.

Church and Models of Church

There are many forms or models of Church, and even within the same denomination there will be wide variances; this has been the case since the time of the early Church. Participation, I believe, can be found in the New Testament in Acts 2.44–7, where everyone cared for the other. This required active participation on the part of the giver and receiver. Is this the case today? In some communities this is the case, but in others, active participation is not encouraged or widely practiced.

Avery Dulles's classic text, *Models of the Church*, identifies the following models through which the Church is spoken about: Institution, Mystical Communion, Sacrament, Herald of God, Servant Role and then a final one, which is Community of Disciples.[8] These models are still of value today, as Dulles recognizes, for example, that institutions are often necessary for the functioning of the Church, but that the Church must be understood in other ways, too, if the Church is to be faithful to its calling. Below, however, I would like to explore the way that 'communities of disciples' often operate, by using Hiebert's notion of 'sets', as this seems to me to be a helpful way of understanding how Churches often exclude young people, but also how young people's participation can be transformed by rethinking the way that Churches operate.

Professor Hiebert[9] identified a way of understanding how Churches operate by using the notion of sets from mathematics; he began with the notion of 'bounded' and 'centred' sets, and later he started to use intrinsic and extrinsic 'fuzzy' sets. Bounded sets are Churches that operate by setting up boundaries by which they

[8] A. Dulles, *Models of the Church*, 2nd edn (Dublin: Gill and Macmillan, 1976).
[9] P. G. Hiebert, *Anthropological Reflections on Missiological Issues*, 3rd edn (Grand Rapids, MI: Baker Academic, 1994).

can determine what is included and what is excluded in those communities. For example, a bounded set may define itself by using a definition of 'Christian', whereby it is easy to determine who does or does not conform to that definition. To be in the set, a person must conform to the boundaries such a definition lays down. If an individual is a Christian, they are inside the boundary, and energy will be put into ensuring that person stays inside the boundary.[10] Church culture can often be seen as being a bounded set, as many in the Church may want to keep things the way they have always been and want to maintain boundaries. One of the problems with viewing the Church as a 'bounded set', however, is that it allows little distinction between the centre and the boundary. It also 'leads inevitably to obsessive boundary maintenance and inquisitorial judgments about whether persons and groups are Christian or not.'[11] For people within a bounded set understanding, 'Church is seen as a gathering of Christians . . . and its unity would be based on uniformity – all Christians would think and act alike.'[12] Such an understanding of Church is problematic, because it encourages a narrowness of mind and justifies a disregard for difference. It is also true that, in reality, Christians do not all think alike, as is evidenced by debate within the Church of England, for example, over women bishops. As such, the notion of Church as a bounded set must be criticized.

Understanding the Church as a 'centred set' means that Christ constitutes the focus, and Church members position themselves in relation to this centre (rather than at the edges or boundary). The centred set focuses on the centre, and allows its boundaries to be more fluid. This often means that fewer people feel excluded from Church life, although it is recognized that there are different stages of becoming and being a Christian.[13] The various levels of participation might be seen as 'seekers, believers, baptized members and elders'.[14] This model is potentially more welcoming of young people, because the Church is presented as being open to people from the outside. It allows for recognition of the fact that the voices of those often outside of boundaries that have been set up, such as young people, count, and that they have a say in the decisions of the Church. A problem with this understanding of Church, it might be argued, however, is that most people feel a need to have boundaries to explore faith. Due to a lack of a boundary, it makes this form of Church a little less secure to do explorations and discuss options. In other words, it could be quite liberal and open, but there is no clue as to what does or does not constitute Christianity.

There are also extrinsic and intrinsic 'fuzzy' sets, which Hiebert also uses for models of Church. The intrinsic fuzzy set is the sort of Church in which people are

[10] Ibid., p. 116
[11] R. E. Olson, *The Mosaic of Christian Belief: Twenty Centuries of Unity & Diversity* (Leicester: IVP, 2002), p. 48.
[12] Hiebert, *Anthropological Reflections*, p. 116.
[13] Ibid., p. 129.
[14] Ibid., p. 129.

still known as Christians. There continues to be some form of adherence to various creeds and doctrines, but it is recognized that people within the Church will have varying levels of commitment to belief and practice.[15] The extrinsic fuzzy Church is a Church in which there is an understanding and allegiance to Christ, with the Church seeking to ensure that its commitment to Christ is resolute. Anyone, regardless of what they believed, would be welcomed to this Church, as long as there was an interest in knowing Christ, which could be developed into a strong belief.[16]

What this means for young people is that, depending on their learning style, there is a place where they could feel welcomed and feel that they could be an active participant, as anything is deemed permissible in this model of Church. The fuzzy sets may also be seen as too restrictive, however, because such sets are also less inclined to view Christ as unique, because Christ does not constitute the centre. This could encourage young people to form an eclectic view of the Christian faith, fusing different elements of faiths together to form their own version with no real commitment to following Christ or his example.

Church explored through the 'sets' idea highlights positive and negative points and identifies the priorities the Church needs to be improving, to become less arrogant and structural, and more open and welcoming.

Within my denomination (C of E) the Church has, in some places, become too structured and too focused on the insiders. What this means for those outside the set (Church) who want to try it out is that there is already a barrier before they have walked over the entrance. Quite often people are left to work out where they are supposed to be reading from in the service books or booklets, and the songs are often too contemporary or too old. It means that the Church needs to recognize that it might operate as a bounded set, and so must, as a consequence, prioritize welcome and change in its work.

To do this, there will need to be a change in attitude by those in the local contexts who think the Church is only for those who have the same beliefs, attitudes or values as those within that local Church. The Church needs to have the attitude that Jesus had to the Gentiles, of being open and inclusive, rather than exclusive to those who have a different value base. An example of this is a Church that welcomed young people who were part of the Goth culture into their Sunday worship service, even though they looked different. The youth worker in that Church acted as a mediator between the different cultures, as sometime has to happen when meeting people of different cultures outside the Church.

Participation and the Trinity

Our way of life, believing and values – our 'habitus'[17] – as Christians comes from our journey of faith, of learning, which includes socialization and being open to

[15] Ibid., p. 121.
[16] Ibid., p. 133.
[17] Adapted from Pierre Bourdieu.

the Holy Spirit. Participating in God becomes our goal, and when we are focused on our journey into a oneness with Christ, a person's individual habitus, which includes others, will be evident. Leonardo Boff argues that because Christians recognize the Trinity as three specific persons who are equal in function in a shared mutuality of love and life, Christians ought to treat everyone in a similar fashion. Indeed, for Boff, '[t]he Trinity is' the model in *this* life for our society in general and our Church in particular.'[18] The Trinity is a social project or programme, which provides a model for everything we do, including 'demanding structures that are characterized by participation, inclusion, equality and respect for differences.'[19] Nichols, writing from a Roman Catholic perspective says, 'if the aim of the Church is to bring members into a personal relationship with Jesus and a participation in the life of the Trinity, then it cannot afford to embrace a social hierarchy that alienates its members, or reduces them to passivity and apathy.'[20] I would argue that this is indeed the case, and I would like to see Churches in which committees are open to everyone and everyone feels their voice will be heard, even those who are not as inclusive as others. Respect is needed on all sides.

However, Miroslav Volf is critical of this understanding of the Trinity as a social programme, as he argues that humans cannot possibly connect with other humans in the same way as the three persons of the Trinity connect with each other. For humanity to have 'life in all its fullness' (John 10.10), there has to be a grounding and sustaining by the Holy Spirit. The Holy Spirit lives within each person, and it is this that connects humanity to God the Father and God the Son. Volf argues that the Trinity should be seen as the 'ultimate normative end towards which all social programs should strive.'[21] He also posits that the love which the Trinitarian persons share is perfect love and that we ought to reflect this mutual love to others. Of course, if this is what Christians ought to be doing, then it follows that the Church ought to be making positive contributions to society in general, as it is called to work together to enable transformation in society. Greenwood talks about the Church being 'here to untie the distorted networks of communication between humanity and creation and to replace them with ways of relating rooted in the Trinitarian image'.[22] If we are made in the image of God (Genesis 1.27) and God is Trinity, then to be human means to be in a mutual relationship with others, and this is a key point when exploring the issue of the participation of young people in Church life. God in Christ calls us to love not only God, but also our neighbours and ourselves. When the question is asked 'who is our neighbour?' the answer for Christians should be everyone, not simply those we like, who are like us, or who we agree with; it includes young people, older people, people with addictions, and

---

[18] L. Boff, *Trinity and Society* (Maryknoll, NY: Orbis, 1988) p. 393.

[19] Ibid.

[20] L. T. Nichols, *That All May Be One*. (Collegeville,MN: The Liturgical Press, 1997), p. 291.

[21] Miroslav Volf, 'The Trinity Is Our Social Program: The Doctrine of the Trinity and the Shape of Social Engagement', *Modern Theology*, 14 (1998) pp. 403–19 (406).

[22] R. Greenwood, *Practising Community*, 2nd edn (London: SPCK, 1996), p. 55.

so forth. In *Mandate to Difference*, Brueggemann proposes, among other things, that 'others belong with us and for us and are welcome as we are welcomed, an alternative so much more healthy than urging exclusivism or pretending others are not there.'[23]

Even when congregations are in favour of including children and young people in Church life, the learning styles and methods used in the Church may not always be empowering for all. This, I believe, must be properly examined in order for the body of Christ to become fully functioning and inclusive, alongside the committee structures already mentioned. Young children who cannot yet read, those who are illiterate, and those who have learning difficulties will be excluded from a worshipping community, which is highly word focused. Likewise, it will partially exclude those who prefer kinaesthetic or pragmatic learning styles.[24] It might also preclude the reflectors among the congregations, if there is no space set aside to reflect on what is being said or sung.

I want to suggest that it is not simply about the full participation of younger people in Church life, but also their inclusion in consultation and decision-making processes, the way worship services are designed and run. Don E Saliers speaks of how a

> deepening sense of 'being Church' is ... part of the unexpected side of the work of inclusion. The movement from adopting an 'inclusive' attitude on the part of the leadership to the actual life of being a place of 'belonging' is itself maturation, both theological and moral. This, I contend, is part of what it means to be a faithful people of God in the world, to 'grow up in every way' into Christ (Eph 4:15). Participating in the movement from inclusivity to the spirituality of belonging to one another is an image of the Christian life itself.[25]

The Trinity shows that God is an inclusive God,[26] not a God who only represents those who believe in certain ways, who behave in certain ways or who belong to a certain Church. At the heart of community is sharing, participation and fellowship, and these values must be positioned at the centre of the Church's practice. This is not just for the sake of young people, as Maslow's hierarchy of needs affirms the generic need among human beings to belong.[27] For Maslow, the need to belong follows after our physical and safety needs have been met, in terms of importance.[28]

---

[23] W. Brueggmann, *Mandate to Difference* (Louisville: Westminster John Knox Press, 2007), p. 67.

[24] Peter Honey Publications, 'The Learning Styles Questionnaire', retrieved from: www.peterhoney.com/content/LearningStylesQuestionnaire.html, accessed 20 July 10.

[25] D. E. Saliers, 'Towards a Spirituality of Inclusiveness', in N. Eiesland & D. E. Saliers (eds), *Human Disability and the Service of God: Reassessing Religious Practice* (Nashville, TN: Abingdon Press, 1998), pp. 19–31.

[26] S. Shakespeare, and H. Rayment-Pickard, *The Inclusive God* (Norwich: Canterbury Press, 2006), p. 108.

[27] Businessballs.com, 'Maslow's Hierarchy of Needs', retrieved from www.businessballs.com/maslow.htm, accessed 11 January 2010.

[28] Ibid.

Community

As has already been suggested, community is about sharing, fellowship and participation. The Trinitarian image of God means that God invites us to be part of an inclusive community, and this carries implications for the participation of young people within the Church.

Too often the attitude in many Churches is that of the bounded set, not a centred set. How young people fit into this kind of culture and community is an important question to be asked, if the Church is serious about building, maintaining and increasing the body of Christ. Church is the one place where community ought to be seen as inclusive, and yet it is very often the place where exclusivity is rife, particularly with regard to young people.

If to participate means to have an understanding of mutuality, or interdependence and, as Fiddes points out, to reflect the Trinitarian values of relationship, community, mutuality and interdependence[29], then participating means including those on the margins.

> Participating in the triune God we find actions which open up space, and interwoven with the kingdom-movement of the Father we discover the movement of the Spirit, opening up closed systems; the Spirit opens new horizons, breaks with taboos, sets new frames of reference, innovates and removes blockages of tradition.[30]

To be included is to be part of the body of Christ, as we see in Galatians 3.28, and although this passage was talking about Jews and Gentiles, it includes all who are marginalized. Inclusion means taking risks, as a welcome has to be given to unknown people who might be different from the majority. Participation for young people is not simply about them handing out hymn sheets or taking the collection, but using their skills and abilities in the tasks and structures of the Church itself. Obviously, this will happen in different ways, and some Churches may and do have structures that already empower young people in this manner. For example, one Church with which I am familiar encouraged young people to organize and run fundraising events for a mission trip to Uganda. The youth leaders empowered the older young people to induct the younger individuals into the ideas so that they could work together to conduct fundraising events and raise money for the trip. Once in Uganda, they established relationships with the local people and helped build houses, schools and hospitals. Another Church actively encouraged young people to organize and run worship services every month, giving them advice when requested, as well as positive feedback. Yet another Church encouraged young people in their vocation to ordained ministry by inviting young people to become servers if they felt a calling from God. This enabled the participants to learn how things are done in different settings in Church services, by shadowing their vicar and asking questions when unclear about something. They

---

[29] P. Fiddes, *Participating in God* (London: Darton, Longman & Todd, 2000) p. 66.
[30] Ibid., p. 100.

are following the call of the Spirit in their lives by becoming active participants and becoming aware of new ways of being a follower of Christ.

When empowered to do so, young people do sometimes have a tendency to think differently from adults, but still need to be actively listened to and cared for at all times. In a recent conference in London, at which we were discussing how we encourage young people to participate actively in the Church, each person in the room talked about people who took time to listen to them and who cared about them unconditionally when they were young people. They were not necessarily talking about youth workers or people who 'usually' worked with young people, but someone who cared enough to ask how they were doing and who prayed for them. We also talked about the importance of empowering young people in active participation. We heard of some young people involved in funding bids for projects who, when it became obvious that the adult working with them genuinely wanted to know their feelings about the bids, opened up and grew in self-confidence because they realized their opinions mattered and were worth something. This is a by-product of participation, and not limited to young people; when anyone is encouraged or empowered, confidence is increased. This often leads to a sense of ownership of the community in which they find themselves, coming to the fore as individuals recognize the importance of standing up for what they want or believe. Community is about all ages, becoming one as in the Eucharist, where we share in the one bread and cup.

Conclusion

Participation for all was the question at the beginning of this chapter, and this has been explored throughout. The other question for this chapter was how children and young people can be empowered to be participative in their own faith journeys and in Church structures, for the good of everyone. This was discussed through exploring the way that core youth work values might contribute to a more inclusive Church, by looking at the Church of England and the youth council, through the models of Church and communication in Church structures and, finally, through using the Trinity as a model for communication and community. For the Church to be completely inclusive is a problem for many people, due to their theological beliefs and understanding of the body of Christ. However, I believe the relationship between the Trinity is a profound relationship, as it teaches us about how we should relate to one another. It reveals that at the centre of all our relationships there should be mutuality and interdependence, not independence. In terms of children and young people, this carries significant implications. It means recognizing the importance of all ages as an equal part of the body of Christ. Although some young people may choose not to participate, for those who do, their confidence may increase, barriers may be broken down and understanding and knowledge of their own faith journey and Church structures may be increased. Unfortunately, research in this area has not been done, and this is one of the things I am currently undertaking as part of my doctoral studies.

It is recognized, though, that young people within the Church have many of the same needs and issues as those outside the Church, and research has proven that confidence and understanding is indeed increased. The main question is whether individuals within the Church can be open to differences and have an awareness of themselves as potential oppressors or liberators. If individuals have this awareness, there is the potential for everyone to be liberated, rather than oppressed.

What is needed is a theology of inclusion and participation that is proactive, open to transformation, so children and young people will not have bad or indifferent experiences of Church, and will therefore stay in the Church. There is evidence to suggest that people are leaving the Church, partly because society today has become a place where consumerism and choice has become the new form of religion, but also, in part, because we all think we know better than the other and so we ignore what others think or believe. Laurie Green writes about 'doing' theology, as opposed to reading and applying theology, and writes, 'A participative theology will not only allow for alternative styles of expression, but will also encourage the pressing issues of the day to be more adequately focused.'[31] This doing and being active participants in theology should enable Christians to look at the issues of today and participate in empowering a transformation of those issues through engaging in the vision of the Kingdom of God. It is true that as a person grows and develops in their understanding and faith, what they believe may change over time.[32] Our place is not to judge or belittle, but to encourage and empower individuals to have new experiences to help more people grow in knowledge and understanding of God.

Our place is to remember that, as Christians, we are all members of the same body of Christ; that we have all been commanded to love God and love our neighbours as we love ourselves (Mark 12.31). If we want to participate, why do we exclude others from doing so?

I. Response to Dot Gosling

Maxine Green

... remember that as Christians we are all members of the same body of Christ, that we have all been commanded to love God and love our neighbours as we love ourselves. If we want to participate why, do we exclude others from doing so?

This is the question Dot puts to us at the end of her chapter. She highlights the deep need to belong, both to God and as part of the Christian community. She also extends a challenge to the reader; if we do want this community of belonging, how can we possibly exclude others from actively being part of this community?

[31] L. Green, *Let's Do Theology* (London: Mowbray, 1990), p. 6.
[32] 1 Corinthians 13.11–12

There are very few Christians who would not agree that we are all the same body of Christ and that we should love God and our neighbours. It is so much at the centre of Christian theology that it is impossible to oppose this while holding Christian beliefs. Drawing on Christian theology and practice, we know that a huge part of being a Christian is joining with others in worship and participating in the life of the Church. So if this is the case, the only reason for pursuing these questions about belonging and exclusion is that it indicates that this is not happening in our Churches, and that there are still some people who are not welcomed into the Christian community. One group that is particularly excluded from the community is young people.

It is sad that this chapter still needs to be written and still needs to be read. *Youth A Part*, a report to the General Synod of the Church of England, was published in 1996, with a central theme of encouraging the Church to embrace young people as full members of the Christian community. Many of the young people who were campaigning for a fuller voice are now married with children of their own. Yet the questions are still being asked, and there are still people engaged with the struggle of obtaining a broader, more participating community of Christians. Dot looks systematically at the various aspects of participation to try and get some sort of purchase on where the blocks are and why the fully inclusive community is still eluding us. Dot defines participation and outlines what it means to be fully active in the life of the Church. She explores theological positions, different models of Church, the behaviour of Church people and leaders, and the operational structures of the Church in trying to elucidate the dynamics and power of exclusion. She also encourages the reader to challenge him/herself in each of these different areas to know their own mind and invites him/her to use this to make their behaviour congruent with their theology, thoughts and feelings.

In her definition of participation, Dot emphasizes that good active participation is not just for the young people themselves, it is for the benefit of the whole Church. A theology of inclusion is not just to stop the decline in Church membership, but to embrace a welcoming, open, Christian theology that is healthy for the Church and the wider society. This is very important, as many Churches hold a limiting belief that there is a finite amount of resource (money, love, power or influence), which has to be apportioned carefully. Dot's theology of inclusion relates to and embraces a theology of abundance in which, when the heart is open, resources become limitless.

Dot explores the structures of the Church and shows that, while there have been some changes and young people now have their own Youth Councils, the structures of the Church are largely resistant to change, and so fail to adapt and allow young people to make strong contributions. She also shows how the behaviour of leaders of the Church can have a big impact. Many adults in the Church seem to lecture young people, rather than treat them as thoughtful, questioning individuals whose exploration can be supported through providing opportunities to explore and reach their own conclusions.

Models of Church also have a large impact on how Christian communities react, and Dot shows how these models affect the way the Church runs and develops. A bounded community has the advantage of keeping beliefs and sacrament intact and safe; however, the disadvantage of this is that it fosters a closed community which can be seen as exclusive and unwelcoming. Dot offers a vision of a Church which is relational, with a strong sense of sacrament, as she says, 'What is needed is a theology of inclusion and participation, that is proactive, open to transformation, so children and young people will not have bad or indifferent experiences of Church, and will therefore not leave the Church'. As well as a *theology* of inclusion and participation, there needs to be a *practice* of inclusion and participation.

The strong community of Church which Dot proposes provides a brilliant starting point to plant the seeds of participation and watch their active and vigorous growth. A loving and caring community is a perfect place for young people to gain skills and responsibilities which will enable them to make important contributions to the life of the Church. Perhaps we should learn to see children and young people as apprentices and our older folk as having a role in providing opportunities and experiences for them to grow. The apprenticeship model could become very powerful, both for young people and for the organization of the Church. As a young apprentice, I would be looking for an institution which was sure of itself, could help me acquire skills and experience, and would also help me find the unique contribution I could make to the institution and to the world. A good mentor would support the apprentice by giving carefully selected tasks and opportunities to build competence and ability. As competence and ability grow, the apprentice is able to take on more and more responsibility. Another feature of a good mentor is that they allow the apprentice to move beyond their own level of competence. The Church community needs to be able to make similar inspiring opportunities for children and young people so that their talents blossom, both for their own development and to bring about beautiful transformations to the life of the Church. Dot draws out many examples of Churches which supported the development and growth of their young people and have thus enriched the young people themselves and their Churches.

Although the will of many older Churchgoers may be fully in step with the inclusive, welcoming, growing approach outlined above, this is often accompanied by emotions of guilt and fear. People feel that they are not doing enough to support young people, and live under a shadow, where they feel that they could do better and are not doing enough. This sits with a sense of fear and trepidation which can be due to not knowing how to talk to and reach children and young people or, in a more extreme form, young people can be seen as potentially dangerous and violent. Talking to a group of hoodies who hang around the Churchyard can be very frightening for older people. In these circumstances, it feels much easier to play it safe, retire into old practices, smile a lot and hope that children and young people will detect the good intentions that exist under the surface. However, this may be an opportunity wasted in failing to reach others in the community, and when Churches have taken risks, the results are transformative.

Dot has explored some of the thinking and practice that exists in Churches; maybe the block is at a feeling level and the feelings of fear and inadequacy block older people from doing something new or different. It is ironic that there is any fear in our Churches. If anyone can take risks, it should be in a community of faith where there is security in God's love. This links with the limiting belief Churches hold about resources being finite: a theology of scarcity, rather than a theology of abundance. In many Church communities, there is a strong feeling that if children and young people had significant responsibility for the future, they would make inappropriate decisions and squander the Church's resources. An interesting feature of young people being involved in making decisions about resource allocation is that they are mostly incredibly responsible, consider the effects at length and are profoundly interested in the outcome. With young people's increasing participation in statutory services, there is a greater awareness among older people of how responsible young people are. Another feature of young people being involved in decision making is the variety of perspectives they bring and how this enriches the final decision.

Moving the debate into action requires thoughtful consideration of the political, theological and practical dynamics, and Dot's piece provides many tools to reflect on these. What is also needed is for individuals and Church communities to feel secure and confident enough to take risks and explore new ways of building an open and welcoming Church. After all, as we are called to cast all our bread on the water, trying new ways of being Church is not that much of a risk.

II. Concluding Comments

Dot Gosling

There are very few Christians who would not agree that we are all the same body of Christ and that we should love God and our neighbours . . . So if this is the case, the only reason for pursuing these questions about belonging and exclusion is that it indicates that this is not happening in our Churches and there are still some people who are not welcomed into the Christian community.

One only has to look around at many Churches to see that Maxine is correct. That women have still not been ordained as bishops, that young people in many Churches feel excluded by Church structures and practices, that gay and lesbian people often feel marginalization at every level of the Church are just a few examples that illustrate how far from being the same body of Christ we are. They show how far we are from being able to love our neighbours in the positive, affirming way that Jesus commands us to love – love our enemies and love our neighbours as we love ourselves and God.

If, as Maxine points out, 'a huge part of being a Christian is joining with others in worship and participating in the life of the Church', it is important for Churches to find ways to make this possible. Churches can so easily get sidetracked into being concerned with struggling to get people to sit in the same pew or row as someone they do not know, or to find people to be on a working party or the PCC. They perceive the major divisions in the Church to revolve around having several different services to meet the needs of those who prefer the *Book of Common Prayer*, only a Eucharist, only a said service, or only an all-age service. But providing a space for difference and allowing people to be themselves in Church can be seen as positive aspects of being Church, rather than as the major concerns of the day. To pretend that these are the most important concerns for the Church is to ignore the real issues that confront Churches – how to deconstruct the structures and practices that exclude and marginalize so many people. My main concern is with young people, as I believe that, as a Christian community of whatever denomination, we are doing them a huge disservice when we do not attend to the ways in which they experience exclusion from the life of the Church: we are not helping the mission of God to proclaim the Good news and we are not behaving how God, through Jesus, models how we can live. As a final thought, one way forward, towards achieving greater participation of young people in Churches, might be to focus on the role of Church leaders.

Leaders in the Church, I believe, need to be role models for others in how to treat people fairly and equally within the Church and society, and this may be where transformation begins. As Maxine says, 'Many adults in the Church seem to lecture young people rather than treat them as thoughtful, questioning individuals whose exploration can be supported through providing opportunities to explore and reach their own conclusions.' A way forward might be that those training for ordination or reader ministry could be encouraged to think about themselves as role models, and in their training could be provided with the skills to enable them to truly listen to and engage with young people and others within the wider Church whose voices are often silenced or marginalized. If the leader is modelling how to listen, how to treat others with respect, how to encourage others and not simply those the leader likes, it could have a significant impact on the way the congregation responds to the leader and to others in the congregation.

I am grateful to Maxine for her exposition of the idea of an apprenticeship model for thinking about how young people could be mentored in Church and how leaders could be role models. This provides an important point of reference for thinking about the role of leaders (lay or ordained) and how they might facilitate greater participation of young people in Churches. Such a model takes time and energy but, as a youth worker and minister myself, I know that when I have given the time and expended the energy to accompany a young person towards greater participation in the Church, the rewards for that person and for me have been worth it.

Jesus led a diverse group of people, not just his male disciples – women and men, children and young people will have been in the group. However, the disciples behaved as all people do, they disagreed with each other and Jesus. Some of them were arrogant, some rude, some weak, and some strong. In all their diversity, they formed a community, and perhaps Jesus provides an example of how to lead in these situations. He modelled how to live in a community and provided a safe space for people to be themselves, to get things wrong, to make silly decisions and some good ones, and, in all of this, his love for those around him continued. Taking risks to encourage changing the way 'things have always been done' and exploring new ways of being an open, inclusive and welcoming Church is surely to encourage new wine within new wineskins, rather than new wine within old wineskins!

> And no one puts new wine into old wineskins; otherwise, the wine will burst the skins, and the wine is lost, and so are the skins; but one puts new wine into fresh wineskins.[33]

---

[33] Mark 2.22

9 Reflection Towards Inclusion: Using Reflection in Work with Young People

Richard Turner

When the scout group needed some funds, the parents got together to organise a couple of superb fetes which raised a great deal of cash. The parents enjoyed the camaraderie and honed their organisational skills but the scouts were consigned to being 'junior helpers' and quickly lost interest. The scout leader had tactfully to reclaim the fund-raising role, so that the scouts could be encouraged to raise funds by their own efforts, even though they raised less money. They would benefit by learning through first-hand experience.[1]

Taylor includes this scenario as part of a discussion about youth worker and adolescent communication with parents and how to tactfully limit over-involvement by parents to avoid oppression. The scenario also illustrates that inclusion and involvement for one group of people can be exclusion and oppression for others.

Without some form of reflection, it is all too easy to overlook the empowering and educational aspect of young peoples' participation and gratefully encourage the adults' fundraising to the exclusion of the young people. Youngsters may lack the ability to express how they feel and, sensing that the adults may respond with suggestions of ingratitude like, 'don't be silly', which can compound feelings they would prefer not to have, 'voting with their feet' seems understandable. The scout leader has noted the developments, reflected on the situation, recalled the purpose of the work, and intervened on the youngsters' behalf.

The purpose of this chapter is to encourage the reader to reflect and, through scenarios and examples, to illustrate how 'Reflective Practice', the process of experience/reflection/action, can be an approach to inclusive practice with young people.

[1] A. M. Taylor, *Responding to Adolescents* (Lyme Regis: Russell House Publishing, 2003), p. 42.

In youth work, no two incidents are the same. 'There can be no prescriptions for particular situations because the same situation rarely recurs'.[2] '[I]n short there is no neat system by which a worker can learn about different types of behaviour and learn ways of responding to that behaviour.'[3] This is essentially the *raison d'etre* for social practice based on values, principles and ethics, and applying them with thought and reflection to specific situations.

Additionally, as 'people are predisposed to see what is ostensibly the same situation in different ways',[4] you and I will see the same incident filtered through our own lens of experience, values, beliefs, viewpoints, vested interests and presuppositions. In short, the Frames of Reference (FORs) through which our perception and thinking occur effect what and how we think, and how and what we do. This can evolve into favoured repertoires, habitual ways of acting and common sense responses based upon our own perceptions and preferences. If we wish to develop a more inclusive society, then we need to review some of the ideas and practices that our society, and our own constructed unique worlds, are based upon. Beliefs, FORs, preferred roles, repertoires, outdated policies and practice and so forth, all need to undergo regular critical review.[5]

My hope is that the examples illustrated will be critiqued and used to help those working with young people to develop reflective practice in two ways. First, in order to build 'up a repertoire of examples, images, understandings, and actions' so that '[w]hen a practitioner makes sense of a situation he [sic] perceives to be unique, he [sic] sees it as something already present in his [sic] repertoire'.[6] Secondly, 'since practitioners can feel threatened by an idea which directly challenges their own underlying understanding of a situation',[7] the sharing of thoughts and feelings in reflection and analysis of these scenarios will encourage 'a willingness to open up and let go of habitual ways of seeing and doing'.[8]

Theological Reflection and Reflective Practice

Many Christians have favourite Bible verses used at different times for comfort and encouragement. Reflection on verses like, 'I have come that they may have life and have life in abundance' (Jn 10.10); 'If you did it for one of the least of my

---

[2] S. D. Alinsky, *Rules for Radicals: A Pragmatic Primer for Realistic Radicals* (New York: Random House, 1971), p. 138.
[3] G. Wilson and G. Ryland, in Matthews, J. E., *Working With Youth Groups* (London: University of London Press, 1966), p. 102.
[4] J. Bamber, 'Learning, Understanding and the Development of Critical Practice', in *Youth & Policy*, 60 (1998), pp. 30–45 (33).
[5] See J. Bamber for further discussion on FORs and favoured repertoires.
[6] D. A. Schon, *The Reflective Practitioner: How Professionals Think in Action* (New York: Basic Books, 1983) p. 138.
[7] Bamber, 'Learning, Understanding and the Development of Critical Practice', p. 36.
[8] Ibid.

children, you did it for me' (Mt 25.35–45); 'to bring good news to the poor . . .
proclaim liberty to the captives . . . sight to the blind . . . to set free the oppressed
. . .' (Lk. 4.18–19), is one part of theological reflection. For others, these kinds
of themes, biblical or secular, will be the source of motivation and direction of
Christian commitment to action for the oppressed, needy or excluded.

As faith needs works to be useful (Jas 2.20), reflection needs action to be more
than mere thoughts and feelings. It must combine with, and propel us into, active
engagement and immersion with people, individuals, families, communities,
churches and society, in order to challenge, change and transform. Just four words
from Martin Luther King, 'I have a dream . . .' are memorable, but retain their
power because of the actions that followed. Although as Green argues,

> It is important to remember, however, that it would be foolhardy to engage in just any
> old action simply in order to prove ourselves active Christians; we must engage in action
> of faithful quality. But how might we judge that our action is of this standard if not by
> reflection and discernment?[9]

Our actions need a reference point so as not to become cavalier, especially when
feelings are aroused. They need checking to ensure they are sound, ethical, purposeful, loving, empowering, inclusive and transforming. We need to be accountable for our actions and interventions in peoples' lives, even when we have some
form of invitation and permission to intervene, but even more if we do not. In
order to bring about change, reflection will require us to be open to critique and
change of our practice, working towards the development of self *in situ*. It will also
require *reflexivity*, looking inwards at beliefs and value-laden 'luggage' of a deeper
level that affect our actions. Romans 12.2 suggests that we be transformed by the
renewing of our minds.

Laurie Green considers Theological Reflection (TR) as seeking 'to understand
and interpret the world through the eyes of its Christian faith using all the sacramental, creedal and biblical insights that the Church has.'[10] Green explains that
theology is there to serve as a tool in transformation and engagement with people
in their situation, and places TR as a part of the broader task of 'doing theology'.
'This is praxis, a constant marrying of action and reflection, and is key to "doing
theology"'.[11]

Graham et al. outline seven methods of TR, which enable 'the connections
between human dilemmas and divine horizons to be explored'.[12] They draw upon
a wide range of academic disciplines – social sciences, psychotherapy, medical disciplines and so forth – and from among their seven methods of TR, '"Theology-in-
Action": Praxis', is one: the 'knowing that is inseparable from doing' where 'theory

---

[9] L. Green, *Let's Do Theology* (London: Continuum, 1990), p. 100.
[10] Ibid., pp. 11–12.
[11] Ibid., p. 7.
[12] E. Graham, H. Walton and F. Ward, *Theological Reflection: Methods* (London: SCM
Press, 2005).

and practice are inextricably joined', and where 'practice is both the origin and the end of theological reflection, and "talk about God" cannot take place independent of a commitment to a struggle for human emancipation'.[13]

Theological reflection, as praxis, begins with practice, in reflection it draws upon both theology and theory from many academic disciplines, and ends with transformative practice. In this way, it has many similarities with Reflective Practice in the caring professions, which, as praxis, links theory and action in an ongoing process of practice-reflection-practice.

Reflective Practice

Basically, Reflective Practice (RP) is the act of taking a step back to review actions and experiences in order to improve future action. It enables us to look again and make sense of the situations and dilemmas we find ourselves in, to examine our values, beliefs, prejudices, passions, assumptions and preferred viewpoints that influence our decision making.

Janet Batsleer recognizes that the emotions and passions which are powerful motivations for involvement in work with young people often remain hidden. Yet these can and ought to be explored in order to disentangle the worker's motivations and agendas from those of the youngsters. The best way of avoiding imposing personal agendas is to recognize them and offer them up for reflection:

> everyone also has personal passions, preoccupations and prejudices which form a personal agenda. The extent to which these agendas are visible both to the practitioners and to the people with whom they work needs to be a matter for regular reflection. In particular, our ability to recognise and take steps to counter prejudice in ourselves, or to recognise limitations in our knowledge and understanding, is vital.[14]

Batsleer describes reflective practice in terms of 'creating time' and 'creating spaces' for 'a process of creative thinking which involves seeing and engaging from a new point of view'. She goes on to say that 'Creative thinking . . . therefore must involve . . . a letting go of what exists in the present . . . to make room for new forms: a step back from what has been made already in order to see it in a different light, in order to bring about change'.[15]

RP involves a commitment to raising self-awareness, to integrating personal with professional, and, like TR, a commitment to informed and transformative action. In a youth work context, that action must be in the best interests and well-being of young people. This transformation or change may be in ourselves, our practice, our structures, society or in the young people we work with.

---

[13] Ibid., p. 170.
[14] J. R. Batsleer, *Informal Learning in Youth Work* (London: Sage, 2008), p. 38.
[15] Ibid., p. 46.

Models of Reflective Practice

Of the numerous models of RP that can be used to take our work with young people forward, many offer some kind of cyclical approach to reflection.[16] The 'pastoral cycle'[17] developed by liberation theologians and now widely used, evolved from the model used by Fr Joseph Cardijn of 'see, judge and act',[18] and Green's 'pastoral spiral'[19] suggests a process that spirals forward from reflection into action and a new experience. I prefer to see the *process* of reflective practice as a circle which never completely closes; where there is both a spiralling forward and constant growth and understanding which informs and transforms self and situation.[20]

Green's model for 'doing theology' uses *phases* in a cycle of 'Experience', 'Exploration', 'Reflection' and 'Response'.[21] Most models offer *phases* or *stages* of reflection with questions or cues to aid the practitioner. These differ from model to model and have their strengths and weaknesses, yet substantial similarities. They offer a structure or framework to aid the reflection process, but that is all they are – an aid to a process. Familiarity with the different models would allow the worker to adapt a framework, the phases, questions and cues that best assist their process of reflection. Some models focus on learning and some pose questions like, 'what would you do if the situation arose again?'.[22] While these models help in building up a repertoire for future situations and are appropriate if the situation has been resolved, they also seem lacking in a stage if the situation is ongoing or requires further consideration.

Some models encourage reflexivity: the examination of self in relation to the social context or situation.[23] All the models can (or should) be used to lead through from one's own learning and development, change of views, to action, social inclusion or emancipation. Rolfe et al.[24] offer a framework built on Borton's[25] model, further adapted here (Table 1) for youth work, where the *stages* are posed as 'What', 'So what' and 'Now what'.

---

[16] See D. A. Kolb, *Experiential learning: Experience as a source of learning and development* (New Jersey: Prentice Hall, 1984); G. Gibbs, *Learning by Doing: A guide to teaching and learning methods* (Oxford: Further Education Unit, 1988); S. Atkins and K. Murphy, 'Reflective Practice', *Nursing Standard*, 8:39 (1994), pp. 49–56.

[17] Graham et al., *Theological Reflection*, p. 188.

[18] Ibid., p. 183.

[19] Green, *Let's Do Theology*, pp. 24–32.

[20] See YMCA, *Circles of Experience: A Workbook on Spiritual Development* (London: National Council of YMCAs, 1985).

[21] Green, *Let's Do Theology*, pp. 24–32.

[22] Gibbs, *Learning by Doing*.

[23] C. Johns, *Becoming a Reflective Practitioner*, 2nd edn (Oxford: Blackwell, 2004); Bamber, 'Learning, Understanding and the Development of Critical Practice', pp. 30–45.

[24] G. Rolfe, D. Freshwater and M. Jasper, *Critical Reflection for Nursing and the Helping Professions* (Basingstoke: Palgrave, 2001).

[25] T. Borton, *Reach, Teach and Touch* (London: McGraw Hill, 1970).

Table 1   Model of Reflective Practice: 'What, So What, Now What'

Descriptive level of reflection	Theology, Theory, knowledge-building level of reflection	Action-orientated (reflexive) level of reflection
What ... → ↖	So what ... →	Now what ... ↵
← ... is the problem/difficulty/ reason for being stuck/reason for feeling bad/reason we don't get on/etc., etc.?	← ... does this tell me/teach me/ imply/mean about me/the youngster(s)/others/our relationship/our care for YP/ the model of work I am using/ my attitudes/the youngsters attitudes/etc., etc.?	← ... do I need to do in order to make things better/stop being stuck/improve my work with young people/resolve the situation/feel better/get on better/ etc., etc.?
... was my role in the situation? ... was I trying to achieve? In terms of young people's growth, inclusion, learning, empower-ment, relationships, skill ... actions did I take? ... was the response of others?	... was going through my mind as I acted? ... did I base my actions on? ... ethics, values, beliefs, ... theology, theory knowledge can I bring to the situation from youth work, law, social sciences, experiential, personal.	... what options are open to me? ... broader issues need to be considered if this action is to be successful? ... might be the consequences of this action? ... idea, phrase, prayer, or passion will motivate me into action?
... were the consequences · for the youngster(s)? · for myself? · for others? ... feelings did it evoke · in the youngster(s)? · in myself? · in others?	from my beliefs, Bible, God, Christian & professional colleagues, history? ... could/should I have done to make it better?	... can I now do to move this forward? (now do it !)
... was good/bad about the experience?	... is my new understanding of the situation? ... broader issues arise from the situation?	

The stages of 'What?', 'So what?', and 'Now what?' are sequential and cyclical. The 'What?' stage is to reflect on the experience/situation in order to describe it and become conscious of it. The 'So what?' stage is key, and draws the worker into analysis and exploration in order to learn, bring clarity and make sense of the situation. The 'Now what?' stage is to evaluate action the options, appropriateness, possible consequences and affect on others. It may involve bold action or gentle presence, but not analysis paralysis. A judgement is now made as to which action is best – what does the situation, the youngsters, God, require me to do? If it is a big task, what smaller steps can I take to move this forward?

Moving outside of our comfort zones can feel threatening, particularly when we understand that these processes can lead to challenging colleagues, churches, organizations and structures. However, the process of TR and RP needs to begin somewhere, and as 'Learning begins with that which immediately confronts the learner',[26] maybe the starting place for reflection on work with young people is with whatever immediately confronts the youth worker. Borton's model is simple and progressive, 'What?', 'So what?' and 'Now what?', and can be used to move reflection through the process into the final stage of 'how can I take this forward?' 'What do I do next?' Exploring Scenario 1 (below) may illuminate the process.

Scenario 1

'Frank is living with his grandma' was the last sentence/line I wrote on my record-ings that night. It had been a stressful evening involving young people with guns coming into the youth centre. Later in the evening I had gone over to the coffee bar for a cuppa.

Rosie, behind the counter, was a caring and helpful source of information – she took an interest in the young people that came to the coffee bar and listened well. Frank had told her earlier that evening that he was 'living with his grandma now'. During my cuppa, Rosie relayed the story to me. I didn't think too much about it at the time, preoccupied with the prior gun incidents.

After the club closed, I wrote a long reflective recording about the guns incidents, the youngsters involved and the possible follow-ups and conversations that might be needed in response to the incidents. Ending, I paused briefly to think about other things that I had seen or heard that night and wrote my final sentence. 'Frank is liv-ing with his grandma.'

No reflection, just a small piece of information, a piece of a jigsaw – I had no idea where it fit.

A few days later, Miriam (a caring, part-time youth worker and gymnast) was running a gym class; she came out of the gym frustrated and annoyed saying 'Frank is creating havoc, he's running around, getting in the way when they're on the equip-ment, it's dangerous. I've told him to bring his gym kit, but he doesn't even bring his trainers, he's still got his school uniform and shoes on, he's doing it on purpose . . . ' During a pause I cut in saying 'Frank is living with his grandmother – maybe she can't afford to buy him a gym outfit.'

Miriam, hands on her mouth, froze – no words or movement. She stared through me in thought, turned, and went back into the gym. There was no need for me to follow; Miriam would deal with it.

The following week, I looked in on the gym class. Frank was there, lined up chat-ting with the other youngsters, waiting to do his exercises on the vaulting horse, but now dressed in a clean pressed set of T-shirt and shorts and a new pair of trainers.[27]

From this scenario, numerous questions can be posed and issues explored. Peer groups, the ethics of charity, the wider poverty issue, the safety of the group

[26] B. Rosseter, 'Youth Workers as Educators', in T. Jeffs and M. Smith (eds), *Youth Work* (London: Macmillan Education / BASW, 1987), p. 53.
[27] Summarized session recording of a youth worker.

over and against concern for the individual. Does disruption continue? Does the structure of the activity need rethinking? Why is he living with his grandma? Do we speak with Frank? All these concerns are worthy of a lengthy discussion in themselves; my intention is to touch on some of these areas as examples of how RP can begin to be applied towards enabling a more inclusive approach to work with young people. So what areas in the scenario need further consideration? And how can we apply the cycle of reflection?

Elements of the beginnings of reflection can be gleaned from a first reading of this scenario. 'What?' Franks behaviour, recognition of the danger to others, Miriam's frustration, her unease with the situation, a possible dilemma of whether to ban or not to ban Frank, Miriam's seeking of advice.

'So what?' Miriam gains more information, considers a wider issue, has a new understanding, draws on her values or beliefs, reconsiders her approach.

'Now what?' She decides to supply the kit and does it.

One could say 'so far so good'. However, the spiral never really ends, and the 'What?' begins again. Frank's behaviour has changed and he is included. Workers have both noted and considered an individual's need among other major concerns at the centre, and there has been collaboration between staff. The recording by the full-time worker has helped recall and identify a possible cause for the problem. A small piece of information about Frank had, I believe, widened Miriam's frame of reference and caused her to make a small paradigm shift of *seeing differently*. Miriam then acted within her own values or beliefs by helping to relieve poverty through a charitable act. This kindness appears, at least in the short term, to have resolved the situation and enabled inclusion.

The key stage now is the 'So what?' where the worker needs to draw down knowledge and theory in order to analyse and build the level of reflection. Sometimes that 'knowledge' is latent and just needs drawing out, sometimes workers need to learn it. Knowledge and theory that we can bring to this stage of reflection can raise awareness; *seeing differently* can lead to new ways of thinking and acting. Reflecting on a particular experience, Covey noted that

'Suddenly I *saw* things differently, and because I *saw* differently, I *thought* differently, . . . *felt* differently . . . *behaved* differently. My irritation vanished . . . . My heart was filled with the [youngsters'] pain. Feelings of sympathy and compassion flowed freely'.[28]

It is in this area of *seeing differently* that youth work begins to flourish. It is essential to the development of both staff and young people that workers aspire to gain deeper insights into their work. Youth work is not just about activities or provision. Anne Foreman made this clear discussing 'Youth Workers as Redcoats'.[29] It is about developing a meaningful relationship within which youth workers seek to engage with young people in purposeful experiences, reflection, and learning,

---

[28] S. Covey, *The 7 Habits of Highly Effective People* (London: Simon & Schuster 1989), p. 31.
[29] Foreman, A., 'Youth Workers as Redcoats', in T. Jeffs and M. Smith, (eds), *Youth Work* (London: Macmillan Education Ltd / BASW, 1987), pp. 12–24.

through which they can examine their values and moral judgements and make informed decisions. It is holistic; concern about their welfare in body, mind and spirit. It seeks to help young people develop through conversation and experiences.[30] It is concerned with the process involved of working *with* youngsters as much as the outcome.[31] It is built on four key principles of equality of opportunity, empowerment, participation and informal learning, all of which require an inclusive attitude and approach. It includes them in the decisions that affect their lives. It begins where young people are, accepts them for who they are, and offers a safe space to be what they are – young people. Activities, then, are just a vehicle through which youth work begins.

Workers need to reflect a little more on their role and the purpose of their work. They need to build relationships with young people so that youngsters feel able to ask for help, learn to listen to youngsters through layers of behaviour and help them develop through participation and learning.

Adolescence derives from the Latin verb *adoare* – 'to grow up'. This growth period is greater than any other period of life after birth and involves biological, physiological, psychological and emotional changes. In a conversation with some youngsters, a youth worker once likened teenage emotions to a volcano. Later, one of the youngsters relayed this with the words 'it's a time of strong *eruptions*! like when it all gets bottled up, you gets lots of feelings in you 'n it just explodes'.[32]

The time of adolescence is also accompanied with dramatic changes to the body: accelerations in height and weight, surges of hormones and so forth.[33] Such changes affect identity, and young people become extremely self-conscious and self-critical. They begin loosening ties with parents, and as they move towards autonomy the desire to be with peers becomes intense, along with the desire to have the same clothes, shoes, music and so forth, with conformity often maintained by the exclusion of those who do not conform.[34]

Some youth workers can recall youngsters whose need to be accepted by their peers means that they will accept the role of joker, mischief-maker or even scapegoat – the butt of putdowns – in order to remain part of a group; any role will do. For some, it is better to be excluded for bad behaviour by an adult than to be rejected by peers.

Peer groups contribute to the social construction of identity, and a consequence of the absence of good relationships with parents can be the compensatory

[30] G. Ingram and J. Harris, *Delivering Good Youth Work* (Dorset: Russell House Publishing, 2001), p. 10.

[31] K. Young, *The Art of Youth Work* (Dorset: Russell House Publishing, 1999).

[32] Teenager – from personal experience.

[33] For further discussion, see J. C. Coleman, *The Nature of Adolescence* (London: Methuen, 1980), pp. 12–17; J. Linden, *Understanding Children & Young People* (London: Hodder Arnold, 2007), pp. 243–57.

[34] J. Head, *Working with Adolescents: Constructing Identity* (London: Falmer Press, Taylor & Francis, 2002), p. 30.

dependence on peers.[35] Unfortunately, other studies indicate that this can create a knock-on effect: lack of good parenting can lead to peer rejection, and peer rejection can predict delinquency and school drop-out in adolescence.[36] Poverty, too, can exasperate exclusion from social experiences and relationships that are available to more affluent youngsters.[37] Fitting in and taking part in activities are important to young people's social participation and development.

There appears to be an interplay of parents, peers and poverty that influence youngsters' inclusion, and all three could be related to Franks' situation. The lack of parental attachment can lead to exclusion from peer groups when inclusion is needed most.[38] Even when family relationships are good, poverty and lack of resources in low-income families for transport, equipment, and entry fees and so forth restricts the opportunity to develop the friendships and social networks youngsters need. Clothing and fashion, whether we as adults like this or not, comprise a key issue for young peoples' sense of esteem, inclusion and acceptance among peers.[39]

Frank's words and behaviour must 'ring bells'. Workers need to be aware of possible signs of exclusion relating to poverty and parental attachment, and the consequences of banning young people. Youth workers need to listen to and make note of both words and behaviour, while at the same time not assuming that the *eruptions* of young people are anything more than part of adolescence. Empathy, tolerance, listening and understanding can be as inclusive as participation in an activity.

Extending work towards greater social inclusion with young people, like Frank, may involve the youth worker contacting families and other agencies. But, 'In the rush to combat social exclusion, children have sometimes been left behind as participants'.[40] Before contacting other agencies, we need to reflect on one of the ethical principles in youth work: 'Respect and promote young people's rights to make their own decisions and choices, unless the welfare or legitimate interests

[35] Ibid., p. 29.

[36] L. F. Katz citing research by Ladd, Price and Hart 1990 and Coie, Lochman and Terry, in Katz, L. F. 'Living in a Hostile World: Toward an Integrated Model of Family, Peer, and Physiological Processes in Aggressive Preschoolers' in K. A. Kerns, J. M. Contreras and A. M. Neal-Barnett, (eds), *Family and Peers – Linking Two Social Worlds* (London and Westport: Praeger, 2000), pp. 115–36 (124).

[37] T. Ridge, 'Childhood poverty: a barrier to social participation and inclusion', in E. K. M. Tisdall, J. M. Davis, M. Hill and A. Prout, *Children, Young People and Social Inclusion – Participation for What?* (Bristol: The Policy Press, 2006), pp. 23–38 (23).

[38] J. M. Contreras and K. A. Kerns, 'Emotion Regulation Processes: Explaining Links between Parent-Child Attachment and Peer Relationships', in K. A. Kerns, J. M. Contreras and A. M. Neal-Barnett (eds), *Family and Peers – Linking Two Social Worlds* (Westport & London: Praeger, 2000), pp. 1–26 (2).

[39] Ridge, 'Childhood poverty', pp. 24–9.

[40] J. M. Davis and M. Hill, 'Introduction', in E. K. M. Tisdall, J. M. Davis, M. Hill and A. Prout, *Children Young People and Social Inclusion: Participation for What?* (Bristol: Policy Press, 2006), pp. 1–22 (5–6).

of themselves or others are seriously threatened'.[41] There may be times when we need to act without youngsters permission; even so, we can still consult and be accountable to them. In scenario 1 the response to the question 'how do I take this forward?' has to include: 'ask Frank'.

Ethical principles like these need to be reflected upon during our work with young people, particularly if we are considering discussing a youngster's family situation with others. If not, we, too, can be party to exclusion and of contravening the UN Convention on the Rights of the Child – the right to have a say about decisions that affect them (Article 12) and the right to privacy (Article 16).

Social exclusion is multi-dimensional, and our 'So what?' reflection stage needs to draw upon a range of understandings to ensure that responses enable young peoples' inclusion:

- Understanding the purpose of youth work; adolescent development, the importance that peer groups play in belonging and socializing.
- The importance of sound and caring adults/parents willing to see differently and listen with understanding to young people's words and actions.
- Enabling participation in activities – which may involve subsidies; recognizing the power structures that can lead to exclusion – access, money, equipment, age and so forth – which restricts where they can go and what they can do.
- Extending their inclusion into organizing and decision making to enable their growth, abilities and confidence, and their participation in the decisions that affect their lives.
- Challenging bullying and exclusion from peers, and challenging the social mores and commodification of young people that affect their inclusion.
- Reflecting that, it can be argued, biblical themes highlight the need for a more inclusive approach to the young, poor, helpless, marginalized and excluded.

The final 'Now what?' stage is to focus on how to take this forward. From the scenario, I suggest that the full-time worker needs to take the initiative. By encouraging Rosie and Miriam to continue listening and to establish a process that would enable them to develop their reflective skills and to review programme structures towards inclusion. And if the 'Now what?' includes 'Ask Frank', it is also appropriate to consider who asks. It is a sensitive issue involving the need to consider the young person's dignity and respect. The importance of a good relationship with the youngster may be the guide as to who does this and how this is done.

Internal Work

If we 'ask Frank', he may say 'No', he may not want anyone contacting his grandma or visiting his home. He may feel he has the emotional support and practical

---

[41] NYA. *Ethical Conduct in Youth Work: a statement of values and principles* (Leicester: The National Youth Agency, 2004).

equipment he needs for now. We may not like that response and may feel the need to do more. These are our feelings and our needs and should be taken into critical reflection. There is a danger that we impose our values and feelings into the situation and so some inner work on ourselves to explore our feelings and motives may be needed. Many of the reflective practice models make provision for this.

Mary Crosby's work on 'extending ourselves' and 'the work of attention'[42] may be useful here. I include extracts from Crosby's case studies as examples of 'extending' and 'attending', first from someone named as 'J', working with a group of young women involved in prostitution.

> The behaviour of S and her friends was at odds with J's own beliefs and values. However J realised that she had little understanding or appreciation of how they saw and felt about themselves and their situation and it was important for her to learn about this from S and her friends. . . .
>
> We can see from this example how J's commitment to "extending herself" made it possible for her to work *with* these young women as opposed to working *on* them . . . J's internal work of managing her own values and feelings meant that she was not so much looking *at* the young women "but looking *with* them at what they are seeking to communicate".[43]

Secondly, of 'M' who was working with a group of young men, where 'M' becomes frustrated with the group because they didn't respond to activities that she thought would be useful to them. Reflecting on this through supervision, 'M' realizes that this was

> more about what *she* needed in order to feel that she was achieving something . . . I realised that I was always coming up with my own agenda for them and not actually taking time to find out theirs. I need to spend more time doing their normal activities with them, trying to understand them better.[44]

Crosby makes clear that this can be hard work and that it is easier to stay within our comfort zones and preconceptions, believing we know what youngsters need and not really attending to those we work with. Fear of working with uncertainty and needing a package to deliver often drives this.[45] It can neglect their participation and focus on certificates distributed, boxes ticked or even bums on pews, rather than the longer task of being with and learning about young people, their

---

[42] M. Crosby, 'Working with people as an informal educator', in L. D. Richardson and M. Wolfe, *Principles and Practice of Informal Education* (London: Routledge, 2001), pp. 54–60.

[43] Ibid., pp. 55–6. Crosby quotes from T. Jeffs and M. Smith. *Informal Education – conversation, democracy and learning.* (Derby: Education Now Books with YMCA George Williams College, 1996), p. 19.

[44] Ibid., p. 57.

[45] Ibid., pp. 56–9.

concerns and problems. At its worst, it can have ethical implications, when projects need funds to keep staff employed. The drive towards achievement and outcomes in line with government agencies' requirements make demands on workers that draw them toward a 'tick box' agenda, and the original focus on youngsters fades into the background. Funding becomes the 'tail that wags the dog'.

The Gospels arguably show that Christ didn't just talk about the Kingdom, but also engaged with people's lives by going to homes for meals, bedsides of the sick, walking alongside people and by going fishing with his friends. Being with people allowed new engagements and conversations to emerge, where 'Kingdom values' were shown, shared and debated (e.g. Lk 14.7–14). On some occasions, Jesus goes against the norms of the day, of not 'ticking the right boxes', spending time with the marginalized and upsetting the status quo (Mt 9.10–13; 12.1–14).

Getting youngsters through programmes can become a production line, but often it stems from a lack of understanding of youngsters' needs. In the following scenario, we can glimpse how the focus on outcomes can cloud the awareness of need. We also see how 'L' (a youth work student) recognizes the strength of his feelings arising from this situation and uses recordings and supervision to ensure his feelings don't cloud his decisions.

Scenario 2

I was on placement at a project that works with young adults with learning difficulties. One of our members, 'R', was offered a chance to go on a training programme for young adults run by another agency. He attended for a few days then became upset. We eventually found out that some of the others were skitting at him because he couldn't keep up with the report writing. I was fuming! I just wanted to punch their lights out – not only had we worked hard to get 'R' to go and reassured him it would be ok, he was looking forward to it. But then he was getting putdowns and snide remarks from some of the others 'cause he couldn't understand some of the writing tasks, and the staff just seemed to ignore it. I was just mad.

Lucky for them – my fieldwork supervisor made me write down how I felt and to think of other ways I could sort it out. I ended up doing loads of recordings and had a couple of meetings with my supervisor and tutor and realized they weren't trained youth workers and may not be aware of what was going on. In the end I suggested that we get another student, as part of his fieldwork, to accompany 'R' as a kind of mentor/advocate, to help 'R' with form filling and his journal. I chatted this over with 'R' who thought it would be helpful and then talked about it with the agency staff, and everybody agreed.

With a mentor alongside him, the skitting stopped, the staff seemed more aware of his learning needs and with some guidance on his journal 'R' was able to keep up and got his certificate at the end. We were all pleased, and I was pleased how I had sorted it out – but I still wanted to punch their lights out![46]

---

[46] Student reflections on the benefits of recording and supervision.

The RP cycle can be seen in operation as 'L' identifies the 'What?' – how the youngster feels, the agency's approach and his anger. In the 'So what?' he recognizes his feelings, records, uses supervision, consults and discusses it with the youngster. He draws upon knowledge and understanding and gains objectivity and direction. Finally for the 'Now what?' he considers the options, formulates an idea and makes a constructive proposal to the agency and gains agreement from all involved. It seems to transform a difficult situation, the agency becomes more aware of the youngster's needs and adapts their usual practice, leading to a more inclusive approach and positive outcome for the youngster. Reflective practice really can make a difference to the work of the practitioner (the acts of aggression were curtailed!), but also, and more importantly, to the lives of young people.

New Staff, New Perspective, New Approach: Further Reflections

Sometimes it may need a change in staff before change can take place, someone new arriving with a new perspective, someone who can see and think differently and who can motivate others with a vision of what is possible. A changeover in staff at the Sighthill Library in Edinburgh led to a change from the punitive banning of young people to a more inclusive approach to engaging with them. With new colleagues in place, the staff at the library set out to discover what the young people would like from the library and gradually offered different facilities.[47] The narrative, taken from Linden below, illustrates another example of the way reflective practice, delivering new perspectives, can make a difference to the lives of young people.

> The library service at Sighthill in Edinburgh had suffered from an increasing amount of antisocial behaviour involving young people. The staff team, together with a number of key partners, tackled problems head on by adopting an inclusive and ground-breaking approach to working with excluded children and teenagers. From being plagued by disruptive behaviour . . . and vandalism, they . . . engaged more positively with young people. Together with many partners, including Lothian and Borders Police and the Duke of Edinburgh Award Scheme, they delivered a programme of . . . IT and arts activities . . . a Computer Crazies Club, a football literacy project and graffiti arts events. Since then, the trouble in the area has dropped dramatically – a 60% reduction in recorded antisocial incidents in the community and the library . . . The project successfully removed barriers that were contributing to the social exclusion of young people in Sighthill, giving them the opportunity to access services that have helped them to develop reading, literacy, learning and life skills.[48]

While the stages of the RP process can be seen – that is, identifying the problems, consulting with youngsters and other agencies, drawing upon knowledge, theory and so forth – considering the options and implementing them, enquiries about the library reveal that success involved the attitude and dedication of the staff,

---

[47] Linden, *Understanding Children and Young People*, p. 14.
[48] Ibid.

intensive training in dealing with anger and aggression, consultation with organizations and a commitment to building relationships.

A vision was necessary, but trying to consider all the necessities in advance can lead to analysis paralysis, fear, or the return to one's preferred ways of responding. RP, used appropriately, can bring feelings of fear out to be viewed, identify resources of knowledge and advice and, from the options revealed, identify the one, next step, to move forward. Asking the youngsters seems to be the chosen first step again. Engaging with unruly youngsters can be quite fearful, yet it is inclusive in itself. Their participation in the planning process also means they can be involved in shaping the vision and begin to become part of the solution.

In describing change, it is easy to remember how bad things were (the problem), and how much better it is now (the outcome). The middle stage is often glossed over and the RP process is not always clear. I think this is the case with both the previous and following scenarios. While they give a vision of what inclusive practice is possible, to build our understanding, we need to spend time considering what may have happened in the middle stage of the cycle. Visualizing how experience, theory, knowledge and so forth was drawn upon, as were the processes of consultation and persuasion upwards through management and outwards to colleagues and clients, and imagining smaller daily cycles of reflection that bring about small steps towards transformation.

Sometimes bringing about change may require appealing against adult decisions and challenging them to think again. This may need a thought-out approach, compelling arguments and diplomacy.

Mark Yaconelli describes how the leaders of a Church in Valparaiso, Indiana, were faced with a crisis involving skateboarders and decided to ban them from the church grounds. Acting as advocates on behalf of the skateboarders, the youth ministry team decided to appeal to the church leaders to change their minds and reverse their decision.

> It seemed the [pavements] . . . parking lot and . . . steps of the church had become a popular gathering place for local teen skaters. Every day kids in baggy clothes and . . . baseball caps pushed their wheels' and flipped their boards 'across the church sidewalks' and property. Locals became 'Upset by the damage to the church property, [and] the church leadership decided to replace the steps, install protective devices into the cement to prevent skating and post signs outlawing loitering and skateboarding.
>
> The 'youth director' and other adults supporting the youth ministry, all of whom had been seeking ways to serve the kids in the community, went to the church leadership to ask them to reconsider their decision. 'They asked if the leadership might see the presence of the youth as a blessing' and instead of asking them to leave, find ways to develop and deepen relationships with them.
>
> 'After weeks of prayer and discernment, the church decided to reverse its decision. It left the crumbling and scuffed cement steps and removed the signs outlawing skateboarders and loitering'. The church leaders met with the skaters, told them they 'were welcome to skate on the church property' and that they 'were welcome to use the other church facilities as well. They gave the kids a tour of the church', showed them where

the toilets and kitchen were and took them 'into the church office and introduced them to the staff'.[49]

Yaconelli describes a picture of kids skating up the steps, twirling their boards in acrobatic feats of life and energy; of the church secretaries and pastoral staff stopping to say hello, chat and applaud skaters demonstrating difficult spins; of youngsters running in and out of the church to get water and use the bathroom and to see what it means to share the presence of Jesus with young people.[50]

Some interesting aspects arise in this scenario: not only are the elders asked to reverse their decision, but they are also asked to see things differently, to see the youngsters as a blessing, not a problem, as an opportunity to build relationships with them and to consider inclusive attitudes as well as practice. An inappropriate challenge from the ministry team could have caused the elders to dig their heels in. I believe that the youth ministry team also spent considerable time in the middle stage reflecting on how they would go about appealing, persuading and presenting their case on behalf of the youngsters, drawing on theology, theory and understanding, prayer and patience – we can only speculate. It also appears to have taken several weeks of prayer and reflection by the elders – reflecting in the middle stage – before they reversed their decision and made further inclusive steps of unlocking their minds and hearts, the car park and steps, and the church and toilets – a courageous step of inclusion.

Skateboarding areas often become a meeting place for peers and friends; it's a place to sit and be. Safe public spaces, under some kind of watchful eye of sympathetic adults, are scarce. Spaces like the one offered by the church need protecting.

Conclusion

Monica Barry believes there is now a 'major opportunity to turn the problem of "youth" on its head and to question the extent to which "adults" – their attitudes, policies and practices – ignore and exacerbate, rather than resolve, the problem of young peoples' social exclusion'.[51]

It is exasperating that, in addition to working with demanding young people, youth workers also have to work hard with other adults to get them to reflect and remove some of the barriers. Enabling reflection in adults is needed to bring about the seeing, feeling and doing differently required for them to move towards youngsters' greater inclusion. Youth workers must make a sustained commitment to reflective practice and develop the understanding and awareness to transform their work, and to develop insights into their own internal worlds of fears, passions,

---

[49] Adapted from M. Yaconelli, *Contemplative Youth Ministry: practising the presence of Jesus with young people* (London: SPCK, 2006), pp. 178–9.
[50] Ibid., p.179.
[51] M. Barry, (ed.), *Youth Policy and Social Inclusion: critical debates with young people* (London: Routledge, 2005), p. 1.

beliefs and intuitions to transform any inner baggage into inner resources: the development of self *and* situ. Yaconelli argues that,

'Study after study in the field of youth work makes it clear that the single most important thing that can make a positive difference in the life of a young person is the presence of a caring adult. In spite of that, research shows that most young people don't have enough caring adults in their lives'.[52]

Young people need sound adults as much as they need their peers, especially as they move towards independence. Adults need to be able to guide, listen, include, and encourage youngsters' independence and at the same time be willing to reflect and grow themselves and be mindful that they have the power, resources, access, ability and the keys to the kingdom. However, the starting point must begin with young peoples' agendas. We need to find ways to remove the barriers that maintain their exclusion, overcome the fear of making the first move towards them, begin engaging in their interests, hopes and fears in order to understand, learn from and be with them. We need to include them in programmes at a planning and decision level so they can feel ownership of the projects they participate in, and at the same time develop the skills, capacities and resilience that enable their future inclusion.

I. Response to Richard Turner

John Richardson

Richard's chapter is both refreshing and challenging in engaging in a very difficult area of enquiry – the relationship between work with young people and the need for this work to bring about 'inclusion'. It is his central assertion, that Reflective Practice (RP) and/or Theological Reflection (TR) can be an essential component of any form of work with young people, I wish to explore. It could be argued that RP and TR are different and that, perhaps, we ought not to confuse one with the other. This difference lies in the number and type of 'Voices' involved in the reflection – a point to which I will return.

However, for the moment, a difficulty both RP and TR face in this age of 'Managerialism'[53] is a tendency to be aligned with 'targeted work', 'measured or learning outcomes' and 'evidence-based approaches', not only in practice, but also in the field of education and training of anyone who works with young people. It is inevitable, perhaps, that the whole arena of 'relationships' using 'interpersonal knowledge and skills' will be brought under the microscope to identify the 'product' of such a labour intensive and expensive activity. Although, as Richard argues that this kind of work may be a 'process', rather than a product – there is still some expectation of a 'positive or identifiable outcome', in our case, 'inclusion'. This way

---

[52] Yaconelli, *Contemplative Youth Ministry*, p. 2.

[53] M. Exworthy and S. Halford (eds), *Professionals and the New Managerialism in the Public Sector* (Buckingham: Open University Press, 1999).

of looking at work with people, and especially with young people, may be a product of 'Rationality',[54] a product of approaching work with people from a 'reason-based' or 'scientific perspective'.[55] This can lead to other criteria, associated with this perspective, such as efficiency, effectiveness, value for money, productivity, fit for purpose, quality assurance and so forth – all value-laden and yet all, apparently, morally and ethically, neutral.

Richard suggests that reflection on practice will enable workers to identify what impediments may exist to restrict the process of inclusion. He argues that this approach already exists in notions of anti-discriminatory or anti-oppressive practice in other forms of intervention, such as health, social work and community work. The assumption is that through reviewing the practice of services to minority or disadvantaged groups, practitioners will be able to 'reach' those members of the community who do not, for whatever reason, access services fully.

This is perceived to be a 'good thing', as traditionally 'poor people get poor services', and yet the whole concept of 'inclusion' may be in itself problematic, given that we live in an era of 'postmodernism'[56] or even 'altermodernism'.[57] This implies that the very institutions that can support 'inclusion' – family, community, work, society, school, church, and so forth – are themselves being eroded and so cease to be as important as they once were.[58] It is against this backdrop that we should consider 'inclusion' and what kind of 'inclusion' is possible – what are people being included into?

Richard suggests that 'inclusion' may be facilitated by the use of RP or TR in the practice of those working with young people, and yet this reflection is a journey into the mind, feelings, attitude, beliefs and values of the worker. It is a journey of introspection and self-exploration. As Richard asserts,

> It is in this area of 'seeing differently' that youth work begins to flourish. It is essential to the development of both staff and young people that workers aspire to gain deeper insights into their work. [p. 166]

This 'seeing differently', gaining 'deeper insights into their work', becomes more than reflection; it creates 'reflexivity'[59] in which the thinking and knowing 'subject' (the worker), contemplates an 'object' (the practice of work). If we apply this to the concept of inclusion we have the subject (the worker) contemplating his/her values, beliefs, ethics and so forth about inclusion in and of themselves, and the object (the practice of work) that must in some way incorporate the values

---

[54] Z. Bauman, *Liquid Modernity* (Oxford: Blackwell, 2000).

[55] P. Bourdieu, *Science of Science and Reflexivity* (Cambridge: Polity Press, 2004).

[56] Bauman, *Liquid Modernity*.

[57] N. Bourriaud, 'Altermodern', in Gaskin, Fiona and McSwein, Kirsteen (eds), *Altermodern: Exhibition Guide* (London: Tate Publishing, 2009).

[58] Bauman, *Liquid Modernity* and P. Ward, *Youthwork and the Mission of God* (London: SPCK, 1997).

[59] A. Giddens, *Sociology*, 5th edn (Cambridge, UK, Malden, MA: Polity, 2009), p. 123.

and so forth of the subject, and at the same time effect some kind of change in the nature of inclusion in the world. This separation of subject and object can lead to the 'objectification', 'typification' and the 'commodification'[60] of the practice and, of course, of the young person. The young person becomes something to be 'worked on' on a 'cost benefit analysis', the approach becoming more actuarial in 'risk assessment and so forth' rather than by a thinking, breathing, sentient, complicated and complex human being!

This could be fairly straightforward in terms of state-sponsored youth work, but it becomes more problematic if we look at Christian Youth Work, which, on the surface at least, would seem to include wider concerns and models of 'being human', the person, based in incarnation, redemption and resurrection.

To add to this, and as suggested above, it is important to recognize the presence of 'Voices' that echo and resonate in the construction of RP, TR and FOR's. Indeed, in Richard's chapter there are a number of 'voices' – Green and Batsleer (representing Schon) already identified, and one could identify other 'voices' – from the academic disciplines, from the profession itself and from the policy makers and managers. Thus, 'reflection' is not a monologue, but a number of dialogues; indeed, it is a collection of conversations based around the nature of the subject (the worker; who or what is he/she exactly?) and around the nature of the object (the practice; what exactly is the work?).

For example, is there a voice of 'professional practice' of work that speaks of the embodiment of theories of appropriate knowledge, of values and ethics, indeed that has a degree of 'objectivity' in identifying a 'human subject' upon whom the 'practitioner can reflect'? One could argue that a dominant Voice is that of 'the Professional'.

In all of these developments, the reality of the lives of workers and young people are represented as if both the human being and the human activity can be viewed as objects, we begin to approach the debate 'objectively' and, indeed, we begin to take the subjectivity of 'being human' out of the equation. If we take this further it could be argued that the very process of reflective practice is an attempt to 'control' and 'limit' the possible discourses around the practice itself. If we wish to challenge this, then we need to ask four kinds of questions:

- 'who' the 'worker' may 'be'? – is an ontological question;
- 'how' they know what they do? – is an epistemological question;
- 'what' they do? – is a methodological question;
- and 'what kind of inclusion'? – is a political question.

There is not the space to develop these questions fully, but it is important to understand that they are not sequential, but rather are constantly interacting with one another in almost a circular fashion. However, if we examine them briefly

---

[60] R. H. Roberts, *Religion, Theology and the Human Sciences* (Cambridge: Cambridge University Press, 2002).

- the ontological question; we are faced with a question of what is the 'being' in human being – the 'being' that is active in youth work, and of course, if we reflect theologically, there is the question of the 'being' of God, immanent or transcendent, involved in this reflection. How is the 'being' or 'Being of God' encountered in this reflection, and how can we conceptualize this activity?
- this leads to the second question – if we accept that God is at work, then how do we know that God is at work? It is an epistemological question, in that we are to ask, how do we know that we know. Other epistemologies are available!
- the methodological question is identified in asking what methods do youth workers use to 'find out', to seek 'facts' that can be constructed as evidence for what they know.

These questions collide when we explore the political question through a quotation that Richard himself uses:

Study after study in the field of youth work makes it clear that the single most important thing that can make a positive difference in the life of a young person is the presence of a caring adult.[61]

There are a number of issues around this 'caring adult' and their role in the life of a young person. It is suggested that the 'caring adult' has a role to play in bringing about a positive difference, but we are left wondering what the implication may be if this 'caring adult' is not present in the lives of young people. What kind of 'inclusion' is enabled by the act of 'Care'? It may be that the 'work' of the 'caring adult' is practised over a number of fields with different specialism – youth workers' specialism being 'youngsters' – and the very definition of the specialism determines some answers to the questions suggested above.

For youth workers, Richard argues that this 'caring adult' is

developing a meaningful relationship within which youth workers seek to engage with young people in purposeful experiences, reflection, and learning, through which they can examine their values and moral judgements and make informed decisions. It is holistic – concerned about their welfare in body, mind and spirit. It seeks to help young people develop through conversation and experiences.

It is concerned with the 'process' involved of working with youngsters as much as the outcome.

The 'caring adult' finds expression in 'meaningful relationship', but one would need other terms – 'engage, purposeful, informed, body, mind and spirit, help, process and outcome' – to be clearly demarcated and defined to be more than a 'good thing' that speaks for itself or that it is 'common sense'.[62] If we put all these issues and challenges into Richard's concept of 'Frames of Reference' we can begin to see that the terrain of debate is there to be captured by dominant voices, and it

[61] M. Yaconelli, *Contemplative Youth Ministry: practising the presence of Jesus with young people* (London: SPCK, 2006), p. 2.
[62] P. Bourdieu, *Language & Symbolic Power* (Cambridge: Polity, 2009).

is here that we can see the difference in reflective practice belonging to the professional youth worker and theological reflection belonging to the practical theologian. These differences are not only internal, in that there are different voices
involved in the construction of the discourse, but also external, if the outcome is
some form of action. As Richard argues,

> reflection needs action to be more than mere thoughts and feelings. It [reflection] must
> combine with, and propel us into, active engagement and immersion with people, indivi-
> duals, families, communities, churches and society, in order to challenge, change and
> transform. [p. 160]

If, as I suggest above, the very institutional 'solids' of the 'social world' – individuals, families, communities, churches and society are melting, how are we to
find the language to account for this 'new relationship' created by engagement and
immersion? How does this relationship connect with challenge, change and transformation, if it is not to be located within the current structure?

In order to try to explain this dynamic and organic activity, many writers argue
that the language of science is inadequate to describe 'cause and effect' in terms of
this 'relationship'. There is no simple 'cause and effect' – *if we do this, then this will
happen*... Perhaps, in this context, we cannot predict anything, and indeed it has
always been impossible to predict – we just assumed that we could!

Maybe if we begin to use the language of art and art forms, we may find some
possibilities. If we 'see' work with young people as an artistic activity and the 'FOR'
of art as more appropriate, then we can begin to recognize that in these reflections
there is a listener – a hearer – one who listens to the voices identified above. This
'hearer' is us as we are, in the moment, in the dynamic, in space and time, and it
is exciting because we 'hear' music, 'see' pictures, 'smell' the world, 'touch' each
other, and so forth, as well as think! – all in one moment. The language of inclusive work with young people and the relationships around it could be described
as forms of poetry, music, dancing, fashion, painting, sculpture, and architecture.
Incidentally it is how young people 'see' the world!

II. Concluding Comments

Richard Turner

John, many thanks for your response to the chapter. You raise some important
and interesting questions, many of which would involve a chapter in their own
right in order to adequately respond to. Some are difficult concepts to absorb and
will need grappling with to understand. Nevertheless, the encouragement to think
beyond our habitual *modi operandi* towards the development of Critical Practice
(CP) is apparent in your response.

While I recognize that there are numerous models of Theological Reflection
(TR), the one most closely aligned with my habitus – that of a youth worker

engaged with both secular and faith-based organizations, and training Christian youth workers – is 'Theology-in-Action': Praxis.[63] – a method of TR that overlaps with my understanding of RP, which itself encompasses reflection on my beliefs. Maybe I can explore the craft or art approach you offer. TR is indeed a craft which is honed by long practice; a point worth noting for those just beginning in the arts of RP and TR, 'it is a process of becoming'.[64] Many of your insights and thoughts are, I believe, a result of long experience in practice and reflection.

The process of offering our dialogue for others to read is in some small way inclusive, and the invitation to engage in the critique and analysis encourages reflection. This we can only really do if we accept that there are few (if any) proofs, absolutes and certainties, and maybe, until someone solves the Gettier[65] problem, epistemological questions can never really be answered either.

I warm to your comments about 'how do we know that we know', 'cause and effect', 'impossible to predict' and the assumptions we make. Yet we can hold in tension the need to communicate and act with confidence and belief, and at the same time recognize the uncertainty, complexity and limits of our understanding. We need to hold onto our doubts in what appears to be a dangerous age of certainties. This also seems to be a prerequisite of facilitating learning among ourselves, among youth work students and young people, who

> may be attracted to people who appear to have easy answers to readily available bodies of knowledge neatly stored into packages of theories. In this way they try to escape the unpalatable fact that the world is complex, our understanding of it is limited, and that if we want to find out and learn we have to face being bewildered, confused and anxious.[66]
>
> For if we are too frightened . . . we also shut ourselves off from the perception of something different, from discovering anything new, producing anything fresh.[67]

Similarly, I consider RP to be a learning process – where we never really arrive at any fixed position. The models I offer are for reflection and exploration, not a formula for identifying prescribed and fixed outcomes. As much of RP entails reflexivity, then much of the work is to be done internally, for the only thing we know we can really change is ourselves. This 'internal work' is shown, for example, with two workers, 'J' and 'M', from Mary Crosby's work on 'extending ourselves' and 'the work of attention'.

---

[63] E. Graham, H. Walton and F. Ward, *Theological Reflection: Methods* (London: SCM Press, 2005).

[64] J. Bamber, 'Learning, Understanding and the Development of Critical Practice', in *Youth & Policy*, 60 (1998), pp. 30–45 (43).

[65] E. L. Gettier, 'Is Justified True Belief Knowledge?', *Analysis*, 23 (1963), pp. 121–3.

[66] I. Salzberger-Wittenberg, H. Gianna and E. Osbourne, *The Emotional Experience of Learning and Teaching* (London & New York: Routledge & Kegan Paul, 1983), p. 26.

[67] Ibid., p. 9.

It is appropriate to ask questions about the 'inclusion'. I tried not to argue that inclusion should be the purpose of RP, but similar to the way that reducing crime is not the purpose of youth work – but it can be a by-product of youth work – so RP can lead to 'inclusion'. But I do hope that RP would enable a more open and 'inclusive' attitude and approach to young people.

While there is much that can be improved in youth work, and sadly many of your concerns about the commodification and objectification of young people are pertinent to current youth work, it seems that key values at the heart of the youth work – the desire to build and work through relationships and an acceptance of youngsters for who they are – are being usurped, a view that is reiterated in the current internet debate 'In Defence of Youth Work',[68] and yet may also be one of the dominant voices to which you refer.

I share your concerns that RP can be used as a tool for managerialism; I guess it is the 'ism' part – the belief that certain imposed methods of management are the panacea for work with youngsters. It is easier, uncaring, impersonal, and in many cases ineffective and somewhat dehumanizing. Yet management in youth work is not a new thing. In the Thomson Report it states,

> There is no real mystery about good management. It has four basic aspects: defining objectives, assigning roles, allocating resources and monitoring performances . . . [69]

Recently I had the privilege of attending two youth events. Both had identified their aims and objectives, assigned roles, used a wide range of workers and resources, consulted and involved young people, budgeted, designed interesting and participative workshops and involved young people in the evaluation. Adhering to policies and procedures relating to health and safety and child protection and so forth, and to youth work values and principles. In a nutshell it was well managed.

But it was also a time for young people to have fun, be with their friends, build relationships and to just be. The motivation to organize came from a desire to work with and be with youngsters. This relational process of being with, engaging with, acceptance of and listening to, were the key threads that made all the activity possible – to lose sight of these is to lose sight of the heart of youth work, and when it all comes together, the art in youth work is plain to see. '[T]he greatest gift that we can give is to "be alongside" another person'.[70] It is this simple, kind warmth, genuineness and giving of time to young people from the mass of volunteers and part-timers that still makes up the bulk of youth work.

---

[68] http://indefenceofyouthwork.wordpress.com/2009/03/11/the-open-letter-in-defence-of-youth-work/, accessed 17 January 2010.
[69] Thompson Report. *Experience and Participation*. (HMSO, 1982), p. 74.
[70] M. Green and C. Christian. *Accompanying young people on their spiritual quest* (London: The National Society/Church House Publishing, 1998), p. 21.

Bibliography

Al-Alawani, T. J., *Towards a Fiqh for Minorities: Some Basic Reflections* (London and Washington: The International Institute of Islamic Thought, 2003).

Al-Faruqi, I. R., 'Common bases between the two religions', in A. Siddiqui (ed.), *Ismail Raji al-Faruqi: Islam and Other Faiths* (Leicester: The Islamic Foundation and The International Institute of Islamic Thought, 1998), p. 231

Ali, A. Y., *The Holy Qur'an: Translation and Commentary* (Beirut: The Holy Qur'an Publishing House, 1985).

Alinsky, S. D., *Rules for Radicals: A Pragmatic Primer for Realistic Radicals* (New York: Random House, 1971).

Allen, C., 'Justifying Islamophobia: A Post-9/11 Consideration of the European Union and British Contexts', in *American Journal of Islamic Social Sciences*, 21:3, (Summer, 2004), pp. 1–25.

Althaus-Reid, M., *Indecent Theology. Theological Perversions in Sex, Gender and Politics* (London: Routledge, 2001).

Ansari, K. H., 'Negotiating British Muslim Identity', in M. S. Bahmanpour and H. Bashir (eds), *Muslim Identity in the 21st Century: Challenges of Modernity* (London: Book Extra, 2000).

Aquinas, T., *Summa Theologiae, Volume 37, Justice*, trans. Thomas Gilby (London: Blackfriars,1974).

—. 'Question VI: On the Cause of Faith', Pegis, A. C. (ed.), *The Basic Writings of Saint Thomas Aquinas*, vol. 2. (Indianapolis: Hackett Publishing, 1997), pp. 1115–18.

Arneson, R. J., 'What, if Anything, Renders All Humans Morally Equal?', in *Singer and His Critics* (Oxford: Blackwell, 1999), pp. 103–28.

Atkins, S., and K. Murphy, 'Reflective Practice', *Nursing Standard*, 8:39 (1994), pp. 49–56.

Augustine of Hippo, *The Fathers of the Church*, trans. M. A. Schumacher (New York: Catholic University of America, 1957).

—. *On the Trinity*, ed. Gareth B. Matthews; trans. Stephen McKenna (Cambridge: Cambridge University Press, 2002).

Avalos, H., S. J. Melcher and J. Schipper, (eds), *This Abled Body: Rethinking Disabilities in Biblical Studies* (Atlanta: Society of Biblical Literature, 2007).

Bacon, H. 'A Very Particular Body: Assessing the Doctrine of Incarnation for Affirming the Sacramentality of Female Embodiment', in J. Jobling and G. Howie (eds), *Women and the Divine: Touching Transcendence* (New York: Palgrave Macmillan, 2009), pp. 227–52.

—. *What's Right with the Trinity? Conversations in Feminist Theology* (Farnham: Ashgate, 2009).

Baker, C., *The Hybrid Church and the City–Third Space Thinking*, 2nd edn (London: SCM Press, 2009).

Bamber, J., 'Learning, Understanding and the Development of Critical Practice', *Youth & Policy*, 60 (1998), pp. 30–45.

Barry, M., (ed.), *Youth Policy and Social Inclusion – critical debates with young people* (London: Routledge, 2005).

Barth, K., *Church Dogmatics* (Edinburgh: T&T Clark, 1956–1975).

Batsleer, J. R., *Informal Learning in Youth Work* (London: Sage, 2008).

Bauman, Z., *Imitations of Postmodernity* (London: Routledge, 1992).

—. *Liquid Modernity* (Oxford: Blackwell, 2000).

—. *Identity* (Cambridge: Polity Press, 2004).

Bellah, R., et al., *Habits of the Heart: Individualism and Commitment in American Life*, 3rd edn (Berkeley: University of California Press, 2008).

Bertens, H., *The Idea of the Postmodern* (London: Routledge, 1996).

Bevans, S., *Models of Contextual Theology* (New York: Orbis Books, 2007).

Boff, L., *Ecology and Liberation*, trans. John Cumming (Maryknoll, NY: Orbis, 1995)

—. *Cry of the Earth, Cry of the Poor*, trans. Philip Berryman (New York, Orbis, 1997).

Bordo, S., *Unbearable Weight: Feminism, Western Culture, and the Body* (Berkeley, Los Angeles, London: University of California Press, 1993).

Borton, T., *Reach, Teach and Touch* (London: McGraw Hill, 1970).

Bourdieu, P, *Science of Science and Reflexivity* (Cambridge: Polity Press, 2004).

—. *Language & Symbolic Power* (Cambridge: Polity, 2009).

Bourriaud, N., 'Altermodern', in F. Gaskin and K. McSwein (eds), *Altermodern: Exhibition Guide* (London: Tate Publishing, 2009).

British Broadcasting Corporation, 'Mother defends rugby suicide son', retrieved from http://news.bbc.co.uk/1/hi/england/hereford/worcs/7677706.stm 18 October 2008, accessed 11 January 2010.

Browning, G., *Lyotard and the End of Grand Narratives* (Cardiff: University of Wales, 2000).

Brueggemann, W., *Mandate to Difference* (Louisville: Westminster John Knox Press, 2007).

Businessballs.com, 'Maslow's Hierarchy of Needs', retrieved from www.business-balls.com/maslow.htm, accessed 11 January 2010.

CAFOD's Response to *Building Our Common Future* (London: CAFOD, 2009).

Cahoone L., (ed.), *From Modernism to Postmodernism: An Anthology* (Oxford: Blackwell, 2003).

Caritas Internationalis, *Climate Justice: Seeking a Global Ethic* (Vatican City State: Caritas Internationalis, 2009).

Carr, D., 'Gender and the Shaping of Desire in the Song of Songs and its Interpretation', *Journal of Biblical Literature* 119:2 (2000), pp. 233–48.

Catholic Bishops' Conference of the Philippines, *What is Happening to our Beautiful Land, A Pastoral Letter on Ecology* (1988).

Chadwick, D. H., 'Investigating a Killer', *National Geographic* 207:4 (2005), pp. 86–105.

Chew, S. C., *The Crescent and the Rose: Islam and England during the Renaissance* (New York: Oxford University Press, 1937).

Church of England, 'Church of England Youth Council', retrieved from: www.ceyc.org/, accessed 20 July 10.

—. *Youth-A-Part* (London: National Society/Church House Publishing, 1996).

Clough, D., *On Animals: I. Systematic Theology* (London: T&T Clark/Continuum, forthcoming).

Coleman, J. C., *The Nature of Adolescence* (London: Methuen, 1980).

Contreras, J. M., and K. A. Kerns, 'Emotion Regulation Processes: Explaining Links between Parent-Child Attachment and Peer Relationships', in K. A. Kerns, J. M. Contreras and A. M. Neal-Barnett (eds). *Family and Peers: Linking Two Social Worlds* (Westport, Connecticut & London: Praeger, 2000), p. 1.

Covey, S., *The 7 Habits of Highly Effective People* (London: Simon & Schuster, 1989).

Creamer, D. *Disability and Christian Theology* (New York: Oxford University Press, 2009).

Crosby, M., 'Working with people as an informal educator', in L. D. Richardson and M. Wolfe, *Principles and Practice of Informal Education* (London & New York: Routledge Falmer, 2001), pp. 54–61.

Dando, N. 'The Victim', *Times* (30 September 2009), p. 26.

Daniel, N., *Islam and the West* (Oxford: Oneworld Publications, 1993).

Davi Kopenawa Yanomami, *Open letter from the Yanomami people concerning development* (Boa Vista, 25 February 2008).

Davis, J. M., and M. Hill, 'Introduction', in E. K. M. Tisdall, J. M. Davis, M. Hill and A. Prout, *Children Young People and Social Inclusion: Participation for What?* repr. 2008, (Bristol: Policy Press, 2006), pp. 1–22.

de Waal, F., *Good Natured: The Origins of Right and Wrong in Humans and Other Animals* (Cambridge, MA: Harvard University Press, 1996).

—. *Chimpanzee Politics: Power and Sex Among Apes* (Baltimore: Johns Hopkins University Press, 2000).

Deane-Drummond, C., *Chimpanzee Politics: Power and Sex Among Apes* (Baltimore: Johns Hopkins University Press, 2000).

—. *Ecotheology* (London: DLT, 2008).

—. *Seeds of Hope: Facing the Challenge of Climate Justice* (London: CAFOD, 2009).

—. 'Deep Incarnation and Eco-Justice as Theodrama', in S. Bergmann and H. Eaton (eds), *Ecological Ethics: Exploring Religion, Ethics and Aesthetics*, (London: LIT, Verlag, 2010).

Derrida, J., and D. Wills, 'The Animal That Therefore I Am (More to Follow)', *Critical Inquiry* 28:2 (2002), pp. 369–418.

DfID White Paper, *Building Our Common Future* (London: DfID, 2009).

Dimmock, A. F., *Cruel Legacy. An Introduction to the Record of Deaf People in History* (Edinburgh: Scottish Workshop Publications, 1993).

Dinnerstein, D., *The Rocking of the Cradle and the Ruling of the World* (New York: Harper and Row, 1977).

DiNoia, J. A., *The Diversity of Religions: A Christian Perspective* (Washington, DC: Catholic University of America Press, 1992).

—. *The Theology of John Calvin* (Grand Rapids: Eerdmanns, 1995).

Dirlik, A., 'The Global in the Local', in B. Ashcroft, G. Griffiths and H. Tiffin (eds), *The Post-Colonial Studies Reader*, 2nd edn (London: Routledge, 2004), pp. 463–7.

Dobson, A., *Justice and the Environment: Conceptions of Environmental Sustainability and Dimensions of Social Justice* (Oxford: Oxford University Press,1998).

Dulles, A. *Models of the Church*, 2nd edn (Dublin: Gill and Macmillan, 1976).

Eiesland, N., *The Disabled God: Toward a Liberatory Theology of Disability* (Nashville: Abingdon, 1994).

Equality and Human Rights Commission, *Disability Discrimination Act: Guidance on matters to be taken into account in determining questions relating to the definition of disability* (London: The Stationary Office, 2005).

Etzioni, A., (ed.), *The Essential Communitarian Reader* (Maryland: Rowman & Littlefield, 1998).

Exum, J. C., *Song of Songs: A Commentary* (Louisville: Westminster John Knox Press, 2005).

Exworthy, M., and S. Halford, (eds), *Professionals and the New Managerialism in the Public Sector* (Buckingham: Open University Press, 1999).

Featherstone, M., *Undoing Culture: Globalization, Postmodernism and Identity* (London: Sage Publications, 1997).

Fiddes, P., *Participating in God* (London: Darton, Longman & Todd, 2000).

Finnis, J., *Natural Law and Natural Rights* (Oxford: Clarendon Press, 1980).

Fiorenza, E. S., *Sharing Her Word: Feminist Biblical Interpretation in Context* (Edinburgh: T&T Clark, 1998).

Fontaine, C. R., ' "Be Men, O Philistines" (1 Samuel 4.9): Iconographic Representations and Reflections on Female Gender as Disability in the Ancient World', in H. Avalos, S. J. Melcher and J. Schipper (eds), *This Abled Body: Rethinking Disabilities in Biblical Studies* (Atlanta: Society of Biblical Literature, 2007), pp. 61–72.

Ford, D. F., 'Gospel in Context: Among Many Faiths', paper presented at the Fulcrum Conference, Islington, Friday, 28 April 2006.

Foreman, A., 'Youth Workers as Redcoats', in T. Jeffs and M. Smith (eds), *Youth Work* (London: Macmillan Education Ltd/BASW, 1987), pp.12–24.

Foucault, M.,*The Archaeology of Knowledge* (London: Tavistock Publications Ltd, 1972).

—. *Discipline and Punish: The Birth of the Prison*, trans. Alan Sheridan (London: Penguin, 1991).

Freire, P., *Pedagogy of the Oppressed*, 30th Anniversary Edition (New York: Continuum, 2001).

Fryer, P., *Staying Power: A History of Black People in Britain* (London: Pluto Books, 1984).

Gandhi, L., *Postcolonial Theory: A Critical Introduction* (Edinburgh: Edinburgh University Press, 1998).

Geivett, R. D., and W. G. Phillips, 'A Particularist View: An Evidentialist Approach', in S. N. Gundry, D. L. Okholm and T. R. Phillips (eds), *Four Views on Salvation in a Pluralistic World* (Grand Rapids, MI: Zondervan, 1995), pp. 213–45.

Gergen, K. J., *The Saturated Self: Dilemmas of Identity in Contemporary Life* (New York: Basic Books, 1991).

Germov, J., and L. Williams, 'Dieting Women: Self-Surveillance and the Body Ponopticon', in J. Sobal and D. Maurer (eds), *Weighty Issues: Fatness and Thinness as Social Problems* (New York: Aldine de Gruyter, 1999), pp. 117–32.

Gettier, E. L., 'Is Justified True Belief Knowledge?', *Analysis*, 23 (1963), pp. 121–3.

Gibbs, G., *Learning by doing: A guide to teaching and learning methods* (Oxford: Further Education Unit, 1988).

Giddens, A. *Sociology*, 5th edn (Cambridge, UK, Malden, MA: Polity, 2009).

Graham, E., 'Redeeming the Present', in E. L. Graham, *Grace Jantzen: Redeeming the Present* (Farnham: Ashgate, 2009), pp. 1–19.

Graham, E., H. Walton and F. Ward, *Theological Reflection: Methods* (London: SCM Press, 2005).

Graham, J. M., *Representation and Substitution in the Atonement Theologies of Dorothee Sölle, John Macquarrie and Karl Barth* (New York: Peter Lang, 2005).

Grant, J., *White Women's Christ, Black Women's Jesus* (Atlanta: Scholars Press, 1989).

Green, L., *Let's Do Theology* (London: Continuum, 1990).

Green, M., and C. Christian, *Accompanying young people on their spiritual quest* (London: The National Society/Church House Publishing, 1998).

Greenwood, R., *Practising Community*, 2nd edn (London: SPCK, 1996).

Greggs, T., *Barth, Origen, and Universal Salvation: Restoring Particularity* (Oxford: OUP, 2009).

—. 'Religionless Christianity and the Political Implications of Theological Speech: What Bonhoeffer's Theology Yields to a World of Fundamentalisms', *International Journal of Systematic Theology*, 11 (2009), pp. 293–308.

—. 'Legitimizing and Necessitating Inter-faith Dialogue: The Dynamics of Inter-faith for Individual Faith Communities', *International Journal of Public Theology* 4:2 (2010), pp. 194–211.

Grenz, S. J., and J. Franke, *Beyond Foundationalism: Shaping Theology in a Postmodern Context* (Louisville: Westminster John Knox Press, 2001).

Grey, M., 'Natality and Flourishing in Contexts of Disability and Impairment', in E. L. Graham, *Grace Jantzen: Redeeming the Present* (Farnham: Ashgate, 2009), pp. 197–211.

Griffith, M. R., *Born Again Bodies, Flesh and Spirit in American Christianity* (Berkeley: University of California press, 2004).

Grisez, G., *The Way of the Lord Jesus*, vol. I (Chicago: Franciscan Herald Press, 1983).

Groothius, D., *Truth Decay: Defending Christianity against the Challenges of Postmodernism* (Downers Grove: IVP, 2000).

Gutierrez, G., *A Theology for Today: the option for the poor in 2005* (CAFOD's Pope Paul VI Memorial Lecture, 2005).

Halteman, M. C., *Compassionate Eating as Care of Creation* (Washington, DC: The Humane Society of the United States, 2008).

Hart, R. A., *Children's Participation*, 3rd edn (New York: UNICEF, 1997).

Harvey, D., *The Condition of Postmodernity* (Oxford: Blackwell, 1989).

Haughton, R., *The Drama of Salvation* (New York: Seabury Press, 1975).

Head, J., *Working with Adolescents: Constructing Identity* (London: Falmer Press, Taylor & Francis, 2002).

Heelas, P., *Spiritualities of Life: New Age Romanticism and Consumptive Capitalism* (Oxford: Blackwell, 2008).

Hennelly, A. T., *Liberation Theology: A Documentary History* (New York: Orbis Books, 1990).

Herman, L. M., S. A. Kuczaj and M. D. Holder, 'Responses to Anomalous Gestural Sequences By a Language-Trained Dolphin: Evidence for Processing of Semantic Relations and Syntactic Information', *Journal of Experimental Psychology: General* 122:2 (1993), pp. 184–94.

Heyward, C., *The Redemption of God* (Washington: University of America Press, 1982).

Hiebert, P. G., *Anthropological Reflections on Missiological Issues*, 3rd edn (Michigan: Baker Academic, 1994).

House of Commons Development Committee, *Sustainable Development in a Changing Climate* (London: DfID, 2008).

Howson, A., *Embodying Gender* (London: Sage, 2005).

Hull, J. M., 'From a Blind Disciple to a Sighted Saviour', in T. Woodcock and I. Merchant (eds), *Fleshing out Faith: A Reflection on Bodies and Spirituality* (Birmingham: Student Christian Movement, 2000), pp. 6–7.

—. *In the Beginning there was Darkness* (London: SCM Press, 2001).

Hunsinger, G., *How to Read Karl Barth* (Oxford: Oxford University Press, 1991).

—. 'A Tale of Two Simultaneities: Justification and Sanctification in Calvin and Barth', in J. C. McDowell and M. Higton (eds), *Conversing with Barth* (Aldershot: Ashgate, 2004), pp. 76–9.

Hunt, A., *Trinity* (Maryknoll, NY: Orbis Books, 2000).

Hussain, I. A., 'Migration and Settlement: A Historical Perspective of Loyalty and Belonging', in M. S. Seddon, D. Hussain and N. Malik (eds), *British Muslims: Loyalty and Belonging* (Leicester: The Islamic Foundation and The Citizen organising Foundation, 2003).

Information Scotland, 'Future of the Profession: Are you down with the kids?', www.slainte.org.uk/publications/serials/infoscot/vol4%286%29/vol4%286%29article6.htm, accessed 17 January 2010.

Ingram, G., and Harris, J., *Delivering Good Youth Work* (Dorset: Russell House Publishing, 2001).

Irarrarzával, D., *Inculturation: New Dawn of the Church in Latin America*, trans. Philip Berryman (Eugene: Wipf and Stock, 2008).

Isherwood, L., *Liberating Christ* (Cleveland: Pilgrim Press,1999).

—. *The Fat Jesus: Feminist Explorations in Boundaries and Transgressions* (London: DLT, 2007).

Jacobson, J., *Islam in Transition: Religion and identity among British Pakistani youth* (London: Routledge, 1998).

Jamieson, A., *A Churchless Faith* (London: SPCK, 2002).

Jantzen, G. M., *Becoming Divine: Toward a Feminist Philosophy of Religion* (Manchester: Manchester University Press, 1998).

—. 'Flourishing: Towards an ethic of natality', *Feminist Theory* 2:2 (2001), pp. 219–32.

Jeffs. T., and M. Smith, *Informal Education – conversation, democracy and learning* (Derby: Education Now Books with the YMCA George Williams College, 1996).

Johns, C., *Becoming a Reflective Practitioner*, 2nd edn (Oxford: Blackwell Publishing, 2004).

Jung, S., *Food For Life, The Spirituality and Ethics of Eating* (Minneapolis: Fortress Press, 2004).

Katz, L. F., 'Living in a Hostile World: Toward an Integrated Model of Family, Peer, and Physiological Processes in Aggressive Preschoolers' in K. A. Kerns, J. M. Contreras and A. M. Neal-Barnett (eds), *Family and Peers – Linking Two Social Worlds* (London and Westport: Praeger, 2000), pp. 115–36.

Kendrick, K. M., 'Sheep Don't Forget a Face', *Nature* 414:4860 (2001), pp. 165–6.

Klein, R., 'Fat Beauty', in J. E. Braziel and K. LeBesco (eds), *Bodies out of Bounds: Fatness and Transgression* (Berkeley, Los Angeles, London: University of California Press, 2001), pp. 19–38.

Kolb, D. A., *Experiential learning: Experience as a source of learning and development* (New Jersey: Prentice Hall, 1984).

Kristeva, J., *Strangers to Ourselves*, trans. L. Roudiez (New York: Columbia University Press, 1991).

Lahutsky, N. M., 'Food and Feminism and Historical Interpretation: The Case of Medieval Holy Women', in Rita Nakashima Brock, Claudia Camp and Serene Jones (eds), *Setting the Table: Women in Theological Conversation* (St Louis, MO: Chalice Press, 1995), pp. 233–48.

Lelwica, M., 'Spreading the Religion of Thinness from California to Calcutta', *Journal of Feminist Studies in Religion* 25:1 (2009), pp.19–42.

Lewis, H., *Deaf Liberation Theology* (Aldershot: Ashgate, 2007).

Lindbeck, G. A., *The Nature of Doctrine: Religion and Theology in a Postliberal Age* (London: SPCK, 1984).

Linden, J., *Understanding Children & Young People* (London: Hodder Arnold, 2007).

Lovejoy, A. O., *The Great Chain of Being: A Study of the History of an Idea* (Cambridge, MA: Harvard University Press, 1942).

Lyon, D., *Postmodernity*, 2nd edn (Buckingham: Open University Press, 1999).

—. *Jesus in Disneyland* (Cambridge: Polity Press, 2000).

—.'Wheels within wheels: Glocalization and Contemporary Religion', retrieved from: http://webjournals.alphacrucis.edu.au/journals/aps/issues-23/wheels-within-wheels-glocalization-and-contemporar/, accessed 13 March 2010.

Lyotard, J. F., *The Postmodern Condition: A Report on Knowledge*, trans. G. Bennington and B. Massumi (Manchester: Manchester University Press, 1984).

—. *The Postmodern Explained: Correspondence 1982–1985*, trans. D. B. B. Maher, J. Prefanis, V. Spate and M. Thomas (Minneapolis: University of Minnesota Press, 1993).

MacIntyre, A., *Whose Justice? Which Rationality?* (London: Duckworth, 1988).

Mason, S., 'Another Flood? Genesis 9 and Isaiah's Broken Eternal Covenant', *Journal for the Study of the Old Testament* 32:2 (2007), pp. 177–98.

Matar, N., *Islam in Britain 1558–1685* (Cambridge: Cambridge University Press, 1998).

Matthai, W., 'Livelihoods, Forest and Climate with Nobel Laureate Ms Wangari Maathai, GBM and Partners', Framework Convention on Climate Change, UN Climate Change Conference, COP 15, Daily Programme, Part Two, Friday, December 11, 2006.

Matthews, J. E., *Working With Youth Groups* (London: University of London Press, 1966).

McCloughry, R., and W. Morris, *Making a World of Difference: Christian Reflections on Disability* (London: SPCK, 2002).

McKinley, N. M., 'Ideal Weight/Ideal Women: Society Constructs the Female', in Jeffery Sobal and Donna Maurer, *Weighty Issues: Fatness and Thinness as Social Problems* (New York: Aldine de Gruyter, 1999), pp. 97–116.

Metz, J. B., *Faith in History and Society: Toward a Practical Fundamental Theology*, trans. D. Smith (London: Burns & Oates, 1980).

Mind Tools, 'Active Listening: Hear What People are Really Saying', retrieved from: www.mindtools.com/CommSkll/ActiveListening.htm, accessed 23 July 2010.

Moltmann, J., *The Trinity and the Kingdom of God* (London: SCM Press, 1981).

Monitoring Minority Protection in the EU: The Situation of Muslims in the UK (London: The Open Society Institute, 2002).

Montoya, A. F. M., *The Theology of Food: Eating and the Eucharist* (Chichester, Oxford, Malden: Wiley-Blackwell, 2009).

Morris, J., *Pride against Prejudice* (London: The Women's Press, 1991).

Morris, W., *Theology without Words: Theology in the Deaf Community* (Aldershot: Ashgate, 2008).

Nasser, M., and H. Malson, 'Beyond Western Dis/orders: thinness and self-starvation of other-ed women', in H. Malson and M. Burns (eds), *Critical Feminist Approaches to Eating Disorders* (London & New York: Routledge, 2009), pp. 74–86.

Nichols, L. T., *That All May Be One* (Grand Rapids, MI: The Liturgical Press, 1997).

Nimmo, P., 'Election and Evangelical Thinking: Challenges to our Way of Conceiving the Doctrine of God', in T. Greggs (ed.), *New Perspectives for Evangelical Theology: Engaging God, Scripture and the World* (London: Routledge, 2009), pp. 29–43.

Northcott, M., *A Moral Climate* (London: Darton Longman and Todd, 2007).

Now, 29 September 2008.

Nussbaum, M., *Women and Human Development: The Capabilities Approach* (Cambridge: Cambridge University Press, 2000).

—. *Frontiers of Justice: Disability, Nationality, Species Membership* (Cambridge, MA/London: Belknap Press/Harvard University Press, 2006).

Nussbaum, M., and J. Glover (eds), *Women, Culture, and Development: A Study of Human Capabilities* (Oxford: Oxford University Press, 1995)

NYA, *Ethical Conduct in Youth Work, a statement of values and principles* (Leicester: The National Youth Agency, 2004).

O'Collins, G., SJ, *Salvation for All: God's Other Peoples* (Oxford: OUP, 2008).

Olson, R. E., *The Mosaic of Christian Belief: Twenty Centuries of Unity & Diversity* (Leicester: IVP, 2002).

The Open Letter: In Defence of Youth Work. http://indefenceofyouthwork.wordpress.com/2009/03/11/the-open-letter-in-defence-of-youth-work/, accessed 17 January 2010.

Orbach, S., *Fat is a Feminist Issue* (London: Hamlyn Press, 1979).

Osborne, C., *Dumb Beasts and Dead Philosophers: Humanity and the Humane in Ancient Philosophy and Literature* (Oxford: Clarendon, 2007).

Palin, D. A., *A Gentle Touch: from theology of handicap to a theology of human being* (London: SPCK, 1992).

Participation Works Partnership, 'National Participation Strategic Vision Launched', retrieved from: www.participationworks.org.uk/news/national-participation-strategic-vision-launched, accessed 5 January 2010.

Partridge, C., *The Re-Enchantment of the West,* vol. 1 (London: T&T Clark, 2004).

Penner, M. (ed.), *Christianity and the Postmodern Turn: Six Views* (Grand Rapids, MI: Brazos Press, 2005).

Pepperberg, I. M., *The Alex Studies: Cognitive and Communicative Abilities of Grey Parrots* (Cambridge, MA: Harvard University, 2000).

Peter Honey Publications, 'The Learning Styles Questionnaire', retrieved from: www.peterhoney.com/content/LearningStylesQuestionnaire.html, accessed 20 July 10.

Philips, A., 'The Resurrection of England', in T. Linsell (ed.), *Our Englishness* (Norfolk: Anglo-Saxon Books, 2000).

Pimental, D., and M. Pimental (eds), *Food, Energy and Society* (Boulder, CO: University Press of Colorado, 1996).

Plantinga, A., and N. Wolterstorff, *Faith and Rationality: Reason and Belief in God* (Notre Dame, IN: University of Notre Dame Press, 1983).

Poole, E., *Reporting Islam* (London: Routledge, 2002).

Pope Benedict XV1, *Caritas in Veritate* (Vatican City: Vatican, 2009).

—. *If You Want to Cultivate Peace, Protect Creation, Message for the Celebration for the World day of Peace* (1 January 2010).

Pope John Paul II, *Sollicitudo Rei Socialis* (30 December 1987).

Pope Paul VI, *Gaudium et Spes, Pastoral Constitution on the Church in the Modern World* (7 December 1965).

—. *Populorum Progressio* (26 March 1967).

Poverty Facts and Stats, http:www.globalissues.org/article/26/poverty-facts-and-stats, accessed on 24 July 2009.

Power, K., *Veiled Desire: Augustine's Writings on Women* (London: DLT, 1995).

Quine, W. V. O. and J. S. Ullian, *Web of Belief*, 2nd edn (New York: Random House, 1978).

Ramadan, T., *To be a European Muslim* (Leicester: The Islamic Foundation, 1999).

Rawls, J., *Theory of Justice*, 2nd edn (Oxford: Oxford University Press, 1999).

Reinders, H., *Receiving the Gift of Friendship: Profound Disability, Theological Anthropology and Ethics* (Grand Rapids, MI, Cambridge: Eerdmans, 2008).

Reynolds, T. E., *Vulnerable Communion: A Theology of Disability and Hospitality* (Grand Rapids, MI: Brazos Press, 2008).

Richardson, R. (ed.), *Islamophobia, Issues, Challenges and Action* (Stoke on Trent & Sterling: Trentham Books, 2004).

Ridge, T., 'Childhood poverty: a barrier to social participation and inclusion', in E. K. M. Tisdall, J. M. Davis, M. Hill and A. Prout, *Children, Young People and Social Inclusion – Participation for What?* (Bristol: The Policy Press, 2006), pp. 23–38.

Riggs, J. W., *Postmodern Christianity: Doing Theology in the Contemporary World* (Harrisburg: Trinity Press International, 2003).

Roberts, R. H., *Religion, Theology and the Human Sciences* (Cambridge: Cambridge University Press, 2002).

Robertson, R., 'The Conceptual Promise of Glolocalization: Commonality and Diversity', retrieved from http://artefact.mi2.hr/_a04/lang_en/theory_robertson_en.htm, accessed on 12 March 2010.

Rolfe, G., D. Freshwater and M. Jasper, *Critical Reflection for Nursing and the Helping Professions* (Basingstoke, UK: Palgrave, 2001).

Rosseter, B., 'Youth Workers as Educators', in T. Jeffs and M. Smith (eds), *Youth Work* (London: Macmillan Education/BASW, 1987).

Ruether, R. R. , 'Augustine: Sexuality, Gender and Women', in Judith Chelius Stark (ed.), *Feminist Interpretations of Augustine* (The Pennsylvania State University: Pennsylvania, 2007), pp. 47–68.

Said, E., *Orientalism: Western Concepts of the Orient* (London: Penguin Books, 1991).

Saliers, D. E., 'Towards a Spirituality of Inclusiveness' in N. Eiesland and D. E. Saliers (eds), *Human Disability and the Service of God: Reassessing Religious Practice* (Nashville, TN: Abingdon Press, 1998), pp. 19–31.

Salzberger-Wittenberg, I., H. Gianna and E. Osbourne, *The Emotional Experience of Learning and Teaching* (London & New York: Routledge & Kegan Paul, 1983), p. 26.

Sawyer, D. F., 'Hidden Subjects: Rereading Eve and Mary', *Theology & Sexuality* 14:3 (2008), pp. 305–20.

Schon, D. A., *The Reflective Practitioner: How Professionals Think in Action* (Basic Books: 1983).

Schreiter, R. J., *Constructing Local Theologies* (New York: Orbis Books, 2008).

Scott, P. M., and W. T. Cavanaugh (eds), *The Blackwell Companion to Political Theology* (Oxford: Blackwell, 2004).

Seddon, M. S., 'Locating the Perpetuation of "Otherness": Negating British Islam', in M. S. Seddon et al., *British Muslims Between Assimilation and Segregation: Historical, Legal and Social Realities* (Markfield: The Islamic Foundation, 2004), pp. 119–44.

—. 'Ancient and Modern Muslim minorities under Christian Rule: A comparative study of Islam in 7th-century Abyssinia and contemporary Britain', in *Crucible: The Christian Journal of Social Ethics* (July–September, 2008), pp. 41–54.

Seddon, M. S., et al., *British Muslims Between Assimilation and Segregation* (Markfield: The Islamic Foundation, 2004).

Sen, A., *Development as Freedom* (Oxford: Oxford University Press, 1999).

—. *The Idea of Justice* (London: Penguin, 2009).

Shakespeare, S., and H. Rayment-Pickard, *The Inclusive God* (Norwich: Canterbury Press, 2006).

Shakespeare, T., 'Cultural Representations of Disabled People: dustbins for disavowal?' in L. Barton and M. Oliver (eds), *Disability Studies: Past, Present and Future* (Leeds: The Disability Press, 1997), pp. 217–33.

Shier, H., 'Pathways to participation: openings, opportunities and obligations: a new model for enhancing children's participation in decision-making, in line with article 12.1 of the United Nations Convention on the Rights of the Child'. *Children & Society*, 15:2 (2001), pp. 107–17.

Siddiqui, M. Y. H., *The Prophet Muhammad: A Role Model for Muslim Minorities* (Leicester: The Islamic Foundation, 2006).

Smart, B., *Postmodernity* (London: Routledge, 1993).

Smith, M. K., 'Young People, informal education and association', retrieved from: www.infed.org/youthwork/b-yw.htm, accessed 23 July 2010.

Sobrino, J., *No Salvation Outside the Poor: Prophetic-Utopian Essays* (New York: Orbis Books, 2008).

Social Issues Research Centre, *Obesity and the Facts: An analysis of data from the Health Survey for England 2003* (February 2005).

Southgate, C., *The Groaning of Creation: God, Evolution, and the Problem of Evil* (Louisville; London: Westminster John Knox, 2008).

Stinson, K., *Women and Dieting Culture: Inside a Commercial Weight Loss Group* (New Brunswick, New Jersey and London: Rutgers University Press, 2001).

Stone, K. A., *Practicing Safer Texts: Food, Sex and Bible in Queer Perspective* (London & New York: T&T Clark, 2005).

Swain, J., S. French and C. Cameron, *Controversial Issues in a Disabling Society* (Buckingham: Open University Press, 2003).

Tam, H, *Communitarianism: A New Agenda for Politics and Citizenship* (Basigstoke: Macmillan Press, 1998).

Tanner, K. 'Creation and providence', in J. Webster (ed.), *The Cambridge Companion to Karl Barth* (Cambridge: CUP, 2000), pp. 111–26.

Taylor, A. M., *Responding to Adolescents* (Lyme Regis: Russell House Publishing, 2003).

Tertullian, *On the Apparel of Women*, trans. Revd. S. Thelwall (Whitefish: Kessinger Publishing, 2004).

Thacker, J., 'Lyotard and the Christian Metanarrative: A Rejoinder to Smith and Westphal', in *Faith and Philosophy* 22:3 (2005), pp. 301–15.

Thompson Report. *Experience and Participation*. (HMSO, 1982).

Townes, E. 'Walking on the Rim Bones of Nothingness: Scholarship and Activism'. Journal of the American Academy of Religion 77:1 (2009), pp. 1–15.

Turner, B. S., *Max Weber: From History to Modernity* (London: Routledge, 1992).

UK Government Report, *Sustainable Development in a Changing Climate* (London: HMSO, 2008).

United Kingdom, *Race Relations Act 1979*. (United Kingdom: Office of Public Sector Information, 1979).

—. *Disability Discrimination Act 1995* (United Kingdom: Office of Public Sector Information, 1995).

United Nations, Food and Agriculture Organization of the United, *Livestock's Long Shadow: Environmental Issues and Options* (Geneva: Food and Agriculture Organization, 2006).

Veling, T., *Practical Theology: 'On Earth as it is in Heaven'* (New York: Orbis Books, 2005).

Volf, M., *Exclusion and Embrace: Theological Exploration of Identity, Otherness and Exploration* (Nashville: Abingdon Press, 1994).

—. 'The Trinity Is Our Social Program: The Doctrine of the Trinity and the Shape of Social Engagement', *Modern Theology*, 14 (1998), pp. 403–19.

Vuola, E., 'Latin American Liberation Theologians' Turn to Eco(theo)logy: Critical Remarks', in C. Deane-Drummond and H. Bedford Strohm (eds), *Religion and Ecology in the Public Sphere* (London: T&T Clark, 2011).

Ward, Graham, 'Bodies: The Displaced Body of Jesus Christ', in J. Milbank, Catherine Pickstock and Graham Ward (eds), *Radical Orthodoxy: A New Theology* (London & New York: Routledge, 1999), pp. 163–81.

—. *Cities of God* (New York: Routledge, 2000).

Ward, L., and B. Hearn, *An Equal Place at the Table* (Published for Participation Works by NCB, 2010).

Ward, P. *Youthwork and the Mission of God* (London: SPCK, 1997).

—. *Participation and Mediation: a practical theology for the liquid church* (London: SCM Press, 2008).

Weir, A. A. S., Jackie Chappell and Alex Kacelnik, 'Shaping of Hooks in New Caledonian Crows', *Science* 297:5583 (2002), p. 981.

Wenham, G. J., *Genesis*, Word Bible Commentary (Waco: Word, 1994), p. 30.

Westphal, M., *Overcoming Onto-Theology: Toward a Postmodern Christian Faith* (New York: Fordham University Press, 2001).

Whitehead, H., *Sperm Whales: Social Evolution in the Ocean* (Chicago, IL: University of Chicago, 2003).

Wittgenstein, L., *Philosophical Investigations* (Oxford: Blackwell, 2001).

World Commission on Environment and Development, *The Brundtland Report, Our Common Future* (Oxford: Oxford University Press, 1987).

Yaconelli, M., *Contemplative Youth Ministry: practising the presence of Jesus with young people* (London: SPCK, 2006).

YMCA., *Circles of Experience: A Workbook on Spiritual Development* (London: National Council of YMCAs, 1985).

Yong, A., *Theology and Down Syndrome: Reimagining Disability in Late Modernity* (Waco: Baylor University Press, 2007).

Young, F., *Face to Face: A Narrative Essay in the Theology of Suffering* (Edinburgh: T&T Clark, 1990).

Young, K., *The Art of Youth Work* (Dorset: Russell House Publishing, 1999).

Zizioulas, J. D., *Being as Communion*, 2nd edn (London: DLT, 2004).

—. *Communion & Otherness* (London: T&T Clark, 2006).

Index

Where authors listed below have a chapter in this book, the page numbers for that chapter are indicated in **Bold**.